PEARSON
mycanadianbuscommlab™

Save Time.
Improve Results.

More than 6 million students have used a Pearson MyLab product to get a better grade.

MyCanadianBusCommLab is an all-in-one learning and testing environment for business communication. The easy-to-navigate site provides a variety of resources including

- An interactive Pearson eText

- Model documents and model document makeovers

- Audio and video material to view or listen to, whatever your learning style

- Personalized learning opportunities—YOU choose what, where, and when you want to study

- Assessment tests to guide you on making the most efficient use of study time

To take advantage of all that MyCanadianBusCommLab has to offer, you will need an access code. If you do not already have an access code, you can buy one online at **www.mycanadianbuscommlab.ca.**

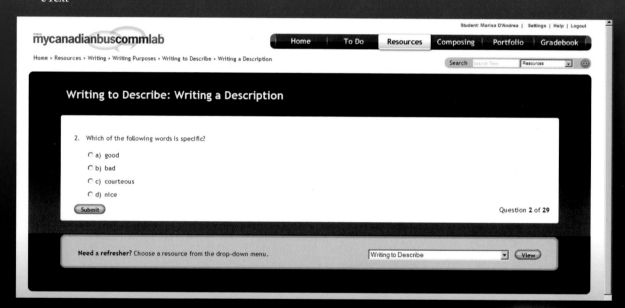

Pearson eText

Pearson eText gives students access to the text whenever and wherever they have access to the internet. eText pages look exactly like the printed text, offering powerful new functionality for students and instructors.

Users can create notes, highlight text in different colours, create bookmarks, zoom, click hyperlinked words and phrases to view definitions, and choose single-page or two-page view.

Pearson eText allows for quick navigation using a table of contents and provides full-text search. The eText may also offer links to associated media files, enabling users to access videos, animations, or other activities as they read the text.

Save Time. Improve Results. www.mycanadianbuscommlab.ca

Get the Writing Help You Need

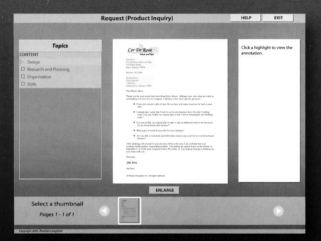

Model Document Practice

In MyCanadianBusCommLab you can see real business-world samples of documents that you will need to write when you begin your career. These "Model Documents" and "Model Document Makeovers" allow you to apply what you have learned.

Help with the Writing Process

MyCanadianBusCommLab provides help with every step of the writing process and will help you prepare to communicate effectively in the business world. Activities include a tutorial on writing formal reports. A "Composing" space provides resources at your fingertips as you research, draft, and revise. You get the help you need when you need it, without ever leaving your writing environment. Improve your writing skills, improve your grade, improve your chances of succeeding in your career.

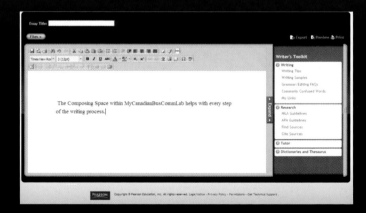

IMPACT!
A GUIDE TO BUSINESS COMMUNICATION

EIGHTH EDITION

MARGOT NORTHEY

JOAN McKIBBIN
ST. LAWRENCE COLLEGE

Pearson Canada
Toronto

Library and Archives Canada Cataloguing in Publication

Northey, Margot
    Impact : a guide to business communication / Margot Northey, Joan McKibbin. — 8th ed.

Includes bibliographical references and index.
ISBN 978-0-13-215886-2

    1. Business communication—Textbooks. 2. Commercial correspondence—
Textbooks. 3. Business report writing—Textbooks. I. McKibbin, Joan II. Title.

HF5718.N67 2011   651.7   C2010-906307-4

ISBN 978-0-13-215886-2

Vice-President, Editorial Director: Gary Bennett
Editor-in-Chief: Ky Pruesse
Acquisitions Editor: David Le Gallais
Marketing Manager: Loula March
Supervising Developmental Editor: Suzanne Schaan
Developmental Editor: Eleanor MacKay
Project Manager: Marissa Lok
Production Editor: Claudia Forgas
Copy Editor: Claudia Forgas
Proofreader: Sharon Kirsch
Coldreader: Laurel Sparrow
Compositor: Aptara®, Inc.
Art Director: Julia Hall
Cover Designer: Miriam Blier
Interior Designers: Miriam Blier and Quinn Banting
Cover Image: Getty Images

For permission to reproduce copyrighted material, the publisher gratefully acknowledges the copyright holders listed on page 241, which is considered an extension of this copyright page.

2 3 4 5   15 14 13 12

Printed and bound in the United States of America.

Contents

Preface and Acknowledgments

In the changing world of business, one aspect is constant—the need for good communication. Although the Internet and other sophisticated technology have increased the speed and ease of getting in touch with others, the consequences of poor or unthinking communication can also have more far-reaching, negative impacts. Repeatedly, the daily news reveals how a poorly phrased message by a CEO can damage a company or how an indiscreet email undermines an employee's career.

This edition of *Impact* reflects students' increased use of technology in their day-to-day lives and the expectation that they will transfer this experience to their jobs, whatever the area. It also reflects our increasingly multicultural workplace. Understanding the nuances of a message and the likely perceptions of the reader or listener is vital to success, whether in motivating fellow employees or in responding to customers. Communicating well means adapting to suit the context.

Despite the changes in society and the workplace, the mandate of this eighth edition of *Impact* remains the same: to provide a small, practical book that is easy to read and easy to use. If you are wary about writing or about speaking in public, this book can help you build confidence and competence. It provides advice on putting words on a page or computer screen. It takes you through the steps of planning and producing good letters, memos, and reports. It reveals strategies for attacking common business-writing problems—ways to address different kinds of readers for different purposes. You will learn how to write with a clear, concise, and vigorous style.

You will also discover the occasions when speaking is more appropriate than writing, and how to make an effective oral presentation, handle a job interview, or run a meeting.

Good writing and speaking reflect good thinking. The explanations and exercises in *Impact* show how thinking through a task and making informed choices will bring you better results. It's a practical approach since, after all, business is a practical matter.

Our thanks to the following for their helpful reviews of this edition of *Impact*: Kendra Carmichael, Acadia University, Cynthis Gagne, Niagara College, Welland Campus, Alison McCuaig, Algonquin College, Sylvia Simpson, Mohawk College of Applied Arts and Technology.

The capable editorial staff at Pearson Education also deserves special thanks: Eleanor MacKay, David LeGallais, Marissa Lok, and freelance editor Claudia Forgas.

Student Supplements

mycanadianbuscommlab

MyCanadianBusCommLab (www.mycanadianbuscommlab.ca). This state-of-the-art, interactive, and instructive solution for business communication is designed to be used as a supplement to a traditional lecture course or to completely administer an online course. See the opening pages of this book for details.

MyCanadianBusCommLab includes a Pearson eText that gives students access to the book whenever and wherever they have access to the Internet. eText pages look exactly like the printed book, offering powerful new functionality for students and instructors. Users can create notes, highlight text in different colours, create bookmarks, zoom, click hyperlinked words and phrases to view definitions, and view in single-page or two-page view. Pearson eText allows for quick navigation to key parts of the eText using a table of contents and provides a full-text search. The eText may also offer links to associated media files, enabling users to access videos, animations, or other activities as they read.

Throughout the book, icons highlight material where related activities or samples are available on MyCanadianBusCommLab:

- Explore dozens of **writing samples,** from letters to emails to reports, that model effective communication.

✱⊣**Explore**

- Practise correcting ineffective communication using interactive **document makeovers.** Feedback guides you to understand problems and find solutions.

✔●⊣**Practise**

- Watch **videos** of simulated workplace communication tasks and real-life business communication issues, and video tutorials on specific topics.

👁⊣**Watch**

A student access card for MyCanadianBusCommLab is packaged with every new copy of the book. Access codes can also be purchased through campus bookstores or through the website.

CourseSmart for Students. CourseSmart goes beyond traditional expectations—providing instant, online access to the textbooks and course materials you need at an average savings of 60 per cent. With instant access from any computer and the ability to search the text, you'll find the content you need quickly, no matter where you are. And with online tools like highlighting and note-taking, you can save time and study efficiently. See all the benefits at **www.coursesmart.com/students.**

Instructor Supplements

Some of these instructor supplements are available for downloading from a password-protected section of Pearson Education Canada's online catalogue (**vig.pearsoned.ca**). Navigate to your book's catalogue page to view a list of supplements. See your local sales representative for details and access.

Instructor's Manual. The Instructor's Manual offers a practical, hands-on approach designed to help you plan your communications course. The manual provides helpful answers and sample responses to the exercises in the book, suggestions for generating class discussion and group work, and ideas for student self-directed learning.

MyTest (www.pearsonmytest.com). MyTest from Pearson Education Canada is a powerful assessment generation program that helps instructors easily create and print quizzes, tests, and exams, as well as homework or practice handouts. Questions and tests can all be authored online, allowing instructors ultimate flexibility and the ability to efficiently manage assessments at anytime, from anywhere. MyTest for *Impact*, 8th edition, includes both Chapter Review Tests and six larger Unit Tests. You can use these as they are or mix and match the questions to create your own personalized evaluations.

Test Item File. This testbank in Microsoft Word format includes all the Chapter Review Tests and Unit Tests from the MyTest version.

CourseSmart for Instructors. CourseSmart goes beyond traditional expectations—providing instant, online access to the textbooks and course materials you need at a lower cost for students. And even as students save money, you can save time and hassle with a digital eTextbook that allows you to search for the most relevant content at the very moment you need it. Whether it's evaluating textbooks or creating lecture notes to help students with difficult concepts, CourseSmart can make life a little easier. See how when you visit **www.coursesmart.com/instructors**.

Technology Specialists. Pearson's Technology Specialists work with faculty and campus course designers to ensure that Pearson technology products, assessment tools, and online course materials are tailored to meet your specific needs. This highly qualified team is dedicated to helping schools take full advantage of a wide range of educational resources by assisting in the integration of a variety of instructional materials and media formats. Your local Pearson Education sales representative can provide you with more details on this service program.

Note to Instructors

Since most students are adept at using the Internet and a variety of Web-based programs, this eighth edition of *Impact* focuses less attention on the technology itself and more on the options and pitfalls when using technology to communicate. The primary emphasis remains where it is most needed—on how to write and talk with clarity, conciseness, and force. We have updated many of the examples and exercises and listened to the advice of instructors who have used the book. The design on this new edition is crisper, with larger typeface and wider margins, giving space for students to make notes. We think you and your students will find it easier to follow and will be able to find what you want quickly. *Impact* has been successful in part because it is deliberately lean. We continue to strive for a practical book that students will want to use and keep. We aim to provide what they need to know in order to be good communicators, without weighing the message down with extra baggage.

This edition of *Impact* also includes updated and expanded coverage of APA style based on the sixth edition of the *Publication Manual of the American Psychological Association* published in July 2009.

Writing and speaking well is challenging, but we hope this edition of *Impact* continues to make the process simpler and the result more satisfying.

About the Authors

Margot Northey was Professor and Dean of Queen's School of Business, Queen's University, from 1995 to 2002. Previously she was a professor and director of Communications at the Ivey School (University of Western Ontario), and, before that, founding director of the Writing Program at the University of Toronto in Mississauga. She has also been a visiting professor at the Helsinki School of Economics.

Dr. Northey is the author of many articles and books, including *Making Sense: A Student's Guide to Writing and Style,* now in its seventh edition, *The Haunted Wilderness: The Gothic and Grotesque in Canadian Fiction*, and *Writer's Choice.* She has served as a consultant and given communications seminars to business and government organizations from coast to coast and previously was on the board of directors of the International Association for Business Communication and of the International Association to Advance Collegiate Schools of Business. Currently she is a director of a number of corporate boards, including Alliance Atlantis Communications, Fraser Papers, Nexfor, Stressgen, and Wawanesa Insurance.

Margot Northey

Joan McKibbin is a Professor at St. Lawrence College, Kingston, where she has taught courses in writing theory, business communication, desktop publishing, and computer applications. She designed and directed a peer writing tutor program at the college and developed a training program in writing theory and practice for peer tutors. She has also held teaching positions at Glendon College (York University) in Toronto and Goddard College in Vermont.

Joan has her own desktop publishing and freelance editing business and has acted as contributing author and technical editor for a number of academic publishers and private-sector authors and publishers.

Joan McKibbin

Thinking about Communication

1

"Good communication is a critical element in making today's fast-paced business run well. It is difficult to have good communication if you are not listening to and understanding the view of your listener."

—Rob Dexter, chairman and CEO, Maritime Travel

"Winning companies will usually have great communication across the organization. But great communication also means listening. One-way talking is not communicating."

—Fred Jaques, former president and CEO, Dare Foods

The prospect of having to write fills many business people with dismay. Owing to the emphasis on quantitative methods in business courses, many students and recent graduates have had little practice writing or speaking formally. As a result, some feel more at ease working with numbers than with words. Yet the ability to communicate effectively is essential in getting to the top in business.

The Importance of Writing

Why is writing so important? The reasons can be summed up in three words: flexibility, power, clarity.

Writing Gives Flexibility

Let's suppose you have an idea for a new product that you want to propose to the managers of marketing and production, two busy and more senior people. You make appointments to see them. First you go to the marketing manager's office and enthusiastically make a brief presentation. Unfortunately, she has had a bad day. The president has come down to see her about declining profits, the latest sales figures are discouraging, and she has just concluded a heated discussion with a major distributor. She responds half-heartedly, makes a few nitpicking points and, while politely showing you to the door, vaguely says she'll think about your proposal.

When you start to talk to the production manager, he is even more distracted. He says one of the expensive new robots in the factory has malfunctioned, causing a production crisis. He apologizes that he is really too busy to think about new ideas at the moment. You leave, feeling unhappy and defeated.

Now, let's suppose you had put your ideas in writing. The two managers could have set your proposal aside to read at a time when they were feeling less harassed. One might even have taken it home to study quietly in the evening. Since the managers would have been reading the proposal at their convenience, they would have been in a more receptive mood—ready to see your suggestion as a possible benefit rather than another headache.

Writing allows this kind of flexibility. It allows readers to decide when and how much they want to read. They have a chance to reread if necessary and to reflect upon a message or proposal.

Writing Has Power

The old saying "The pen is mightier than the sword" suggests the enormous influence the written word has had over people, both individuals and groups. Martin Luther's 95 theses, which ushered in the Protestant Reformation, or Karl Marx's *Das Kapital*, laboured over in the damp rooms of the British Museum, have had more influence than the armed might of most rulers. On an admittedly far less profound level, writing in a business setting can also be a powerful force.

To begin with, writing has staying power. Often a written proposal or report will be shelved because it is ahead of its time or not in line with current policy. Later, sometimes several years later, when conditions are more favourable, the same document can be picked up and made the basis for company action. To stay alive, the spoken idea relies on memory—a notoriously unreliable vehicle—whereas the written word needs only an adequate filing system. It provides a permanent record.

Writing also has travelling power. Young employees of medium-to-large businesses are sometimes surprised to discover that a memo or report they have written has made its way into the president's office before they have. With the ease and access of computers, clearly written ideas or information often travels quickly up the rungs of the corporate ladder. It is not unusual for good writing to catch the eye of a senior manager and lead to speedier promotion for the writer.

Writing Helps Clarify Thinking

Writers often say that the act of putting things down on a page not only records what they have in mind but also helps them sort out their thoughts. Many people who are struggling with a problem or trying to make a decision find that writing it down encourages them to be logical and arrive at a satisfactory solution. You may have heard the expression "How do I know what I think until I see what I say?" Writing can be a valuable aid to thinking.

You will find—or may already have found—that you can analyze complicated business problems more clearly when you try to sort things out on paper. Beyond being a medium of communication, therefore, writing becomes a tool for understanding. It's a tool worth learning to use well.

Communicating in Organizations

⬤─[Watch
BCVL: Effective vs. Ineffective
Communication

It's perhaps not surprising that Marshall McLuhan, the most influential communications expert of the twentieth century, was a Canadian. As a nation, we have been preoccupied with forging communication links among a sparse, widespread population. Year after year we strive to maintain a national radio system that reflects the diversity of our country and builds bridges between regions and two linguistic communities. We also fight hard to maintain our television broadcasting system in the face of pervasive foreign competition.

Canadian companies have been aggressive in entering the international high-tech market with newly developed telecommunications equipment. The ubiquitous BlackBerry is the most obvious example. But even high-tech companies have come to realize that excellence comes not only from technological know-how but also from handling people well. Good managers are usually good communicators, whether the process of communication is systematic or informal.

Communication Systems

As they expand, most businesses create systems or mechanisms for communicating both inside and outside the organization with people who are important to their success. Shrewd managers strive to set up an effective communication system, not as an end in itself but because it's a way of improving overall performance and capitalizing on opportunities.

WRITTEN SYSTEMS

Internal communications are designed for company employees. Email is the most common route, but bulletin boards and face-to-face group meetings also play a part. Today's businesses realize the need for two-way communication between management and staff. Human resources departments, if they are doing their job, are active in seeking feedback from employees and ensuring that they have a voice in the workplace environment.

The aim of external communication is to inform the organization's outside stakeholders (including shareholders, governments, customers, and the public at large) through various written and spoken communications. Building good relations with the media also matters. The growth of public relations departments illustrates the increasing dependence of business on a favourable public image—and the recognition that an organization cannot operate in isolation.

ORAL SYSTEMS

Conversations over coffee, spontaneous meetings, and even casual access to the boss's office down the hall all contribute to an informal communications network. By "wandering around," managers contribute to the sense of openness within the company and help create an environment where employees can voice their concerns and ideas.

The grapevine is a major source of information in most organizations. News about hirings, firings, or layoffs is apt to reach people first through the grapevine rather than through formal channels. Grapevine information may be distorted or based on rumour, but it always travels fast. Managers can learn who the key people in this informal network are and make use of them. They can also anticipate what's likely to spread by rumour and give the official version first.

More organized oral communication can occur in meetings or through teleconferencing, either internally among different branches of a single corporation or externally among people in locations around the world. Today's technology adds a new dimension to oral communication by allowing people to "meet" without having to travel to a common location, and teleconferencing has become increasingly attractive in light of the expense and inconvenience—and sometimes even the risks—of air travel.

BCVL: Management Now

The Flow of Information

Whether communication is channelled through formal structures or an informal network, employees have information needs that must be met if they are to continue giving their best. Roger D'Aprix suggests that employees want answers to three questions:

1. How am I doing and does anybody care? (The need for personal evaluation.)
2. How are we doing? (The need to know group or company performance measures.)
3. How can I help? (The need to contribute meaningfully.)

Managers who are good communicators see that those who report to them have answers to these questions. However, creating good communication in an organization isn't a one-shot effort. Rather, it's a continuous process that requires an ongoing management commitment.

The annual list of Canada's Top 100 Employers, compiled by Mediacorp Canada Inc., bases its rankings in part on communication issues: whether the firm lets employees know if they are performing well; and whether the firm passes on news and information to its employees.

An organization with good communications has an efficient flow of information in three directions: downward, upward, and lateral.

DOWNWARD COMMUNICATION

This flow of communication follows the hierarchical route from superior to subordinate. It may take place at any level. Top executives use this route to explain corporate strategies, to instill loyalty, to recognize success, or to rouse employees to greater effort. Lower-level managers often give job instructions, details of policy, and feedback about employee performance.

Downward communication often is serial—that is, it is transferred from person to person through several levels. The more links in the chain of command it passes through, the more distorted it becomes.

According to Pace and Boren (1973), serial communication has several tendencies:

- The original message can become simplified, with some details such as qualifiers omitted and the remaining parts highlighted or "sharpened."
- Some details are changed according to the predisposition, communication style, or status of the interpreter.
- The order and details of events are adapted according to what is plausible. What one expects to have happened overrides what actually happened.

Serial communication is more likely to be distorted if it is oral, but changes in meaning can occur in any message. A good practice, therefore, is to monitor important messages—to check on how they have been received after passing through several levels, so that any distortion can be corrected.

UPWARD COMMUNICATION

Communication from subordinate to superior can increase productivity and help create a team feeling. Yet too many companies still pay only lip service to it. Participative management, which the Japanese have used so effectively, does not mean that subordinates make all the decisions, but rather that they provide input into the process.

Upward communication takes two forms:

1. Requested feedback to superiors on policies, practices, or performance
2. Unsolicited ideas or suggestions

For either form to work, there must be a climate of trust. Subordinates must feel free to make critical comments or suggest changes without being considered troublemakers. Without a climate of trust, employees will say only what they think the boss wants to hear.

LATERAL COMMUNICATION

This kind of communication moves horizontally across areas that are on the same level in the hierarchy, or sometimes diagonally to a different level. In complex organizations, such communication helps coordinate activities across functions or departments and can produce a spirit of cooperation. When there is little lateral communication—when "the right hand doesn't know what the left hand is doing"—departments often operate at cross purposes. Often companies trying to be more productive reduce some of the layers of management. In this "flattening" of the organization, lateral communication becomes even more important, since each manager will have a wider span of control—that is, a greater spread of people to manage.

Some Help from Communication Theory

A growing body of research and theory exists about various aspects of communication, from semiotics (the study of signs) and linguistics (the study of language) to cognitive psychology and persuasion theory. For communication specialists, these are fruitful areas to explore. However, for those of us interested in the individual acts of writing and speaking in business, the most important feature of modern communication theory is its description of communication as an exchange. Rather than thinking of communication as only the delivery of a message, we should envisage a process in which the receiver of the message matters as much as the sender.

This idea is not new. The ancient Greeks had at the centre of their education system the art of rhetoric. Students learned various techniques for communicating ideas; they practised ways of swaying an audience to the speaker's point of view by appealing to both reason and emotion. In more recent times, however, with the Western world's emphasis on reason, we have tended to overlook the importance of the listener in the communication process. The thinking has often been that since people are reasonable, they will agree with your conclusions, as long as you present them with a reasonable argument. You need concentrate only on the logic of your message.

In the twenty-first century we know enough to correct this mistaken approach. The insights of psychology have made us realize that human reactions are much more complicated than we once thought. In our dealings with others, a simple reliance on reason will not work. Moreover, the insights of linguistics, especially in the area of semantics, have made us aware that meaning itself is a complex matter. Words do not have a fixed meaning; they are only symbols and their meaning may differ with different users and in different contexts. The word *cool* may mean one thing when a meteorologist refers to "a cool temperature"; it has another meaning when a politician bemoans "a cool reception" for his speech; and yet another when a teenager talks about a friend being "a cool guy."

Modern communication theory builds upon these and other insights in studying the ways we express ourselves. It analyzes communication on several levels, beginning with the individual and extending to the interaction among large groups and cultures. It explores the different ways, verbal and nonverbal, that we communicate with each other, from written messages and oral presentations to gestures and body language.

In a book of this size it is obviously impossible to explore the intricacies of communication theory; what follows is simply a summary of some of the key concepts that affect our ability to write and speak effectively as individuals in business.

A Communication Model

In 1949, Claude Shannon and Warren Weaver published a mathematical model of communication based on Shannon's work in the Bell Telephone Laboratories. It described a one-way communication process going from sender to receiver (Shannon & Weaver, 1963). As might be expected, it used terms associated with electronics. Subsequent changes to this basic model have described a two-way process and have a more behavioural emphasis, dealing less with the message itself than with the way people perceive it. Figure 1-1 illustrates a simple two-way model. To accomplish a purpose, a sender encodes a message into signals (words, numbers, or pictures) that are transmitted by a channel (for example, fibre optic cables, satellites, telephone lines, radio waves, or the nervous system) and a medium (such as a telephone, magazine, television, computer, or even a voice). The receiver gets the signal either directly, through the ear or eye, or indirectly, through the medium of technological equipment. The receiver decodes and reacts to the message, and in turn gives feedback, through the same process of encoding and transmitting a signal.

Barriers to Communication

◉─Watch
BCVL: Impact of Culture on
Business: Spotlight on Latin
America

Interference can disrupt any stage of the communication process. The most common types of interference are technical, semantic, and environmental.

TECHNICAL INTERFERENCE

Most people have experienced static on telephone lines, a breakdown of television transmission, websites or servers that are down, or a computer "crash." Some people may have to cope with faulty hearing aids or inadequate eyeglasses. We all know that even minor

Figure 1-1   A Simple Model of Two-Way Communication

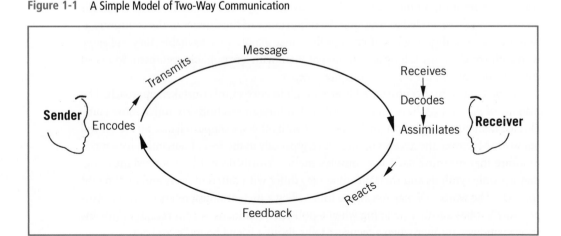

physical ailments can affect communication. If the boss has a headache when sending a memo, the message may be unintentionally abrupt or snappish.

SEMANTIC INTERFERENCE

The problem here stems from words themselves. When faulty diction muddles a sentence, the message may be misinterpreted. "Bypassing" occurs when the same word means different things to different people. For example, if you say that management has made an "aggressive" effort to cut costs, you may mean "enterprising" and "vigorous" but the listener may interpret the phrase negatively as "destructive" or "hostile."

ENVIRONMENTAL INTERFERENCE

Often these barriers have to do with individual or group attitudes. We tend to filter information according to our perception of reality, and that perception may differ from one person or group to the next. In an age where political correctness is a catchword in the workplace, it is important to be aware of possible sources of environmental interference:

1. **Age.**   The term *generation gap* reflects the fact that a difference in age can cause people to see things in a different light. Teenagers are well aware of this phenomenon when communicating with parents.

2. **Sex.**   Jokes or comments acceptable to males may offend females, and vice versa. In addition, perceived sexist attitudes in a message may cloud the reception of a message that ostensibly has nothing to do with sex.

3. **Physical appearance.**   The underlying premise of "dress for success" lessons is that people are judged partly by the clothes they wear. We may not like this kind of typecasting by appearance, but it is not likely to go away. If applicants for a job turn up in untidy or inappropriate clothes, they send an unintentional message. So may someone with nicotine-stained fingers, especially if the prospective employer is a nonsmoker.

   Interference is not confined to personal appearance. A letter containing typos or an email message containing spelling errors may annoy some readers enough to deflect their attention from the ideas.

4. **Cultural attitudes.**   Cultural attitudes, even aside from obvious racial and religious prejudices, can cause interference. Although most groups in our multicultural society share common types of behaviour, we can still see subtle differences based on cultural background. People's ways of seeing things (their perceptual maps) differ from the ways of others in a different cultural group and can affect the reception of a message. In today's globalized business environment, an awareness and appreciation of cultural difference is essential to cultivating a successful business. The following discussion provides some guidelines for avoiding cultural interference.

The Globalization of Business

Whether a large bank or a small manufacturing company, most Canadian businesses are looking beyond our borders. Two major developments have helped foster globalization:

◉ **Watch**
BCVL: Communicating Effectively in the Global Workplace

- **International trade agreements.**   Canada has signed a number of national and international trade agreements, such as the North American Free Trade Agreement (NAFTA) in 1994, that eliminate trade barriers, facilitate the cross-border movement of goods and services, and increase investment opportunities for Canadian business. These trade agreements have made it easier and less expensive to conduct business in foreign markets, and a new model has emerged with small Canadian firms forming global alliances with similar firms in other countries to establish "virtual corporations."

- **International communications technology.**   Rapid developments combined with falling communications costs have allowed small Canadian companies to participate in business generated by the globalization trend. Voice technology makes communication easy and accessible through cellphones, handheld units, and conference-call technology. Developments in information technology have made it possible to transfer complex information almost instantaneously with ftp, pdf, and zip software and to see and hear others across wide distances. It's hard to imagine, now, a business world without email, voice mail, video conferencing, and cellphones with built-in cameras.

The Role of Intercultural Communication

Watch

Perils of Pauline: Intercultural Communication

An increase in global business opportunities has resulted in a heightened awareness of the need to communicate effectively with people of different cultures. As businesses strive to compete in diverse environments, they have recognized the importance of intercultural communication skills for professional success. Resolving issues across cultural and ethnic differences requires an appreciation of cultural diversity and an awareness of intercultural practices. Each year, it seems, the technology improves and the costs decrease.

For instance, attitudes to time vary from culture to culture. North Americans are generally concerned about being on time. In business, "on time" means precisely at the scheduled hour, perhaps even at the scheduled minute. North American executives who have to cool their heels for an hour in the waiting room of a South American associate could be infuriated about "wasting time" if they didn't realize that their ideas about time are not always shared by others.

Attitudes to space also vary. Research in proxemics (the study of the space between people) shows that different cultural ideas of what is "private space" may cause communication problems. For example, South Americans and southern Europeans like to move close when they talk to each other. Northern Europeans and North Americans, by contrast, like to keep about a metre apart in business relationships, moving closer only if the relationship becomes more intimate. The British, with their customary reserve, have a reputation for being the most "standoffish." It's easy for people from these different cultural backgrounds to give offence unknowingly when talking to one another by moving in during a conversation or by backing away.

Attitudes toward the Internet can also reveal cultural differences. A request for digital photographs and biographies of business partners or staff may meet some resistance from Latin Americans, who are reluctant to share personal information with people they do not know; North Americans, on the other hand, tend to see this type of exposure as a good promotional tool.

Email messages, too, can show cross-cultural differences. Asians tend to adopt a very formal tone, writing email messages that are similar to written letters and include openings and closings. North Americans, with their commitment to speed and efficiency, often forgo these formalities. Students sending text messages are used to an even more casual style with shortened spellings and abbreviations, although these are inappropriate in business.

Different cultures practise varying business etiquette and communication styles when negotiating business deals. One study (Hung, 1994) identifies Canadian negotiating styles as individualistic, informal, and direct, with a sequential approach to the handling of tasks and a marked dislike of silence. According to this research, only 15 per cent of the typical negotiating styles of Canadian business executives are appropriate in Pacific Asia, Canada's second most important trading partner after the United States.

Bridging cross-cultural differences has become a fundamental ingredient of successful business communication. When diversity issues are involved, the following guidelines will prove helpful in enhancing communication, both written and spoken.

Writing across Cultures

1. **Avoid the temptation to sound sophisticated or erudite.**   Choose words that are common and may well be included in the English lexicon of a non-native speaker of English. For example, try *rank* instead of *prioritize* or *make* instead of *implement.*

2. **Stay away from any slang or colloquial expressions.**   Terms such as *headhunter* or *bean counter* might create some unintended confusion.

3. **Avoid complex, inverted sentence structure.**   Beginning a sentence with an introductory clause makes it harder for the reader to interpret the message. Try to use simple syntax that places the subject and verb at the beginning of the sentence.

4. **Remember not to use acronyms, contractions, or abbreviations.**   What might be common knowledge to a North American may well be unknown to an Asian or European reader. Writing the phrase in full diminishes the need for any guesswork on the part of the reader.

Speaking across Cultures

1. **Watch for signs of confusion or lack of comprehension.**   Use the nonverbal communication cues discussed below to assess whether your message is being understood.

2. **Be an active listener.**   North Americans have sometimes been told that they have a tendency to talk too much. Be sure to allow ample opportunity for others to ask questions or verify information.

3. **Be a sensitive listener.**   People from different cultures may have an imperfect understanding of English, but this is not a reflection of their thinking. Be sensitive to what is underneath their struggles with your language.

4. **Remember that gesture and facial expression are the most commonly understood means of communication.**   A smile or a raised eyebrow can say a great deal, bearing in mind the cultural differences discussed below.

Nonverbal Communication

Many of the difficulties mentioned above are nonverbal. Although the primary focus of this book is verbal communication, it's important to recognize the part that nonverbal communication plays.

One research study has found that a whopping 93 per cent of the effect of a message on a listener is conveyed by nonverbal means (Mehrabian, 1981). Although the influence of nonverbal elements is certainly less in written communication, presentation still matters. Layout, use of illustrations, typeface, and colour can affect reader response, as experts in direct mail know.

Psychologists have shown that people learn in different ways. For many, visualizing (seeing pictures, charts, and so on) is the primary means of understanding. For others,

◉─ Watch
Perils of Pauline: Verbal and Nonverbal Communication

hearing words and music has a major effect. Still others learn best when they do—by imitating motions or working with their hands. If you think back to your early years in school, you will likely remember that teachers often tried to communicate using all three approaches. If we know a person's favoured learning style, we can often emphasize the preferred method in planning communication.

Nonverbal communication can be classified in various ways, but it falls most easily into two divisions: setting and gesture.

Setting

The colour of an office or its decor can be an important element of communication. For example, we know that green, which used to be so prevalent in hospitals, helps create a relaxed atmosphere. By comparison, red, a feature in the decor of many restaurants, is a stimulant.

The way furniture is arranged can also affect communication. Managers who want to emphasize their status can do so by talking to others from behind an imposing desk. Managers who want to put visitors at ease will move from behind the desk and talk in a conversation area where chairs are arranged more casually. Similarly, if the person chairing a meeting sits at the head of a long table, he or she will more easily dominate the discussion. In contrast, a circular table will encourage conversation among all the participants.

Gesture

Kinesics is a field of research that explores the science of gestures. It has given us helpful insights into the messages people send by using their bodies in a particular way. We all react, often unconsciously, to the signals that people send by their expressions or actions. If we are in the middle of making a point and we see that our listener has raised eyebrows, we infer that he or she has doubts. Similarly, we interpret a frown or scowl as a negative reaction. We wouldn't take long in an argument to move away from a clenched fist or to interpret a handshake as a sign of a truce.

In a North American context, smiling and head nodding communicate a positive response, as do relaxed, open body positions and forward leaning. Eye behaviours, too, are an important element in nonverbal communication. Studies have shown that direct eye contact in this culture creates an impression of competence and honesty, while people who avert their eyes are perceived as less credible (Burgoon, Bullet, & Woodall, 1989, p. 324). Vocal cues are another factor in nonverbal communication: rapid speech is often interpreted as a signal of intelligence and dominance, while a slower rate is perceived as more honest, people-oriented, and benevolent (Nolen, 1995, p. 49).

However, it is important to allow for individual and cultural differences in behaviour. In trying to develop our unconscious understanding of nonverbal signals to the level of conscious interpretation, we should remember two provisos:

1. **Individuals may not fit a common pattern.**   Just as racial stereotyping distorts the truth about individuals, so does the reliance upon a single, prescribed interpretation of a gesture. For example, a listener's crossed arms often signify opposition, but they may also be just a comfortable position. To be interpreted reliably, a specific gesture needs to be considered in context.

2. **Gestures can have different meanings in different cultures.**   When people in Western cultures nod their heads up and down in a conversation, they are generally showing agreement. For some Africans, the same nod means disagreement. For Asians, nodding means "I understand"; it doesn't mean that your listener is in agreement with the

point you are making. Looking a person in the eye also has varied meanings. A young person in most Western cultures is coached to look an adult in the eye as a sign of respect. However, a young North American Indian or West Indian may be taught that this is disrespectful.

As a communicator, you can make many gains by being receptive to nonverbal signals as long as you are aware of their limitations. The key to nonverbal communication is to be observant and sensitive to subtleties. Remember also that the better you know people, the more likely you are to be able to "read" them correctly.

Becoming a Good Listener

Watch
Perils of Pauline: Listening Skills

Listening is probably the most underrated of all the communication skills, probably because it seems so easy. Yet a common complaint from subordinates about managers at all levels is that they don't listen. Research has shown that managers generally rate themselves as better listeners than their employees rate them (Brownell, 1990).

Often a manager's poor listening behaviour reflects the old notion that a manager's job is to tell others what to do and see that they do it. Although good managers do indeed have to spend time talking with others (instructing and advising them), increasingly they recognize the need to involve employees throughout the organization in making suggestions and problem solving, as a way of improving performance and productivity. Such effective upward communication depends on management's willingness to listen.

What are the guidelines for effective listening? First of all, it helps to understand Carl Rogers' (1995) distinction between passive and active listening.

Passive listening means listening without giving a response, other than the odd nod or show of comprehension. It's appropriate when the talker merely wants to let off steam or muse out loud. *Active listening*, by contrast, creates a constant interaction between speaker and listener. By directly responding to what the speaker says, through comments and questions, the listener helps direct the conversation. An active listener can, in fact, retain control of a conversation.

If you want to be an active listener, according to Rogers, you need to have *empathy*—an understanding of the speaker's perspective and feelings. Empathy is not the same as sympathy or feeling sorry for the speaker, but rather implies awareness. Four kinds of "mirroring" techniques will help you show this awareness:

1. **Paraphrasing,** in which you restate in different words the speaker's point: "You mean . . ."
2. **Clarifying,** in which you ask for a restatement or fuller explanation: "What exactly do you mean by . . . ?"
3. **Reflecting feelings,** in which you respond to the emotions behind the words: "It sounds as if you're feeling . . ."
4. **Summarizing,** in which you pull together the speaker's points: "What I hear you saying is . . ."

Beyond mirroring the speaker's remarks, here are some ways to become a good listener:

1. **Stop talking.**   Sometimes this is a hard thing for busy managers to do, especially those used to giving orders. Don't be afraid of silence. Give others time to collect their thoughts. If they take time getting to the point, be patient. Don't interrupt to finish sentences for them. Wait until they pause, and then clarify or try to draw them out.

2. **For a lengthy discussion, pick a spot where neither of you will be distracted.** Telephone calls or other disruptions can interrupt the flow of a discussion. Clear your mind of other matters so that you can concentrate on the conversation.

3. **Show by your posture and expression that you are attentive.** Leaning forward, for example, can show concern for the other person, as can facing the speaker squarely rather than turning partly away. Eye contact also helps signal that the listener is attentive, although staring or glaring will certainly not encourage relaxed conversation.

4. **Be open rather than judgmental.** Try not to let preconceptions or biases about the speaker shape what you are hearing. Concentrate on the substance rather than the style. At the same time, try to get some sense of the pattern and direction of the speaker's remarks.

5. **Be alert to nonverbal cues.** The speaker may betray deeper or more conflicting feelings than the words indicate. Nonverbal cues can often alert you to areas where you should probe deeper to find a hidden message.

Sometimes we assess the speaker by the pace of the speech. A fast talker may be impatient with a slow talker, or a slow talker may be suspicious of someone who speaks at a fast clip. The typical difference in speed between "fast-talking" Northerners in the United States and the slower "drawl" of Southerners has affected attitudes in many a conversation. On the whole, a listener who matches the speed of the speaker's talk will produce a more positive atmosphere in the conversation. There are exceptions, however. For example, people who are upset or excited often talk faster than usual, sometimes at a breathless pace. We can help calm them down by responding in a slower, more moderate way—a technique doctors use with agitated patients.

Listening to Understand

Although much of this discussion about listening involves strengthening a relationship with others, there are times when the point of your listening is simply to understand some information, as when you are receiving instructions, finding out background information to a problem, or attending a speech or lecture. Often in these instances it's useful to take notes, as long as getting down details doesn't prevent you from catching the overview or "big picture." Don't try to put everything into notes unless you are skilled at shorthand or are able to review your short-form scribble immediately afterward. Instead, try to concentrate first on understanding the flow of the talk and the main argument before attending to the details.

It can be helpful to write the speaker's key points in one column on a page and the examples or justifications in another column to the right. You might also try leaving space at the right of the page to fill in your own comments after the talk. That way, at a later date you can easily review at a glance the speaker's ideas and your response to them. Personalizing the information will help you to remember it.

Listening as a Critic

Occasionally your task as listener will be to evaluate—to assess the information critically. For example, you may need to assess a sales proposal or respond to an employee's plea for a change in procedures on the factory floor or work site. The danger here is that you can become so intent on finding weak spots or problems that you don't really hear what is being said. Sometimes your own biases and emotions can get in the way, so that you unwittingly "tune out" the speaker's message. In either case, the result is distortion or misunderstanding.

Instead, try to concentrate on coming to a full understanding before reaching evaluative conclusions. Brief note-taking can help. You might also jot down beforehand questions that are central to your assessment, so that after you are sure you have understood the presentation you can use them as a guide for your evaluation. If you have only a general idea of what the topic will be, here are some basic questions that can help you evaluate:

- What is the main strength of this idea?
- Are there any factual errors or distortions?
- Is the point of view balanced? Is there an underlying bias?
- What are the alternatives to the proposal, and have they been adequately considered?
- What are the short-term and long-term implications of the ideas?
- How could the ideas be implemented practically? What are the barriers to their implementation and could they be overcome?
- As a result of this speech, what needs to be changed, re-examined, or explored further?

Remember that a speaker cannot talk as fast as your brain can process the information. There's a lot of "empty time" when, as a listener, you can easily be distracted. A more useful alternative to daydreaming is to use that time to review or summarize the sequence of ideas, to consider implications, and to anticipate where the talk is heading. It's worth reiterating, however, that your first duty, even as a critic, is to listen carefully to what is being said.

Approaches to Questioning

Effective questioning clearly fits hand in glove with effective listening. Asking the right questions helps us reach the right answer or solution to a problem. Some kinds of questions ease the flow of communication; others hinder it. This list illustrates the effect of different kinds of questions:

1. **An open question** allows the receiver to respond in a variety of ways. It often begins with "How," "Why," or "In what way." It helps to probe the listener's opinions, eliciting a thoughtful or in-depth reply:
   - How can we improve this setup?
   - Why do you think this is a problem?
   - In what way will this affect our performance?

2. **A closed question** asks for a limited response—often yes or no. It's useful for getting specific information or for checking the accuracy of something:
   - Are you saying you'd like more support?
   - Should we mail the report?
   - Have we covered all the dimensions of the issue?

3. **A hidden assumption or "loaded" question** makes it difficult for the receiver to answer without admitting something. It's a trap that puts the receiver on the defensive, and journalists often use it to try to get business leaders or politicians to acknowledge an error or weakness. Clearly, it impedes free-flowing communication:
   - Why haven't you done anything to stop this massive pollution?
   - Is it really that difficult to keep costs down?
   - When will we get a report from you without mistakes?

4. **A hypothetical question** asks "What if?" It is a useful sort of question when people are doing free-form planning or trying to think up creative ways to address an issue:

   - What would you do if your budget were cut by 15 per cent?

   - If you were in charge of this group, what changes would you propose?

   On the other hand, a hypothetical question can be troublesome if it is directed at you as a kind of accusation. A question such as "If your product is found to contain dioxin, what do you intend to do about it?" leads away from the known facts to supposed ones and can deliberately inflame an issue.

5. **A two-part question** is really two questions in one. It can confuse, or make it difficult for the receiver to know which part to answer:

   - How should we react and is this really the whole problem?

   - How can we better deploy our sales force as well as increase our promotional efforts?

   The questioner would be better to split the question and ask each part separately. Following these guidelines will help you get the feedback you need promptly and efficiently.

Internet Issues

Today email is the norm in businesses and organizations of any size. It encourages people to communicate more frequently and respond more quickly. Using email, some people feel free to make suggestions or take the initiative; they are more comfortable keying a message onto their computer screen than they are dealing with another person face to face. While computers are liberating, don't let the electronic environment lure you into some common pitfalls. Here are a number of guidelines for using email effectively:

1. **Remember the human side.** This is the cardinal rule of communicating in an electronic environment. Just as you visualize your reader when you are writing a letter, remember the intended recipients of your email and imagine their responses to your message.

2. **Be succinct.** The ease of keying in text makes it all too common for writers to become unusually long-winded when they sit down at a computer screen. As most of us know, having to wade through lengthy emails is tedious and will certainly not help to make your reader more receptive to your ideas.

3. **Avoid short-form symbols.** Although smiley faces and other typographical and spelling short forms common in text-messaging work with friends, keep your business writing free of them. They undermine the seriousness of what you are communicating.

4. **Pay attention to appearance and format.** The environmental interference discussed in this chapter is often overlooked in the speed and haste of electronic environments. Take the time to spell check, edit, and proofread your outgoing email to avoid the embarrassment of seeing a mistake just after you click "Send."

Do remember, though, that spell checkers aren't foolproof. They often cannot identify a "commonly misused word" (see Appendix) that is spelled correctly but used incorrectly, and they often don't identify grammatical problems.

Exercises

1. Analyze two company publications, such as brochures, magazines, or newsletters. How would the contents improve internal communications, whether upward (employees to management), downward (management to employees), or lateral (among equals)?

2. Popular cartoons and comics in the daily newspapers often focus on communication problems. Find one or two such cartoons or comics and analyze the interference in the communication process.

3. Give a brief outline or a one-minute talk describing the oral and written communication skills needed in one or two of the following jobs:

   - insurance sales representative
   - doctor
   - computer programmer
   - internal corporate accountant
   - store manager
   - payroll and benefits supervisor
   - affirmative action counsellor
   - bank manager
   - administrative assistant
   - receptionist

4. For each of the following scenarios, identify the nonverbal message being sent and indicate if the sender and/or receiver should handle the matter differently:

   a) While you are talking to a client, she starts drumming her fingers on her desk.

   b) You are a new employee attending your first group meeting. When a man arrives after the meeting has started, others stand up to offer him a chair.

   c) When you make a suggestion at a group meeting, a colleague rolls her eyes.

   d) You need to speak with the internal controller. When you enter his office, you see that he sits with his back to the door, facing the window. He motions you to sit down and continues working for a minute before turning to face you.

   e) At a meeting you've requested with your boss, she closes the door after you've entered and forwards all calls to her secretary.

   f) A prospective employee sits facing you. She hunches her shoulders, fiddles with her ring, and bites her lip throughout the interview.

   g) You hear there is a new engineer your age down the hall and go to his office to welcome him. While you sit talking to him across his desk, he continually rocks back in his chair and presses his fingers together in a "church steeple" position. He smiles with his mouth but his eyes don't smile.

   h) Three days after you have reprimanded an employee, she refuses to look you in the eye when you meet in the corridor. She returns your greeting in a clipped voice.

    i) On your work site, a supervisor doesn't respond when you mention the email you sent about a possible environmental hazard.

5. Identify the mirroring technique shown in each of the following conversations:

    a) "When I suggested that idea, no one responded, but when Beth suggested it, the same people were enthusiastic."

    "You feel that you don't count?"

    b) "The problem with this project flows from the group dynamics."

    "I'm not sure what you mean."

    c) "I mentioned he was a good prospect two weeks ago, and no one has contacted him yet. It's the same with other leads. We have to get more action."

    "You want us to follow up on leads a lot faster."

    d) "This department can't handle the workload. Management wants us to increase the number of direct mail campaigns and add to the number of special events. We can't possibly do all this with our present resources. We're strapped in this department, and if they're going to keep dumping stuff on us like this we need a lot more money."

    "To do the added work effectively, you need an increase in the departmental budget."

6. It is Monday morning, and you have promised to have a draft report ready for your supervisor to look at. The truth is that you had some distractions over the weekend and you don't have the draft ready. You consider trying to get your supervisor to agree to a new deadline by asking

    a) an open question

    b) a closed question

    c) a loaded question

    d) a hypothetical question

    e) a two-part question

    Draft one question of each type. Which is likely to be the most effective? What response would you expect to each question?

7. Suppose that in some organization you belong to—such as a business, an athletic team, a social club, a student group, or a volunteer group—you have been asked to help hire a part-time employee. Create a list of four or five attributes needed to do the job well. For each attribute, create an open question for candidates that will help reveal whether they have that attribute.

8. Select a partner, and each of you take careful notes during a lecture you both attend. A day or week later, review your notes together. Do they still make sense to each of you? Did you miss any important points? Could they be better organized or laid out so that key ideas stand out from less-important details? Have you made any evaluative comments, personalized the ideas, or considered practical implications beyond those presented by the speaker?

9. Analyze the barriers to communication in the worst classroom in your school or the worst room in your office building. Compare these conditions with those in another area of your school or office where communication is easier and more effective.

Consider the size, shape, and colour of the room, as well as the lighting, seating arrangements, furniture, acoustics, and other influences.

10. Increasingly, businesses are aware of the importance of public relations and fostering a good corporate image. Examine the advertisements in a mass-market business publication (for example, *Canadian Business, Enterprise,* or *Report on Business*), paying attention to those that are not selling a specific product. Assess three or more advertisements. What do you think is the particular message of each ad, and what perceptions on the part of the reader is it trying to influence or correct?

11. Think of someone you have worked for in any organization (perhaps a business, a school, or a volunteer group). Analyze the effectiveness of communication between you and the other person. Consider these questions:

   ■ What direction did the flow primarily take?

   ■ How formal or informal was the communication?

   ■ How at ease were you in the communication and why?

   ■ How relevant was this communication to your concerns about the job?

   ■ To what extent did the organization foster good internal communication?

12. Give a three-minute oral presentation or write a few paragraphs discussing how one or more of the following changes might affect business communication, either inside the organization or with the public:

   ■ increased decentralization in business

   ■ increased business competition from China

   ■ greater job security provisions in contracts

   ■ affirmative action programs

   ■ promotion or recognition of multicultural goals

   ■ increased public suspicion of corporations

13. Select two people in the class who hold opposing views on an emotionally charged political or social issue, for example, private medical clinics, mandatory retirement, legalization of marijuana, or patients' right to die. Have them present their views to the class, and then have everyone write a brief assessment of the discussion. Compare your assessment with that of others in the class. Are there differences? Does the listener's own bias account for some of the differences? To what extent does this exercise reveal barriers to communication?

   Then select two more opponents to discuss a different issue. Listeners should merely summarize the side of the argument they least agree with. Compare summaries. Are the differences fewer or greater than in the first part of the exercise? Why? To what extent does the tendency to evaluate interfere with the listening process? In what business situations might this tendency hinder effective communication? What are the possible remedies?

14. Singly or in a group, through research or visits, compare the process of communicating in a fairly small company (up to 100 employees) with that of a large one. Consider the downward, upward, and lateral flow of communication. Try to draw some conclusions about the different communication needs in a large organization as opposed to a small one.

15. Think of a possible improvement in your program or work site. Consider why it matters. Reflect on a potential objection from the person you want to address it to. Then write a short email message that makes your case to a specific boss or person in authority.

Strategies in Planning for Writing and Speaking

2

"The most effective messages are those crafted with the audience foremost in your mind. I try to think about what the people I'm talking or writing to know of the topic and how I might make my message useful to them."

—Jane Peverett, corporate director and former CEO, British Columbia Transmission Corporation

The Importance of Planning

In business, mistakes in communicating can have dire consequences. Hardly a week goes by when we don't hear or see how a slip of the tongue, a tasteless remark, or poor wording can cause havoc in the lives of politicians, corporate leaders, and other public figures. The ease of sending incriminating information via email and blogs means that slip-ups can instantly reach a wide audience. And you don't have to be a senior executive to get caught in this negative exposure. Even within an organization, bad news seems to spread faster than good news.

Planning can help you avoid many of the risks of poor communication. It makes sense, then, to give forethought to what you are communicating. Planning is especially important if you are writing. In ordinary conversations you can afford to be spontaneous, since the instant feedback of the person you are talking to allows you to correct any mistakes immediately. An angry or skeptical look, or even a raised eyebrow, will point the way to changes. With formal oral presentations you need to prepare carefully, but at least the audience's reaction helps you gauge the impact of what you are saying.

Writing does not give you that kind of instant feedback. Since correction is more difficult once a message has been delivered, it's important to try to avoid misinterpretations beforehand. Careful attention to planning and editing is your best insurance against misunderstanding. Rather than dashing off the first thing that comes to mind, think of writing as a three-stage process in which planning, drafting, and editing receive equal time.

Even though email messages are usually short, they are a common source of misunderstanding. Because they are so easy to send, we tend to write them very quickly. Less time to write can often mean more time to regret. Whenever you are tempted to respond quickly, especially when you are angry or frustrated, give yourself a grace period before you click "Send." If you can, sleep on an emotionally charged message. If it cannot wait, at least take the time to consider the effect of your message on the person who will receive it and on the long-term relationship you may have to maintain.

Much of the advice on planning in this chapter, and on drafting and editing in later chapters, is directed at writing, but it can apply as well to formal speech. Chapter 9 will focus specifically on formal oral presentations.

Putting Communication into Context

Watch
BCVL: Business Etiquette

It's useful to think of business communication as presenting a problem for which there may be no single solution. As a communicator, you will often have to choose from a variety of options. To decide wisely, consider the context of your communication, as outlined in Figure 2-1. Ease your way into the task by asking the most basic questions first: What is the reason for communicating? Who will be the receiver? What is his or her environment?

Considering the Reason and the Desired Result

Explore
Letter 23: Giving a Negative
Performance Review

Business communication usually has one of two general purposes: to inform or to persuade. However, in devising an initial strategy you need to be more specific about your reason or reasons for communicating. Failure to do so has resulted in many unsuccessful exchanges—the sales agent who describes the features of the product but forgets to ask for the order; the customer service clerk who sends a requested refund but annoys a customer in the process; the job applicant who, in listing qualifications, inadvertently supplies ready-made reasons for being turned down. In figuring out exactly why you are communicating, remember that you may have more than one purpose, in which case you need to distinguish the primary reason from the secondary ones. Here are some of the most common reasons why people in business communicate with others. Some are action oriented, geared to a specific business objective, while others have more to do with getting a general response from the receiver:

- to ask for or give information
- to explain (whether a new company policy or a drop in revenue)
- to issue instructions
- to advise or recommend

Figure 2-1   Basic Communication Process

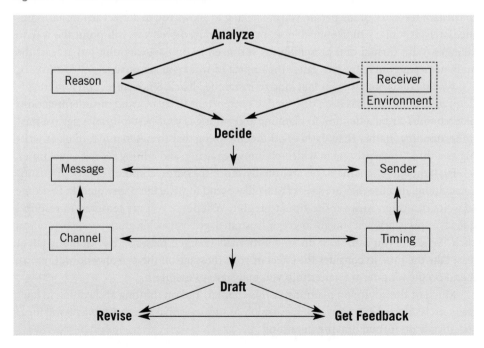

- to create a record
- to persuade (whether in a sales pitch or a job application)
- to thank or congratulate
- to foster an atmosphere of goodwill
- to improve the company's image
- to create a good impression of oneself

In considering the reasons for communicating, go beyond what you want to do and focus also on the result you want from the receiver. Unless your writing is a matter of pure record keeping, you usually want the receiver to do something—to act, decide, or approve—or simply to think in a certain way. Before you begin, try completing this sentence: "As a result of this communication, the receiver will . . ." and list all the results you want.

As you will see later in this chapter, determining specific reasons and desired results helps you decide how to focus and organize your message. It helps both you and your reader to avoid wasting time on unimportant details or irrelevancies. Anticipating receiver response also helps you word your message so that it creates the impression you want and doesn't foster misunderstanding.

Assessing the Receiver in Context

Socrates' prescription for understanding is first to "Know thyself." For business communication, that wise dictum might be amended to read, "Know your audience." The most frequent and serious of all mistakes in business correspondence comes from an incorrect or inadequate assessment of the receiver. Too often people communicate as if to thin air or to some faceless machine, or else they assume that the receiver will think the same way they do. As a result they produce letters or reports that are *writer based* rather than *reader based* and speeches that miss their mark with the audience. (Flower [1993] discusses these terms in detail.) Don't fall into this communication trap; spend time assessing your receiver. And since people don't exist in isolation, consider also the environment, or context, which may influence the receiver's response. Ask yourself the following questions:

1. **How will the receiver benefit?**   In a routine memo, the benefit may simply be that the reader will be better informed, but in correspondence in which you are making suggestions you need to figure out specifically what benefit there is to following your proposal. By pointing out the benefit, such as increased savings, higher profits, or improved company morale, you have a better chance of interesting the receiver in what you are saying—and of getting results.

2. **What is the receiver's position and responsibility?**   Is he or she your superior, your subordinate, or an associate? Considering the receiver's position may help you decide the level of formality to use. Determining the exact area of responsibility will help you decide the kind of detail to include.

    Suppose you have an idea for a new product and want to sound out others in the company about its feasibility. Clearly you would want to have a different emphasis and a different set of questions for the marketing manager than for the plant manager or the controller. Where one person would be most concerned with potential markets and sales, another might be concerned with production problems or costs. In the same way, if you are composing application letters you should stress different aspects of your qualifications, depending upon the different responsibilities of the people who will receive them.

3. **What is the receiver's knowledge?**   Considering this question will help prevent you from being either condescending or confusing. Most business people have a specialized understanding of certain aspects of their business. If you give them information that they already know, you may annoy them. It would be condescending for a surveyor to write to a lawyer, "A survey by a registered surveyor has legal authority," or for a manager to send a memo to a new assistant saying, "I require my letters to be properly formatted and free of typographical errors." (The manager should speak to a new employee anyway, rather than send a memo.)

On the other hand, avoid "bafflegab"—giving receivers information they will not understand or issuing instructions they will have difficulty following. Technical experts frequently make the mistake of giving highly specialized information to managers who are confused by it and, as a result, often get annoyed. By thinking about the receiver's field and level of knowledge before you begin, you will be better able to decide what technical or specialized information you should include.

4. **What interests and concerns the receiver?**   It's not necessary to play psychoanalyst here, but do use your practical understanding of human nature and of the particular reader to establish what will create interest or concern. How will the receiver likely react to your information or suggestions? Is he known as a stickler for details or as someone who is impatient with particulars? As someone impressed by creativity or nervous about quick change? Will an older employee feel threatened by the ideas of a young "upstart"? What specific objections will the receiver likely raise?

5. **What is your experience with the receiver?**   If you have dealt with the receiver before, you can benefit by recalling what was positive or negative in the relationship. You can try to avoid potential areas of friction and repeat what worked. Occasionally, you might even decide to send correspondence elsewhere.

A junior employee in an auditing firm learned this lesson early in her career. She had a manager who was repeatedly critical of her inattention to details. When she wrote a memo to him presenting an imaginative idea for saving time on a large auditing account, he dismissed the concept with the comment that she was just trying to avoid detailed work again. Some time later, she presented the idea to a different manager, who both accepted the idea and offered her high praise. The moral is that past experience can colour thinking and influence the reception of a message.

Past experience may also be company experience. If you are trying to collect money owed, for example, you should see if the creditor has been delinquent with prior payments and what the response has been to previous appeals. Similarly, if you are writing a promotional letter to customers, you should find out how they reacted to earlier promotions.

6. **What is the receiver's environment?**   Diverse cultural backgrounds create different expectations. In our multicultural society, with its growing international trade, understanding the receiver's cultural environment will reduce the chance of friction in communication. Although one cannot become an instant expert on other cultures, being aware that there are differences in business communication styles will at least help you avoid the arrogance of assuming that others will or should react as you do.

The political and economic climate can also shape communication needs. Widespread public concern about pollution might affect a report to a manager on the purchase of new machinery. An economic downturn, or the threat of one, might shape a sales letter to a customer or an internal proposal for an expensive acquisition.

Understanding the broader environment of the receiver can in many instances make a dramatic difference to the effectiveness of communication.

7. **Will the correspondence reach secondary readers?**   In some cases, a secondary reader can assume major importance. For example, a performance evaluation may become a lawyer's weapon in a lawsuit for wrongful dismissal. An internal report on a chemical spill might somehow find its way into a press exposé of pollution. "Be prepared" is the best motto. Consider who *might* read the communication as well as who definitely will read it.

    Again, emails pose a special danger. Even between close associates in your workplace, never assume that emails are private. Although they may be deleted, they can usually be traced. Forgetting this warning can have far-reaching consequences. Recently in the news we have seen that traced emails have led to lawsuits and even criminal convictions. An email that goes astray and reaches an unintended recipient can ruin a friendship or even a career.

    In situations where confidentiality matters, remember that what you write down, whether in a paper document or an email, has a long life.

It may seem that this detailed list of questions is too elaborate to bother with. In fact, getting a precise fix on the context of the communication task is really not very time-consuming. With a routine letter or memo to a familiar associate, you will gauge your receiver quickly. Even if the task is more complex, you will soon discover that spending a few minutes considering these questions will prevent false starts and discarded drafts—or unwanted results. Your analysis will help you create receiver-based communication that gets results (see Figure 2-1).

Deciding on the Sender

You may not always be the best person to carry out the communication, even if you are responsible for handling the issue. You need to decide whether you are the person most likely to get the desired results from a specific receiver. Would a superior have more influence? Or would an associate with different experience have more credibility? You may decide in some instances to have someone else write or speak, or you may draft correspondence that will go out under another person's signature.

Choosing the Best Timing

Sometimes it's a good idea to delay awhile. You may be in a hurry to get results, but the receiver may be immersed in other matters. For example, a president worried about giving an important report to the board may not be instantly responsive to your latest marketing idea. Employees in the midst of a layoff process may not react favourably to a motivational memo.

With some tasks, you may even decide to create a sequence of correspondence over a set period of time. The process of collecting delinquent bills usually follows such a sequence.

Whatever the communication, timing can affect its chance of success.

Selecting the Channel and Medium

⊙–Watch

BCVL: Technology and the Tools of Communication

There are no hard and fast rules about which channel of communication to choose. Whether you should speak or whether you should write depends on the context. Decisions about communicating, either to an individual or to a group, may depend on the personalities of the people involved. Nevertheless, it's possible to establish some guidelines based on common sense.

You write when

- you or the reader wants a record of the communication
- you don't need an answer but are simply supplying information
- the receiver is preoccupied with other pressing matters
- the information is complicated or detailed
- it's difficult or impractical to arrange a meeting or a telephone conversation

You talk when

- you want to encourage discussion
- you need a quick response
- you want to foster a personal relationship
- you want to build group rapport
- you are dealing with a personal or sensitive matter

Aside from whether you write or speak, the particular medium you choose can affect how others receive your message. The term *medium* overlaps the term *channel* but usually has a more specific meaning, referring to the technologies used for communication, for example, email, meeting, video conference, telephone, or memo. When Marshall McLuhan said, "The medium is the message," he may have overstated the case, but no doubt the choice of medium influences how messages are interpreted.

One way of attacking the problem of choice is to think about the "richness" of the medium, that is, the number of different ways a message can be relayed or reinforced. For example, a telephone is a richer medium than a newsletter because the receiver can listen to the tone as well as the words and can question the sender. Similarly, television is richer than radio because it permits seeing as well as hearing. Lengel and Daft (1988) have suggested that the more nonroutine the information, the richer the medium you should use. As Figure 2-2 shows, a memo will work well for a routine message, but for news about plant layoffs a face-to-face meeting is better.

Figure 2-2   Choosing the Best Medium

Media Richness		Message Type
Highest .... .Physical presence (face-to-face)		.Nonroutine
↑ .... .Interactive media (telephone, video conference)		
.... .Personal static media (memos, letters, email, tailored computer reports)		↓
Lowest .... .Impersonal static media (flyers, bulletins, group email, generalized computer reports)		Routine

*Adapted from Lengel & Daft (1988).

Considering the Proper Tone

Although tone is one of the subtler aspects of communication, an inappropriate tone can certainly cause problems. Tone is the emotion or attitude that is conveyed by voice or language. In everyday conversations with people we know well, we probably unthinkingly use a variety of tones, and our friends are probably not upset if we're occasionally sarcastic or irritable. But with business colleagues we do not know as well, we need to be more careful—especially in a letter, where lack of instant feedback rules out quick correction. The following guidelines will help you set the proper tone.

BE COURTEOUS

The fundamental rule of business communication is to adopt a courteous tone. Your letters, memos, and reports can quite properly have other characteristics, such as enthusiasm or pride, but courtesy is the foundation. Even if you are angry for good reason, you will be more effective if you don't make discourteous remarks. What does *courtesy* mean? A number of synonyms come to mind—*consideration, politeness, tact*—but perhaps the common feature of them all is sensitivity to the feelings of others.

Consider the following memo, sent by the manager of a restaurant to the employees:

✗ This is to tell you that you shouldn't talk to other employees about nonbusiness matters while you are working. Surely you realize that a lot of trivial chattering is inappropriate business behaviour.

If you want to keep your job, limit your unimportant conversations to the times when you are on a break. Pay attention to customers when you are working and the restaurant will be more profitable.

If you were one of the employees, what effect would this memo have on you? Would you react differently to a more courteous version such as this?

✓ Keeping our customers satisfied is the most important element in running a successful and profitable restaurant.

We provide a long lunch break to enable members of our workforce to enjoy some leisure time and look after personal concerns.

Please remember to give our customers your undivided attention during work hours, as we depend on them to keep "Herrington Court" busy and prosperous.

Benjamin Franklin knew the importance of courtesy. Renowned as an international diplomat, he once said, "You catch more bees with a drop of honey than with a pint of gall." In businesses where you will be dealing with people you don't know well, it can be hard to undo the damage of impolite, belittling, or sarcastic comments. When you are working with people of different ages, personalities, and backgrounds, you will avoid offending anyone if you treat everyone with courtesy.

CHOOSE THE RIGHT LEVEL OF FORMALITY

Although courtesy is the basis for a pleasing tone, you also need to decide the appropriate register, or level of formality. A moderately informal tone is usually best for business correspondence as well as business presentations, but not always. Occasionally a very informal tone can work well—though you should think twice before littering your correspondence with slang expressions.

Consider this notice, written by an employee in a large company. At his suggestion, management has recently provided employees with an exercise room and changing areas, but maintenance staff are now complaining that the mess in the men's changing room adds to their workload. Recognizing that the people using the facility are mostly young employees like himself, he posts this message on the changing room door:

✕ Guys, this locker room sucks! It's getting so you can't see the floor, and the place stinks!

 The Maintenance Department is freaking out, and if we don't get our act together, I won't be surprised if management does a number on us and closes the joint. So don't trash it—stash it or take it home and wash it!

The writer uses an informal, slangy tone because he wants to be a "buddy" rather than an authority—but not all of the male employees are young, and others might be offended by his locker-room humour. A safer message could still use an informal tone but avoid the slang:

✓ We're lucky to have these excellent new facilities, but we're in danger of losing them if we don't take care of them.

 We've been creating extra work for the Maintenance Department by leaving clothes and equipment lying around.

 Let's keep our changing room respectable so we don't lose our privileges.

The trouble with slang is that it is usually short-lived; slang words move in and out of fashion quickly. Twenty years ago no one would have used terms such as "spin doctor" or "ezine," and in another 20 years these expressions may well be forgotten. Another problem with slang is that it is often limited to a certain age or cultural group. What is common among 20-year-olds may be misunderstood by 60-year-olds. Moreover, the slang of Vancouver may be different from the slang of Montreal or St. John's. For most business writing, therefore, you should try to stay away from slang.

At the other extreme from slang is highly formal language. Some writers adopt an overly elevated style when they are producing large or important documents that will be read by a number of people. They think that formality lends an air of authority to what they are saying, but they end up sounding pompous instead. In this departmental memo, a supervisor resorts to inflated language in an attempt to establish authority and sound impressive:

✕ The report attached hereto is considered by management to comprise the final recommendations devised by the Public Relations Committee.

 All staff are reminded that adherence to the procedures stated herein is considered mandatory in all circumstances.

The wording and tone of this memo make the message confusing, and the writer also runs the risk of alienating readers. The supervisor would communicate more effectively if he or she were to adopt a clearer, more informal tone:

✓ Our Public Relations Committee has published the attached report on advertising policy.

 Please pay particular attention to the eight recommendations on page 3, as they are effective immediately.

Unfortunately, writers who try to be formal in their language sometimes create an air of affectation instead. A great many formal reports are burdened with wordy, cumbersome prose. In short, they're deadly to read.

A guide for most business writing, therefore, is to avoid the extremes of formal and informal language. Choose a middle level, one that is moderately informal. For letters, emails, memos, and internal reports (reports sent to people inside your organization), be conversational. Choose the kind of language you would use if you were talking to an associate. Here are some tips for creating a conversational writing style:

1. **Stay away from old-fashioned words and archaic legalisms.**   In wrongly thinking that formality is the essence of good business writing and that old legal documents are the model to copy, one businessman regularly began his letters: "Your favour of the 28th received and contents duly noted, and in reply to same would state . . ." Nowadays such an opening is pretentious and affected as well as being virtually incomprehensible. Business writers should stay away from words such as *heretofore* and *aforementioned* and expressions such as *duly noted, the undersigned,* and *in reply to same.* A good rule of thumb is to avoid opening and closing statements beginning with words ending in *ing* ("referring to your letter"; "trusting you will agree").

2. **Use personal pronouns.**   Business communication is often boring because it is impersonal; we don't know which person is behind the idea or action described. The writer may say "it could be argued" or "a decision was made" rather than "I would argue" or "we decided." Similarly, students sometimes scrupulously avoid putting an *I* in any academic essays. If this is your habit, it's best to change it, except for certain kinds of formal reporting. In your everyday business correspondence, use personal pronouns freely. Refer to *I, me, you,* and *we,* as you would in conversation. Personal pronouns emphasize that communication is between people rather than faceless automatons:

✗ A discussion of sales figures for the appliance division will take place on Monday.

✓ We plan to discuss the sales figures for your division on Monday.

You is the most important pronoun of all. As you will see in Chapter 4, it focuses attention on the reader rather than the writer, heightening the reader's interest.

In trying to avoid personal pronouns, many writers slip into the habit of using expletives—putting *it is* or *there is* at the beginning of a sentence. Occasionally these are efficient phrases, but more often they add clutter and dullness and may make your message unclear. See if you can eliminate them.

✗ It is hoped that all supervisors can attend the meeting.

✓ I hope you can join us at the meeting.

✗ There are two ways to recover the costs.

✓ You can recover the costs in two ways.

3. **Use contractions.**   Just as you use contractions in speaking, except on the most formal occasions, it's appropriate to use them in business writing when you want to establish an informal rapport. In your letters and memos particularly, consider writing *can't* rather than *cannot, it's* rather than *it is, I'm* rather than *I am,* and *we're* rather than *we are.* This advice holds only if you feel natural with these contractions. If the occasion is more formal than the usual business communication, or if your writing seems peppered with apostrophes, use contractions more sparingly. In any case, if you write in a way that is as natural to you as possible, you're likely to put your reader at ease.

Some businesses or institutions may require you to write more formally at times, for example, when you're writing a report for another company or when you're preparing a

Figure 2-3   Characteristics of Different Levels of Formality

Formal Tone	Moderately Informal Tone	Very Informal Tone
sounds solemn	sounds conversational	sounds chatty, familiar
can use archaic or legalistic phrases	avoids archaic and legalistic phrases	can use slang
avoids individual names	uses individual names	uses individual names
avoids personal pronouns	uses personal pronouns	uses personal pronouns
avoids contractions	uses contractions	uses contractions
uses complex sentences	uses shorter sentences	can use point form or sentence fragments

formal policy paper. If that is the case, you may have to disregard some of the guidelines for informal writing listed above. Specifically, you may have to

- avoid contractions, since these give writing a chatty quality
- avoid individual names, since the focus is more likely to be on policies or procedures— on the requirements themselves—than on the individuals who work with them
- avoid first-person pronouns. Keep in mind, however, that *I*-free reports are becoming less common since they often produce passive, convoluted writing. Chapter 8 on formal report writing discusses this problem and suggests alternatives.

Figure 2-3 compares a formal tone with a moderately informal and a very informal tone.

 # Internet Issues

Perils of Pauline: Using Email Effectively

Rapid changes in technology mean that the best way of communicating today may be surpassed by a new type of medium tomorrow. Generally the advances have not only increased the ease of communicating but also reduced the cost, and exploiting the possibilities of new technology can increase our effectiveness as communicators. Like other forms of writing, electronic communication should observe certain guidelines:

1. **Consider the medium.**   Remember that email, although it is fast and efficient, is asynchronous—it does not occur in "real time." Although this has its advantages—for example, it eliminates the frustration of telephone tag—it does not allow us to pick up on verbal cues or to create tone through inflection or gesture. In personal email messages you may choose to use emoticons like smiley faces to convey humour. However, these symbols do not have a place in most business correspondence. In all but the most casual notes, you need to observe the principles of good writing to create an appropriate tone. Be careful not to "flame" (express a strong opinion or criticism) or "shout" (create emphasis with uppercase expressions), as this might be misinterpreted in a "cool" medium such as email. If you are in doubt, you may want to use a different medium such as a telephone call or a face-to-face meeting to convey your message.

2. **Begin by addressing the recipient.**   With its emphasis on speed, email can often sound abrupt and impersonal. Always take the time to personalize your message and create a link with your reader.

3. **Maintain privacy.**   If you are sending a message to a group of people, you may want to put individual recipients' names in the blind carbon copy (bcc) field so that their identities are not revealed to others. In addition, although it is quick and easy to forward a message, never do so without the author's permission. And, most importantly, don't send confidential messages via email as you cannot guarantee their privacy.

4. **Maintain your email credibility.**   Don't be guilty of "spamming"—sending unsolicited advertising messages or junk mail—as this is a major violation of cyberspace etiquette.

5. **Be clear.**   Whatever the new developments, one thing is certain: technology cannot make a muddled message clearer or an annoying one more pleasing. You will always need to consider carefully what you send as well as how you send it.

Exercises

1. Compare two advertisements for different brands of the same kind of product (for example, cars, liquor, shampoo, perfume, soap). Analyze the intended reader, the message, and the tone of the ad as well as the effectiveness of its words and images in creating its appeal.

2. Assume that you want to start your own small business and are looking for some start-up money. You plan to create a written proposal. Think of two different types of people you might approach and do a receiver analysis for each, based on the questions suggested in the section "Assessing the Receiver in Context." (You might, for example, approach a personal loans officer, a wealthy friend, or a relative.) What are the implications for the way you would write each proposal?

3. Which communication channel and medium would you choose in the following situations? Discuss the advantages of your choices.

   a) You have an idea for a new promotion but are not sure how it fits into the marketing manager's plans.

   b) You want department heads to know of modifications in procedures for laying off unsatisfactory employees.

   c) You are the recent replacement for an autocratic manager in a department where morale is low. You want the employees to know about your priorities.

   d) You suspect an employee of padding his expense account.

   e) You want to know whether supervisors in five different departments can attend a planning meeting on Friday at 9:00 a.m.

   f) As assistant to the president, you have received a favourable offer to buy a warehouse your company has for sale. Either the president or the chief financial officer needs to sign the offer-to-purchase document but both are attending a convention at a large hotel in another city.

   g) You want to reduce the expense accounts in a department you've been put in charge of. Most of the employees have been there for many years.

   h) Your plant manager is preparing for a visit from head office executives and you need to give him recent sales figures.

   i) Two new factory employees are producing work of inferior quality; they will be laid off if they do not improve.

   j) You discover racist jokes on the washroom wall and suspect that one or two of the employees working for you are responsible for them.

   k) As the office manager, you receive complaints that a calendar on an employee's office wall is offensive.

   l) As manager of the Sales Department, you want to congratulate your staff since the department surpassed sales targets for the month by 50 per cent.

   m) Your employer's specifications for a construction job are too vague to allow you to proceed confidently.

4. Revise the following sentences so that the tone is courteous and conversational:

   a) There will be considerable cause for concern if the billings are screwed up by the Accounting Department with respect to our most important client.

b) Although I hate to disturb anyone who is sleeping, it would be a pleasure to have our order filled by your department on time for a change.

c) If the girls in Human Resources want prompt payment for overtime, they should come to visit me on the fourth floor before Friday.

d) With respect to your letter of August 9, please be advised that you neglected to send the camera, which prevents us from assessing your allegations of poor performance.

e) Mr. Miller, that customer must be on crack—but let's touch base about how to sweet-talk him so he doesn't call it quits.

f) Pursuant to my previous memo of the 28th, the new instructions for the photocopying machines should henceforth be duly distributed not only to supervisors in the Marketing and Sales departments but also to all personnel using the aforesaid machines.

g) Since I'm busy with important matters, instead of having our usual weekly meeting just let me know if your department will have the page proofs ready on time for a change.

5. For each of the following sentences, assess the level of formality on a scale of 0–10, with 0 being extremely informal and 10 being exceedingly formal. In each case, rewrite the sentence using a register that you consider to be appropriate in a business setting:

a) With reference to your request, an extension to your warranty has been arranged.

b) This no-good boss of mine is definitely out of the loop.

c) If you think our service stinks, why don't you get lost?

d) It is imperative that this conundrum be resolved by Tuesday.

e) It is the opinion of the regional managers, upon close perusal of the document, that the duration of the warranty has indeed expired.

f) If you keep being so sloppy and think you can stay on the payroll, you can forget it.

g) The utilization of maximum precaution in the sanitization of any culinary utensils is forthwith mandatory.

h) Okay, you guys, let's get our butts in gear and get back on schedule before the boss goes ballistic!

i) The intention of this document is to ensure that we minimize communication problems and ensure optimum service to our clients.

j) I wish the manager would just chill and take a pill.

6. Revise this impersonal email message from a senior human resources manager so that it has more personal pronouns. What is the effect of the revision?

It is important to note a change in the dental plan for all Tricorp employees. As of July 1, there is an opportunity to recover 50 per cent of the cost of orthodontic work. Details are set out on the attached form. The eligibility extends not just to employees but also to their spouses and dependants.

This improvement in benefits reflects the company's continued interest in the well-being of its workforce.

7. Fill in the blanks with words or phrases close in meaning to those provided, according to the level of formality in each column.

Formal	Moderately Informal	Slang
expired	died	_____
domicile	_____	place
_____	sick	under the weather
regurgitate	vomit	_____
converse	_____	rap
disorganized individual	messy guy	_____
reprimand	_____	blast
_____	help	give a hand
tiresome	boring	_____
purloin	steal	_____
_____	crazy	wack
intoxicated	drunk	_____
_____	fired	canned
acquiesce	agree	_____
wealthy	rich	_____
sycophant	flatterer	_____
fabrication	lie	_____

Notice how quickly slang becomes dated and how moderately informal words are usually the plainest and most familiar.

8. Here is an example of a formal invitation to be sent to business clients. Change it to a moderately informal email invitation for a prereception lunch on the same day for members of the firm.

John H. Charlesworth, LLB,
Senior Partner,
requests the honour of your presence
at a reception
to celebrate the fiftieth anniversary
of Holden & Gunn
on Thursday, June twentieth
at six o'clock
in the Empire Room, Regency Hotel.

R.S.V.P.
Grace Philips
(905) 924-3289

9. The External Relations Committee of your college has agreed to help raise funds for visually impaired residents in the community by undertaking a charity car wash on Saturday and Sunday afternoons. Despite some publicity, only a few students have volunteered to help so far.

   Three members of the committee each draft an email to all students to encourage greater participation (see below). If you were the head of the committee, which one would you pick? Analyze all three and give specific reasons for selecting one and rejecting the others. Take into account the intended receiver and reason for writing as well as tone and wording.

   a) People have to take responsibility in this world. Taking part in the college's charity car wash this weekend is the way to show that you are a responsible member of society. It should be brought to your attention that volunteer work is not something you get paid for but something you contribute to others. Having a lot of studying to do or essays to write is really no excuse for not helping those who are less fortunate, such as the blind in the community. Become a responsible member of society and join the college charity car wash! Sign up today! Give to the blind!

   b) After all the trouble the External Relations Committee has taken to organize the charity car wash for this weekend, it's indeed depressing that so few students have volunteered to help. The car wash is the most important function of the committee this year, and it can make an inestimable contribution to the disabled in the area. We have put in a lot of hours to arrange it, so get off your duff and help! The participation rate in this college is the pits. Do something about it and volunteer! We need more bodies! We need you!

   c) The charity car wash is our college's way of helping the blind people in the area. By giving just a few hours of your time on Saturday or Sunday afternoon this weekend, you can support the college and support the blind. We need more volunteers to fulfill our commitment to raise funds. Please help! Join the car wash team. Give a few hours and have the satisfaction of helping others in this community. We need you—and so do they!

10. Jie Chan works in the Promotion Department of a Calgary toy manufacturing company trying to establish itself in western Canada. Last year, before joining the company, she staged a skating show in the city, with the proceeds going to the local Society for Special Needs Children. Since the show had a sellout audience of 4 200 and netted $30 000 for the charity, the society has asked if she will produce the show again in April. Jie thinks she needs a week off work to do the job properly. Her supervisor suggests that she email the general manager, Philip Donaghue, asking the company to donate a week of her time to the show. Although Jie doesn't know him well, she is aware that the manager has a marketing background and a good eye for business opportunities.

   a) Create a point-form assessment of both the reason for writing the memo and the intended reader.

   b) Based on your assessment, evaluate the following draft of the memo:

To:	Philip Donaghue, General Manager
From:	Jie Chan, Promotion Department
Subject:	Company Donation to Skating Show
Date:	January 10, 2011

Last year I produced a successful skating show in Calgary, which wowed the crowd. You may be interested to know it made big dollars for charity: $30 000, to be exact.

I've been asked to produce another show in April for the same charity—the Society for Special Needs Children. Since I would have to work like a dog to do the show properly, I would like to have a week's paid leave. Obviously it is a worthwhile cause and will benefit disabled children. I'm sure you realize that business has a responsibility to contribute to society as well as make a profit.

Please let me know your decision as soon as possible.

c) Rewrite the memo, following the strategies discussed in this chapter.

11. Consider how a business leader or public figure, or even someone you know personally, has been a victim of poor communicating. What were the consequences? What might the instigator of the communication have done differently?

PEARSON mycanadianbuscommlab

Visit www.mycanadianbuscommlab.ca for everything you need to help you succeed in the job you've always wanted! Tools and resources include the following:

- Composing Space and Writer's Toolkit
- Document Makeovers
- Grammar Exercises—and much more!

Writing with Impact

Learning Outcomes

This chapter of *Impact* will help you to

1. understand the principles of plain language;

2. use simple, concrete words when you write;

3. be concise and specific in expressing your ideas;

4. use active verbs to create forceful, energetic writing;

5. avoid jargon and clichés;

6. write well-constructed sentences;

7. construct clear, well-developed paragraphs;

8. compose clear, well-written email messages;

9. write effective Web documents.

"There is a risk in the enormous volume of information we are required to communicate today. It has therefore never been more important to focus on the audience and be clear, concise, and timely in distilling the key messages."

—Bev Park, president and chief operating officer, Couverdon Real Estate

Since business writing is practical, an effective business style is not fancy but functional. It's simple and straightforward. Some writers deliberately fill their writing with exalted terminology and elaborate phrases, thinking that such a style will make them seem more intelligent or sophisticated. Don't make this mistake. Complicated writing is often confusing and may make you seem confused. On the other hand, if your writing is lucid you will appear a lucid thinker. It follows that if you really want to impress your most discerning associates, you will begin by making your writing clear.

In Canada and around the world, a plain-language movement has gained momentum as businesses, employers, and legal and medical practices have recognized the need for clear communication. Plain language is language that your reader can easily understand. It saves time and money because it communicates the message without the risk of confusion or misunderstanding. Whether you are describing a procedure, giving directions, writing a report, or training staff, you need plain language to communicate effectively. Increasingly, manufacturers have recognized the risks posed by instructions that are difficult to follow or labels that don't communicate clearly to consumers. Businesses can't afford to put employees at risk through badly written safety procedures or lose clients as a result of communication problems. Today, banks are holding plain-language workshops to improve their customer relations, and government agencies are sponsoring plain-language programs and publishing plain-language guidelines on websites. In the business world, plain language creates efficiency and economy—an obvious asset in today's competitive and fast-paced environment.

Readers infer writers' personalities from their writing styles. A ponderous, boring writing style suggests, rightly or wrongly, a ponderous, boring person. Conversely, a lively style suggests a lively person. If you, like most people in business, want to create the impression that you are energetic and forceful, you should try to develop an energetic, forceful style. Such a style is especially suited to management, where vigour and decisive action are virtues. In any business, you will clearly make more of an impact if you write with impact.

Good writers can elicit a positive response or win support for their ideas by expressing them with energy and conviction. How can you give your writing this kind of impact? Consider the following suggestions.

Choosing Clear, Concise Wording

In selecting words, it's worth remembering the difference between the dictionary meaning of a word (its **denotation**) and the associative meanings or range of suggestions it calls up (its **connotations**). The words listed as synonyms in a thesaurus do not always mean the same thing. Some words have positive or negative associations, while others are more neutral. For example, the adjective *economical* is grouped in a thesaurus with *cost-effective*, *efficient*, *cheap*, *profitable*, *frugal*, and *prudent*. But who wouldn't prefer to be called "frugal" rather than "cheap"? Take care, therefore, that the subtle shadings of the words you choose get your message across.

Below are some strategies for choosing words that communicate effectively.

Using Plain Language

Through the centuries, English speakers have adopted and adapted a great many words from other languages, especially French and Latin. Yet the most common words in the English language are usually the oldest. The words children first learn are derived from the same Anglo-Saxon stock used for more than a millennium. Whether we recognize the reason or not, we usually choose these words for our conversations, since they seem most natural. Plain English words are also generally short—another good reason to use them.

By contrast, a lot of foreign derivatives, even if they have been in our vocabulary for years, still feel less natural. This is not to suggest that you never use an unusual or long word. Used occasionally, an uncommon word can be effective. Nevertheless, a string of them will make your writing seem artificial or pretentious.

French derivatives, for example, may give an aura of class. Every copywriter knows that you sell a fine wine by its bouquet rather than its smell and a perfume by its fragrance. Every ad for upper-level real estate seems to mention residences with foyers rather than houses with front halls. Even if you consider yourself a plain "meat and potatoes" kind of person, you surely would feel inelegant at a restaurant if you asked for pig rather than pork (from *porc*) or cow rather than beef (*boeuf*). The point is that in business writing you may choose French-based words or expressions for a particular effect, but you will generally avoid a lot of them if you don't want to seem phony. Notice the natural, direct quality of the words in the second column, compared with those in the first:

French Derivatives	Plain Language
request	ask
desire	want
assist	help
endeavour	try
dine	eat
pursue	follow
commence	begin

You should also avoid a lot of Latinate words. Even if you have never studied Latin, you will recognize Latinate words by the attached prefixes (such as *pro, anti, ante, sub, super, ad, ab, ex, con, pre*) or suffixes (*ism, ent, ate, ite, ise* or *ize, tion*). Such attachments are useful in science, since they add precision to the description of structures and processes.

(Think of common scientific verbs like *evaporate, crystallize, react, ingest, absorb,* and *liquefy*; or noun forms like *condensation, magnetism,* and *coagulation.*) Even in a formal but non-scientific context, the occasional Latinate word can add a feeling of scholarly dignity.

The trouble comes with too much: writing that is full of Latinate words is dense and difficult to understand. Business people who want to appear scientific often mistakenly fill their writing with unnecessary Latinisms and nearly kill their meaning (to say nothing of their readers). Unfortunately, the Latinate disease is spreading, but you should try not to catch it.

1. **Be wary of newly formed** *ize* **words** (or *ise* words, if using British rather than American spelling), for example, *incrementalize, prioritize, sensitize, finalize, operationalize, optionalize.* Although words like *maximize* and *minimize* have taken such firm root in our vocabulary that they are unlikely to be weeded out, it's a good idea to use plain language substitutes when you can.

Latinism	Plain Language
finalize	finish, complete
operationalize	start
maximize	increase
optionalize	allow choice
prioritize	rank
utilize	use

2. **Avoid lengthy nouns that end in** *ion* **and are formed from verbs,** especially when the verb has an *ize* ending. Notice how the wording in the three columns becomes progressively more complex—and weaker—through the use of Latinisms:

Plain	Latinate Verb	Noun Form
order	systematize	systematization
toughen	desensitize	desensitization
start	operationalize	operationalization
make aware	familiarize	familiarization

    Increasingly in the working world, we converse with people whose first language is not English. Simple language can help avoid misunderstanding.

Using Concrete Language

In business, we often need to discuss complex concepts such as economics, profitability, inflation, solvency, management, leadership, responsibility, and security. These are abstract terms, because we cannot discover them through any of the senses. We understand them only through intellect. By contrast, what is concrete we can see, hear, touch, or smell. For example, we cannot grasp "insolvency" through the senses, but we can see or touch "an empty wallet" or "an empty till."

Our ability to reason allows us to generalize—to think abstractly. But since concrete words are more sensuous and need little intellectual effort to be understood, they make reading easier and more vivid than a string of abstractions would do. To explain moral concepts, Jesus used parables—stories about individual people. Similarly, ancient philosophers often used analogies—comparisons with familiar situations—to make complex ideas more accessible. Economists, too, use analogies—"guns and butter" or "bread and cheese"—to demonstrate economic principles.

What is the guide for business writers? Use concrete language wherever you can. If you have a choice between an abstract word and a more concrete one, choose the concrete. When you do need to use a lot of abstractions, balance the mix through examples, analogies, or illustrations. This is one instance when a few words added to your writing will improve it.

Eliminating Clutter

Watch
Grammar Video Tutorial: Wordiness and Redundency

Just as removing deadwood in a forest makes the remaining trees stronger, getting rid of dead or useless words makes sentences more vigorous. Wordiness weakens. Thin out common cluttering phrases, such as the following, or omit them altogether:

Cluttering Phrases	Alternatives
at this point in time	now
due to the fact that	because
with regard to	about
it is possible that	maybe
it is probable that	probably
as a matter of fact	actually
for the purpose of	for
in the near future	soon
consensus of opinion	consensus
in accordance with	as
on the occasion of	when
in the eventuality that	if
when all is said and done	(omit)
in all likelihood	likely
on a regular basis	regularly
in view of the fact that	since, because
be of the opinion that	think, believe
until such time as	until

Using Adjectives and Adverbs Sparingly

The shotgun approach—scattering modifiers in the hope that one will hit the mark—rarely works. One well-chosen adjective or adverb is more effective than several closely related ones:

✕ He proposed an extraordinarily daring and bold procedure.
✓ He proposed a daring procedure.
✕ Her campaign was imaginative, original, and creative and thus was highly acclaimed.
✓ Her innovative campaign was highly acclaimed.

Qualifying or intensifying adverbs should also be used sparingly. Strange as it may seem, *very* or *extremely* in front of an adjective is usually less forceful than a precise adjective by itself. "She is an imaginative person" packs as much wallop as "She is a very imaginative person"—and it avoids the risk of sounding overdone. Qualifiers such as *rather* and *quite* are also often unnecessary. Why say "rather costly" when you mean "costly," or "quite effective" when you mean "effective"?

Be ruthless with redundant adverbs. *Very unique* or *completely finished* makes as much, or as little, sense as *rather bankrupt* or *quite dead*.

Being Specific

To keep readers from having to second-guess you, be as exact in your words as you can be. You can often replace vague, "all-purpose" verbs such as *involve, concern,* and *affect* with ones that are not as open to misinterpretation. In addition, use specific names, dates, times, and amounts to increase the clarity of a message. Admittedly, when you are referring to a group it may be impractical to list each member or item. When you have a choice, however, be specific rather than general:

✗ We are concerned about the environmental factors that affect two provinces.

✓ We are worried about (or we are studying) the acid rain that threatens the lakes of Ontario and Quebec.

✗ Management is concerned that your costing expert be involved in the planning process for the renovation.

✓ Hugh Willis wants your costing expert, Sheila Moore, to do estimates for the renovation.

✗ Since you were involved in the report, I'd be interested in knowing about it sometime.

✓ Since you prepared the report, please call me next week to discuss it.

✗ Aitlin had a significant rise in sales recently.

✓ Aitlin's sales have increased 10 per cent in the last six months.

Remember also that the pronoun *this* or *it* must refer to a specific noun. Writers often use one or the other in a vague way, so that it is unclear what exactly the reference is. Here is an example:

✓ We completed the project this week by working until late Friday night and by bringing in an extra technologist. This pleased our client.

What does "this" refer to?

✓ Our extra effort pleased our client.

✓ Our client appreciated our promptness.

Using Active Verbs

Verbs are the most energetic of words. Writers known for their forceful style usually use only a light sprinkling of adjectives and adverbs, but a variety of strong, specific verbs. The relative energy of the four main types of words can be charted:

strongest ◄─────────────────────────────────► weakest

verb   noun   adjective   adverb

Moreover, an active verb has more energy than a passive verb, as the terms themselves suggest. With an active verb, the subject does something as an active agent:

The engineer **discovered** that the casing was faulty.

We **decided** to sell our shares.

I **expect** an upturn in the bond market.

With passive sentences, the grammatical subject does not act but is acted upon. Sometimes a human agent is missing or buried in a modifying phrase. It's not always clear who does what:

The faulty casing **was discovered.** (Agent missing)

It **was decided** that the shares would be sold. (Agent missing)

The faulty casing **was discovered** by the engineer. (Agent in modifying phrase)

An upturn in the bond market **is expected** by us. (Agent in modifying phrase)

If your writing seems flat, it's probably filled with passive verbs. Try replacing most of them. Use active verbs to create "whodunit" sentences, in which the subject *has done*, *is doing*, or *will do* something.

Passive verbs *are* appropriate in four instances:

■ When the focus is on someone who is the victim or unwilling recipient of an action:

The workers were let go when the plant was shut down.

■ When you want to emphasize the thing acted on rather than the person acting:

The unsafe machine must be replaced.

■ When you want to avoid an awkward shift of focus in a sentence or paragraph:

When fumes seeped into the cafeteria, they were first noticed by the cashier.

■ When you want to avoid placing blame or seeming accusatory:

The bill hasn't been paid.

Unless one of these exceptions applies, use active verbs.

Choosing Verbs over Noun Phrases

Nouns, although stronger than adjectives and adverbs, are still less dynamic than verbs. Writing that is heavy with noun phrases can be a burden on the reader. Try replacing noun phrases with verbs for a more energetic style:

✗ Since they had an expectation of higher profits, the managers made a decision in favour of increased remuneration for the workers.

✓ Since they expected higher profits, the managers decided to pay the workers more.

As well, avoid clusters of nouns used as adjectives. In this instance a reordering, even if it adds a word, will make understanding easier.

✗ employee benefits payroll deduction forms

✓ payroll deduction forms for employee benefits

✗ plant energy conservation project

✓ project to conserve plant energy

Avoiding Jargon

Most areas of knowledge have special terms that help experts communicate with each other. The terminology allows them to say quickly and precisely what they mean without having to resort each time to definitions or explanations. Scientists in particular rely upon technical terms, as a doctor does when describing a patient's medical condition to a colleague. The difficulty comes when people unnecessarily use jargon—complicated or unfamiliar terms—perhaps in an attempt to appear scientific or sophisticated. Rather than clarifying an issue, they obscure it.

Here's an example:

✕   Should you require clarification regarding new procedures in your department pursuant to recently adopted policy changes, further information can be provided upon request to the director's office.

Here's a plain language revision:

✓   Please contact Beryl Smith's office if you have any questions about how the new policy will affect your department.

People in business sometimes make the mistake of cluttering their writing with jargon to demonstrate their "insider knowledge." Instead of following this approach, remember that the brightest minds are those that can simplify a complicated issue, not complicate a simple one. The guideline is straightforward: use specialized terms if they are a kind of short form, making communication easier. Avoid jargon when plain English will do.

Avoiding Clichés

Clichés are truths so well worn they are threadbare. Originally, many of them were colourful metaphors or similes, but through overuse they have lost their power. How does one determine what has become a cliché? If someone can supply the ending to a phrase, the phrase is a cliché. Apply this test to the following passage:

> At this point in _____, when inflation again threatens to rear its _____ _____, it goes without _____ that government spending should be curbed. In point of _____, the nation as a whole should tighten its _____. Of course, this is easier said _____ _____. It stands to _____, however, that those in the government corridors of _____ should lead the _____. If they take drastic _____ to nip spending _____ _____ _____, then slowly but _____ our economic health will be _____. With all due _____, those economists in their ivory _____ who encourage government deficits must beat a hasty _____. Otherwise, without a _____, inflation will again increase by leaps _____ _____. There is no time like the _____. Government must strike while the iron _____ _____ to restore the faith of Canadians in a land of _____. If our leaders do not act, we will all suffer for generations to _____.

If a politician were to give this speech, we'd pity the listeners.

As well as being tiresome, some clichés are redundant. Sadly, many of these redundancies find their way into business writing:

mutual agreement	advance planning
end result	serious concern
future prospects	genuine opportunity
serious crisis	each and every
best ever	all-time record
exact same	first and foremost

Writing Clear, Effective Sentences

Making Important Ideas Stand Out

👁‑[Watch
Grammar Video Tutorial: Sentence
Fragments

👁‑[Watch
Grammar Video Tutorial: Run-on
Sentences

One good way to make writing forceful is to emphasize important ideas and de-emphasize unimportant ones. You can achieve this kind of weighting in several ways.

1. **Place key words in strategic positions.**   The most emphatic parts of a sentence are the beginning and the end. Writers often naturally put a key idea at the beginning of a sentence, since this is the usual order of speech. It's less natural, but often more effective, to put a key word or phrase at the end. Notice the difference in impact between the following two sentences:

✗ The hydro contract will be a moneymaker, despite our early concerns.

✓ The hydro contract, despite our early concerns, will be a moneymaker.

In the first sentence, the key word, "moneymaker," is buried in the middle. The second sentence ends with more force.

When a word or phrase is taken out of its usual place and put at the beginning, it becomes more noticeable. When put at the end, it gets even more emphasis, especially if set off by a comma or dash. Compare these three sentences:

She usually gets along with the manager.

Usually she gets along with the manager.

She gets along with the manager—usually.

2. **Subordinate unimportant facts—or those you want to hide.**   Put a fact you want to stress in an independent or main clause (one that makes sense by itself) and put one you don't want to stress in a subordinate clause (one that makes sense if attached to another).

In the following example, you avoid drawing attention to increased costs by putting them in the subordinate clause and the positive news, new clients, in the main clause:

✓ Although the advertising cost more than we anticipated, it brought many new clients.

If you put both facts in independent clauses, they will have equal stress, as in this sentence:

✗ The advertising cost more than we anticipated, but it brought many new clients. (Two independent clauses are joined by a coordinating conjunction.)

It's generally a mistake to put a "negative" fact in the main clause and a "positive" one in a subordinate clause, unless you want to stress the negative.

✗ Although the advertising brought many clients, it cost more than we anticipated.

3. **Enhance important information.**   Using upper case, italics, or boldface to make key words stand out is the simplest trick of all. (Note that italics has replaced underlining in print material today.) Used sparingly, these typographic features can be an effective way of stressing information. However, don't use them as a substitute for other, less intrusive ways of creating emphasis.

4. **Use contrast.**   Just as a jeweller emphasizes the sparkle in gems by placing them on dark velvet, so you can highlight your points through contrast. Read this unadorned sentence:

   ✕   We won this contract through hard work.

   Now consider the impact of this contrast:

   ✓   We won this contract not through luck but through hard work.

   Similarly, compare the force of these two sentences:

   ✕   The machine keeps breaking down because of faulty operators.

   ✓   The machine keeps breaking down, not because of faulty parts but because of faulty operators.

5. **Use repetition.**   The rhythm created by repeating a key word or phrase can build the drama of a sentence. Because of the emotional force of this device, it should be reserved for special events or issues:

   To reach our profit target, we analyzed the product, we analyzed the market, and we analyzed the competition, but most of all we analyzed our own method of managing.

6. **Vary sentence length.**   Short sentences are emphatic. Long sentences, which meander gently, winding their way to a conclusion, are more reflective. In earlier days, when reading was largely confined to the leisured classes, readers were accustomed to extended sentences that would weary the typical reader today. The average sentence length 200 years ago was about 50 words. Responding to the need to transfer information quickly and easily, good journalists and good business writers now favour shorter sentences. Experts today recommend an average sentence length of 15 to 20 words.

   A block of long sentences may put your reader to sleep. On the other hand, if every sentence is short, your writing may seem immature, like the staccato prose of a child's reader: "Look at Jane. See her jump." The moral? Check for variety when you are editing a passage, and break up blocks of long sentences. For special emphasis use a very short sentence, occasionally even a sentence fragment. Like this.

Making People the Subject

Remember the "personality principle": we relate more to other people than to objects or abstractions. Newspaper editors know that human interest stories attract attention. Readers turn to a story about a particular laid-off worker before reading a statistical analysis of unemployment. A picture of a starving child has more impact than any abstract discussion of food shortages. Similarly, if you refer to individuals, your business writing will be more interesting:

✕   We met two supervisors last night.

✓   We met Susan Arthurs and Harry Jones last night.

   or

✓   We met the supervisors, Susan Arthurs and Harry Jones, last night.

For greater stylistic impact, try to make people the grammatical subject, so that it's clear who has been doing what.

✗ It was discovered that staggered hours were unacceptable to our supervisory staff.

✓ We discovered that our supervisors did not want staggered hours.

Business writers trying to be objective sometimes begin a sentence with an impersonal "it is" or "there is." Although these phrases, called expletives, can be useful, they more often contribute to lifeless prose. Where it's easy to do so, avoid them.

✗ It is necessary for her to arrange new financing.

✓ She needs to arrange new financing.

✗ There are several remaining options for increasing office space.

✓ Several options remain for increasing office space.

Avoiding *Which, Who, That* Clauses

A string of clauses beginning with *which*, *who*, or *that* can make a sentence seem cluttered. In many cases these clauses can be reduced, often to a single word:

✗ The shops that are damaged will be renovated by two carpenters who are unemployed.

✓ The damaged shops will be renovated by two unemployed carpenters.

✗ The two proposals, which were outlined earlier, will increase staff in the departments that have employees who are overworked.

✓ The two proposals, outlined earlier, will increase staff in the departments with overworked employees.

✗ The data that were received last month should be published by the Information Technology Department on the company website.

✓ The information technology team should post last month's data on the website.

Creating Logical, Well-constructed Paragraphs

Paragraphs are difficult to define because they have so many shapes and sizes. They are needed, however, to help the reader follow the development and shift of ideas. These guidelines for creating paragraphing will help you maintain a sense of clarity and order in your writing:

1. **Create a new paragraph for a change in idea or topic.**   Paragraphs develop and frame ideas. By creating a new paragraph, you signal to a reader that you have finished developing one idea or an aspect of it and are switching to another. Of course, it is possible to outline several ideas in a single paragraph—for example, if you are briefly listing a number of reasons for some action. If you discuss an idea at any length in a paragraph, however, you should create a new paragraph when you move on to another idea.

2. **Make the first sentence the main point.**   The human mind prefers order to disorder and always struggles to make sense out of an array of facts. If you immediately provide that order by stating the key point first, the reader (or listener) can more readily fit together the particulars that follow. The assimilation of information is easier.

Read the following paragraph. Notice that the main idea is at the end. Although this indirect order is perfectly reasonable, the busy or impatient reader will more readily catch the drift of the paragraph if the last sentence becomes the first one.

From 1990 to 2010 in Baytown, the percentage of our citizens over 65 years of age doubled, and demographic analysis suggests that this trend will continue. Many seniors live lonely, isolated lives. Over a third are on small pensions and living below the poverty line. Our municipal government should assume more responsibility for identifying the particular needs of our seniors and coordinating services for them.*

We need a coordinator of Seniors' Services for Baytown to help improve the quality of life of our older people.

Admittedly, not all paragraphs in good prose have a beginning key point or topic sentence; nor does every topic sentence have to appear at the beginning. In creating a persuasive argument, for example, you may want to lead indirectly to the key idea by starting with particular facts and later pulling them together with a general statement. Yet for most of your business writing, begin each paragraph with the main point. Do a quick check on the sequence of paragraph beginnings in your writing. If you get a clear idea of the line of your thinking, your writing will likely seem well ordered and logical to other readers.

3. **Vary paragraph lengths.**   The trend in business writing is toward short paragraphs. They look less dense than long ones and are more inviting to read. Follow this trend and avoid long paragraphs. When you see a chain of long paragraphs (each more than eight or ten lines), try splitting some at an appropriate spot. On the other hand, a string of one-sentence or two-sentence paragraphs can make your writing seem choppy and undeveloped. Clearly, a single-sentence paragraph can effectively begin a letter or call attention to an idea, and short paragraphs are appropriate for news releases and brief correspondence. However, for reports or other complex discussion, the ideas need more development if they are to be accepted. Typical ways to develop an idea in a paragraph are by

- illustrating the idea
- classifying the parts
- revealing cause or effect
- giving a solution to a problem
- comparing or contrasting with another idea

Of course, you may want to take more than a paragraph for any of these methods of expansion, but make sure that your paragraphs go beyond a simple point to a discussion of that point. If readers have commented that you need to explain your ideas more fully, the list above provides good ways to do so.

Good writing in business usually comprises a range of paragraph lengths, from short (two or three sentences) to moderately long (seven or eight sentences), with most paragraphs somewhere in between. When considering your own paragraphs, try for variety; it's as much the spice of writing as of life.

4. **Keep the focus.**   Some paragraphs may not seem focused, even though the sentences are all on one topic. The reason may be that they are constantly shifting the grammatical

subject. Notice the difference in these two paragraphs (the grammatical subjects are in bold in each):

✗ Business **analysts** have noted the different ways managers operate. Sometimes all the **decisions** are made by a manager, and **employees** are given orders or procedures to follow. The success of this kind of manager is not long-term, since leaders are not developed as potential successors. The opposite **type** is the manager who avoids making decisions, tending to delay by forming committees and requesting endless studies. **Managers** of this sort are also not effective. **Employees** find themselves between these extremes with managers who encourage their participation in planning. **Responsibility** for making the final decision remains in the bosses' hands. **These** are effective managers.

✓ As business analysts have noted, modern **managers** have different ways of operating. **Some** tend to make all the decisions, giving employees orders and procedures to follow. In the long term **they** are ineffective since they do not develop leaders who can succeed them. Other **managers** avoid making decisions, tending to form committees and request endless studies. **They** are also ineffective. In between these two extremes are **managers** who encourage employees to participate in planning, but who take final responsibility for decisions. These **managers** are effective.

The second paragraph is clearer and easier to read because it is better focused; more of the grammatical subjects are the same—managers.

You may wonder: If the grammatical subject is always the same, how can a paragraph not be boring? Here are two tips, both followed in the second paragraph above:

■ Use substitutes such as **pronouns** and **synonyms** to avoid repetition of the subject. An example is the use of "some" and "they" to replace "managers" in the example above.

■ Put something in front of the subject. Although the grammatical subject is most often at the beginning, it can also come later in a sentence. Putting a word, phrase, or clause in front of the subject ("As business analysts have noted," "in the long term," "in between these two extremes") makes the subject less noticeable.

5. **Link the ideas.**   Some words and phrases have a linking function, signalling to the reader the relationship between different parts of a sentence. They provide the logical connections and transitions between ideas. Correct use of the common linking words and phrases listed below will help make your paragraphs clearer and more coherent.

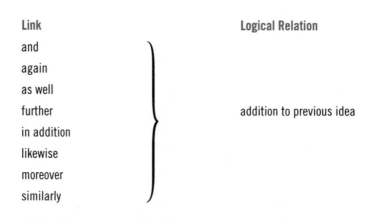

Link	Logical Relation
and	
again	
as well	
further	
in addition	addition to previous idea
likewise	
moreover	
similarly	

as a result of because since owing to	explanation of previous idea (cause and effect)
although but yet by contrast despite even so however in spite of nevertheless on the other hand rather	change from previous idea (reversal)
accordingly consequently for this reason hence so therefore thus	summary or conclusion

Numerical signals, such as *first*, *second*, *third*, are also useful linking words.

Editing with Care

◉⊣Watch
Grammar Video Tutorial: Using Style and Grammar Checkers

What "correct" means is sometimes open to dispute. Acceptable grammar and punctuation are really conventions or customary practices; the way educated people speak and write over a period of years and throughout a wide area becomes known as "standard" English. Although the standard gradually changes and will continue to change, following a standard is useful in business writing. It enables people from a variety of areas and backgrounds to understand one another readily. Most of the rules of grammar and punctuation are a way of making sense—of communicating efficiently.

While correctness is an important part of good writing, if you are constantly worried about corrections when you sit down to write you may freeze at the switch and have difficulty getting started. A solution is to forget about grammar, spelling, or any kind of mistake and simply get your ideas down on the page. Many experienced writers find that working straight through the first draft is the best way to begin. Only after they've finished writing do they start revising and editing. This method will help you avoid writer's block. You will have to leave a lot of time for editing and revision, however. Even if you revise as you go, you need to spend time editing.

A useful order for editing is to "start big and finish small." That means to begin with the organization and development of ideas at the paragraph level. Then move to sentence style and word choice as it affects the flow and vitality of your writing. Finally, check the mechanics of grammar, punctuation, and spelling, as well as the graphical elements—typeface, headings, and illustrations. By starting with the big picture rather than the details, you will better address the reader's first question, which is "Do the ideas make sense?"

The Appendix at the end of *Impact* explains the important rules of grammar and punctuation, providing examples and exercises. If your knowledge of the rules is scant or rusty, refer to the Appendix. You can also take advantage of your ears and eyes:

1. **Listen to what you say.**   Practise reading your work out loud in a firm voice. Listen carefully. Children learn language not by rules but by ear; writers also need to use their ears. If something doesn't "sound right" to you, chances are it will also be confusing to your reader. If you find yourself stumbling over a sentence, try to reconstruct it in a simpler way. If you have to catch your breath several times in the middle, the sentence is probably too long. Break it up. Reading out loud, although it takes more time than a silent skim, will make you a better critic.

    Reading aloud also helps you catch errors such as typos, agreement problems, and spelling mistakes because it forces you to slow down and really see (and hear) what is on the page.

2. **Do a spot check.**   Eyes are a second line of defence against sentence errors. Try to remember the kinds of mistakes you made in the past and check especially for them. If you learn to spot your mistakes when you are editing, you will soon find that you make fewer of them.

Internet Issues

Writing Email Messages

👁—Watch
Perils of Pauline: Using Email Effectively

The speed and efficiency of email sometimes results in slapdash messages that are poorly formatted and edited and consequently open to misinterpretation by the recipient. In the fast-paced environment of today's business world, it is tempting to send an email as soon as the message is on the screen, without properly checking for clarity, tone, format, and correctness. Try to develop a routine for email correspondence just as you would for other forms of written communication; remember that it takes more time to clarify a misunderstood message than it does to proofread and revise it before you send it. Short forms that work in simple emails among friends, in text messages, or on Twitter aren't acceptable in business writing.

For routine business messages of a sentence or two, a quick proofreading may suffice; for more complex, lengthy, or important messages, consider these guidelines:

1. **Send the email to yourself first.**   Looking at it as the reader rather than the writer is often a useful exercise and allows you to see the effect of line division and formatting as well as possible editing problems.

2. **Print a hard copy before you send.**   Most people proofread with greater acuity from a printed page than they do from a computer screen. Taking the time to print a copy of your message might save you the embarrassment of sending an email containing

typos. Remember, too, that reading aloud will help you make corrections since you are relying on two senses instead of one.

3. **Don't forget to use paragraphs.**   We have all had the experience of trying to wade through long emails that are written as a single paragraph. Remember that a new paragraph, onscreen as well as on paper, is a visual cue to your reader and makes your message easier to read.

4. **Be wary of trends such as the use of Internet acronyms, abbreviations, and emoticons.** You'll frequently see acronyms such as LOL (laughs out loud) as well as abbreviations like WRT (with regard to) or emoticons such as the smiley face :-) or its opposite :-(in chat rooms, social networking messages, and text messages. Participants use them in an effort to convey their intended tone or attitude toward a subject under discussion. Although these shortcuts may have their place in informal messages, avoid using them in a business context. Rely instead on your good writing to communicate your intended meaning.

Writing for the Web

Writing for an online audience requires special care, as most readers find reading online more difficult than reading print. Estimates suggest that our reading speeds are 25 to 50 per cent slower for online documents than for printed material (Goldsborough, 1999). Consequently, keep online documents short—50 per cent shorter than their print counterparts, one study suggests (Mitternight, 1998).

Since processing electronic text is more taxing, readers tend to scan rather than read the text word by word. This scanning tendency creates a real challenge for the writer, who must be sure that the message is clear. Here are some tips for writing online documents and messages:

1. **Use key words** that alert readers and communicate information to them quickly. Make sure you avoid abstractions and jargon.

2. **Keep sentences short,** using vertical lists and bullets as visual cues to help the reader process the material.

3. **Create short paragraphs,** organizing the text in chunks to help the reader "see" the content of your message.

4. **Present the material graphically** by using headings to divide the information into sections, which are easier to process than large blocks of type.

These practices for electronic documents will reduce the demands placed on your readers and ensure that your message gets through.

Exercises

1. Suggest plain English words or phrases for these more elaborate ones:

proceed	edifice	attempt
signification	equivalent	approximately
indisposed	inalterable	equitable
accumulate	expedite	beneficial
humorous	facilitate	domicile
materialize	reimburse	occasion
conceptualize	sufficient	inform
construct	transmit	remuneration

2. The meaning of a word depends in part on its associations for the receiver. The same word, therefore, may not have exactly the same connotations for everyone.

   Reorder the following groups of adjectives so that the words that for you have the most positive connotations come first and those with the most negative connotations come last:

   a) eccentric, strange, weird, unusual, individualistic

   b) strong, determined, domineering, confident, aggressive, tough

   c) subdued, meek, shy, reserved, retiring, nonaggressive

   d) rash, daring, venturesome, audacious, headstrong, impetuous

   e) cunning, shrewd, artful, wily, astute, sharp, sly

   f) sensitive, warm-hearted, sentimental, soft-hearted, impressionable, perceptive, thin-skinned

   g) firm, steadfast, stubborn, inflexible, fixed, uncompromising

   h) curious, inquisitive, inquiring, prying, nosy, thirsty for knowledge

   i) courteous, polite, refined, soft-spoken, obsequious, ingratiating

   j) talkative, fluent, verbose, eloquent, chatty, glib, long-winded

3. Revise the following sentences, replacing many of the Latinisms, unnecessary noun phrases, and jargon with plain language:

   a) It is incumbent upon our sales representatives to make overtures of a positive nature to prospective clients prior to the finalization of their respective sales forecasts.

   b) In accordance with managerial policy, any intensification of effort on the part of employees leading to a maximization of production will be met with commensurate compensation.

   c) It is the decision of supervisory personnel that, with respect to employees, attendance charts will be maintained on a monthly basis.

   d) It should be noted that greater utilization of the company manual, which provides an outline of factory hazards, will have as a consequence an improvement in our safety record.

e) We would be obliged if you would give an indication of the parameters of the delivery problem so that we can interface with suppliers about this strategic matter in the interest of effectuating an improvement.

f) At this point in time we do not have plans under consideration for the termination of employees, but the bottom line is that in this period of decreased economic activity the profitability factor must have top priority.

g) All employees should endeavour to familiarize themselves with the new fire regulations so that personnel can be mobilized with due haste should there be an occurrence of fire in the vicinity of our offices.

4. Rearrange the following sentences so that something appears in front of the subject:

a) We cannot afford to hire a new secretary this month.

b) I finished the report last Friday and sent it to be photocopied.

c) She is very good at selling, despite her quiet manner.

d) We should be able to complete the assessment by June 30 at the latest, and possibly even earlier.

e) I plan to stick with my quote, whether or not it is underbid by competitors.

f) I was selected, along with three other supervisors, for the special project team.

5. The following response to a report was written by a highly trained business manager. In groups of three:

a) record the time it takes to read the paragraph and understand its message;

b) underline all the words with prefixes and suffixes, except those suffixes showing tense (*ing* and *ed*);

c) rewrite the paragraph in plain language. Exchange your group's revision with another group's and compare the time it takes to read and understand the revision with the time it took to do the same with the original.

> While the initial study committee has made a skilful and in-depth analysis of the alternative resource mixes as they relate to the proposal in question, the optimal functions as selected by the committee's thematic projections would suggest a nonaffirmative response if the executive office were forced to make an immediate decision. In view of the paramount importance of the multifaceted aspects of the proposal, it is my recommendation that a special task force be created with the assigned responsibility of appropriately developing sound administrative options to the proposed implementation decision. Reliable and tested administrative procedures would enhance the practicality of the proposal and add to the incremental viability factors essential for the type of creative innovation that functions within established guidelines.

6. From any publication, pick two or three paragraphs in which the wording is murky and difficult to understand. Try revising them. (You may want to look at business, legal, educational, or sociological articles—or government publications.)

7. Use appropriate *transitions* (linking words) to join each group of sentences into a single sentence.

a) Many brides insist on a lavish white wedding.

Forty per cent of marriages end in divorce.

b) The client was late.

Appointments started to back up.

The supervisor had to see some clients herself.

c) I enjoy coffee.

I get really tired when I drink too much.

It keeps me awake all night long.

d) You get a headache when you use your computer.

You should have your eyes tested.

e) Sadie is a conscientious worker.

She does not always solve problems effectively.

She is not very creative.

f) Ahmed is a very good student.

He gets terribly nervous during tests.

He gets poor marks at the end of term.

g) You faint at the sight of blood.

You aren't a very good candidate for medical school.

h) Leslie really likes going to movies.

It costs her a fortune every time she goes.

She usually ends up watching TV instead.

i) There was an attendance policy in effect at the college.

Students were inclined to miss classes on Fridays.

The teachers decided to have all of their exams and tests on Friday afternoon.

j) The lawyer decided not to represent his client.

The client told his lawyer that he had murdered his girlfriend's husband.

8. The following paragraph has blank spaces where linking words or phrases would be useful.

a) Read the paragraph aloud as it now is.

b) Fill in the blanks with appropriate logical connectors.

c) Read the paragraph aloud again and note the difference in coherence.

d) Not all the blanks need to be filled. Consider which ones benefit most from logical connectors—those signalling added information, explanation, reversal, or conclusion.

> We need more entrepreneurs, _____ they are the great job creators in our economy. _____ many people who say they would like to start their own business are really dreamers. They have an urge to open a restaurant, an antique shop, or a travel agency, or even to produce some new household product _____ they are unlikely to act. _____ many of those who do try to get going haven't really determined the unique service or benefit they would provide in order to compete successfully. To be an entrepreneur isn't easy. _____, you need an idea that will sell. _____, you need expertise in the area. _____, you need to work long and hard for little initial return. If you have doubts about your idea, you

will probably have difficulty selling it to customers or clients. _____ you will probably have difficulty raising the necessary capital. _____ if you are confident in the idea, and have the competence, discipline, and drive to carry you through the rough beginnings, you will probably succeed.

9. The following paragraph is well focused, but it is boring because so many sentences start the same way. Revise it by substituting pronouns or synonyms for the subject or by putting something in front of the subject.

> The Excalibur photocopier has many advantages. The photocopier is fast, producing a page in half the time of our present one. The photocopier can print in colour, unlike our present one. The photocopier is reliable as well, and has a six-month warranty on parts and service. The photocopier produces high-quality reproductions so that much of the work we now send elsewhere could be done here. The photocopier will therefore have paid for itself in a year. The Excalibur photocopier is, in my opinion, the best buy for our needs.

10. In each of the following sentences, decide which of the two independent clauses should have the main emphasis, and then change the other clause to a subordinate one. For extra emphasis, try putting the main clause last.

    a) The safety inspector came, and we stopped work.

    b) I have worked outdoors, but I have no experience as a forest manager.

    c) He didn't have anywhere to stay, and I invited him home.

    d) The costings are accurate, and they are later than anticipated.

    e) She is disciplined and hard-working, and I think we should hire her.

    f) He will welcome your opinions, and he must decide himself.

    g) I got a raise, and I will take you out to dinner.

    h) The report was badly organized and difficult to read, and it did not please Mr. James.

    i) In reports prepared for me, I expect careful work but I am not a nitpicker.

    j) You will learn a lot, and you may be under a lot of pressure working for Ann Hall.

11. Vary the position of the boldfaced word in each sentence to give it more emphasis. (In some sentences you may have to alter the wording slightly.)

    a) John found that firing incompetent employees was the most **distasteful** of all the jobs he had to do.

    b) In the end, he convinced the workers by his **actions**, not by his words.

    c) Most members of our team respect Mary's **ability**, whether or not they like her sharp tongue.

    d) When the firm was small, our work seemed more **stimulating**, because we were always doing a variety of tasks.

    e) Mr. Marks is clever, but he is a pompous **bore** in his speeches, I think.

12. Reduce the relative clauses beginning with *which*, *who(m)*, or *that* in these sentences:

    a) The boy whom we saw yesterday is one of the applicants for the job that was advertised on Sunday.

    b) The project that is most important this week is the proposal for the government contract that Lee hopes to get.

   c) I hope that the errors that we made in the report will not have repercussions that will be serious.

   d) That woman, who wore a leopard skin coat and large hat that matched, drove a red sports car that had a convertible top.

   e) I'm sure that the problem, which is complicated, will finally have a solution that is simple.

13. In the following sentences, put active verbs in place of the nouns ending in *ion*, or any other nouns:

   a) Boris made a suggestion favouring the acquisition of a new coffee machine.

   b) There is a recommendation from the investigator favouring the continuation of payments to the centre.

   c) Our hope is that the introduction of fitness programs by the company will bring about an improvement in employee health and a reduction in absenteeism.

   d) It is the boss' expectation that, when we have an increase in the sales staff, we will have an increase in earnings.

   e) Now that I've made an arrangement for the installation of new carpets in the office, I have an inclination to get the walls painted.

   f) Despite the engineer's plans for the inspection of the building, his delays in the introduction of changes allowed a continuation in the deterioration.

   g) After an investigation of options, it is our intention to make a quick decision about the method of organization for the seminar.

   h) We have no indication that the lawyers have yet made an allocation of the proceeds realized from their settlement of the lawsuit.

   i) Although we asked for clarification and elaboration of the data by the controller, we made no attempt at verification.

14. Use simpler or more energetic substitutes for the phrases in bold:

   a) **It is our understanding** that the packaging division **maintains approximately** 10 chequing accounts; **it is recommended** that these be consolidated **at an early date**.

   b) **Subsequent to** our investigation, a report will be provided **for the purpose of** outlining procedures for **the procurement of** new equipment.

   c) **It is our opinion** that **in order** to **achieve a reduction in** overdue accounts you should require a deposit **in the amount of** 20 per cent **prior to** delivery.

   d) **In view of the fact** that the control checks **were not performed in accordance with** the **aforementioned** guidelines **on a regular basis**, our decision must be **held in abeyance**.

   e) **There are possibilities** for our delaying the contract **until such time as** we can **arrange a better allocation of** resources.

   f) **As per our discussion** last week, **it is likely** that we will **make a submission of** budgets **on a quarterly basis**.

15. Make the following sentences more forceful. Get rid of clichés and clutter (some of it jargon), and use personal subjects and precise, active verbs.

   a) It is to be hoped that our sales figures for the month of February will show a consistently steady improvement.

b) Considerable concern existed on the part of the directors that our expenditures would be in excess of revenue and that the end result would be bankruptcy.

c) June Briant was quite involved in the planning of our campaign and her contribution has been recognized by us as a factor in its success.

d) Due to the fact that permission has been granted by head office for employees to have an extra day of holiday over Christmas, Christmas parties for all departments should be completely restricted to hours not normally part of the working day.

e) The problem of employee dissatisfaction has been increased by the unwillingness on the part of the supervisor to conduct an investigation into the complaints made by employees with regard to ventilation.

f) If an expansion of the plant is to be made in the near future, the inclusion of day-care facilities should be a matter for immediate and serious consideration by management at the planning meeting that will be held in January.

g) At this point in time, there is a decision to be made by Jim about hiring a full-time accountant, in view of the fact that the work of the accountant who is part-time entails a considerable number of overtime hours.

h) An announcement was made in the speech of the president that the result of management's introduction of robots in the factory, which is scheduled for this year, will not be the termination of employees.

i) It is anticipated that the full total of the damage that was caused by the fire can only be assessed by engineers who are specially trained, but we have made a very rough guess of approximately $220 000.

j) If it is the immediate priority of the manager to effect an increase in sales, then it stands to reason that an interface session with key employees should be instituted on a regular basis to discuss the parameters of the sales effort.

k) There is a valid reason why the aforementioned trespasser, who was discovered by the security guard in the vicinity of the computers prior to the fire, was not submitted to a rigorous police interrogation using tried and true methods.

16. Identify any passive verbs in the following sentences and change them to active verbs. Rewrite each sentence using active verbs and eliminating any unnecessary wording so that each sentence is clear and concise.

a) It was felt by the members of the board that the financial crisis had been improperly handled by the company president.

b) The decision to close the Princess Street office was made by Jeffrey Johnson, and it is the opinion of the staff there that insufficient knowledge of the situation was made available to him at the time.

c) Last year's financial report was found by the auditors to be grossly inaccurate; consequently the treasurer was demoted by the company to the position of division manager.

d) There seems to have been a terrible mistake on the part of the directors in allowing the company to be bought by a large foreign corporation.

e) Charges were laid by Mrs. Maverick that concerned discrimination against her for religious reasons, but they were totally ignored by the Personnel Department.

f) The attendance policy was considered too harsh by the students, so it was decided by the teachers that a more lenient policy should be adopted by the college.

g) It was stated in the annual report by the directors that increased absenteeism on the part of the employees was to be monitored by the new Committee on Human Resources Management.

h) The reason I am writing you this letter is because the recent purchase of 100 computers by our firm has placed us in an insecure financial position that must be reviewed by management before further decisions regarding the spending of more money are made.

i) It was thought that Mr. Terry's absence was brought about by his frequent use of alcohol, but it turned out that he was advised by his doctors to remain at his place of residence for the remainder of the month.

j) Accusations were made by several female employees who said that overtly threatening remarks had been made to them by Mr. Harrison, but the charges were denied by the man who had been accused.

17. Jake Hardy has written this draft of a letter to a long-time friend and business associate, Martin Field. Hardy is replying to an invitation to a lunch celebrating Field's promotion to marketing manager at Warren Enterprises. In groups of three, discuss the weaknesses in wording and style. Improve the letter.

> Dear Martin
>
> Regarding your new job at Warren Enterprises, it's indeed a pleasure to learn that you are now marketing manager. In this day and age of cutthroat competition, it's extremely gratifying when a man of very great talent and tried-and-true ability gets his just deserts, so to speak.
>
> It's a genuine disappointment that I cannot be present at your celebration party, which will be held on Monday, the twelfth of July, due to the fact that I will be otherwise engaged at a meeting. The meeting, which has been scheduled since last month, is with a wealthy investor, who is from New York and who is coming here for the purpose of making an investment in a business. When all is said and done, it's to be hoped that the final result is worth the expenditure of effort on my part at this point in time.
>
> Let me repeat my regret at the impossibility of my presence on that occasion of joyous celebration. In my absence please extend my sincere best wishes to your better half.

18. The following sentences contain abstractions or generalized statements. In a sentence or two, help to clarify each statement or make it more vivid by adding a concrete illustration or example.

a) Pensioners suffer when inflation is high.

b) Many Canadian entrepreneurs have already penetrated the American market.

c) A country's deficit cannot keep increasing without causing severe problems.

d) The media have too much influence on the political process.

e) Expanding public transit makes more economic sense than expanding the road system.

f) We need more pollution controls to protect a deteriorating environment.

19. Consider the following paragraph. Where is the most important idea? Could it be placed in a different position? Ensure that the sequence of sentences allows a busy reader to easily get the point of the paragraph.

Our research has discovered that the Apex plants have outdated manufacturing processes. Senior management, which is highly centralized, autocratic, and secretive, has walled itself off from operations' employees, while allowing little local decision making. Not surprisingly, the employees are not highly motivated and the company has not been as productive or profitable as the competition. It makes little sense to invest in Apex until its processes and management have changed.

20. The following passage should contain more than one paragraph. Where would you begin new paragraphs?

Our department met yesterday to discuss the proposed language testing for all incoming students. The director and all language teachers were present, and the director began the discussion by announcing that he had budgeted $10 000 to purchase the test materials. It soon became clear that six out of eight teachers oppose standardized testing on the grounds that it creates a negative atmosphere in the classroom and causes unnecessary stress for students. They also argued that the test instrument is invalid; it tests vocabulary that our students never encounter and assesses reading ability on the basis of students' ability to recall factual information. More importantly, the test does not include a writing sample, which the teachers feel is the only reliable way to evaluate a student's writing ability. Despite their objections, the director will impose compulsory testing for all incoming students; in addition, he will institute exit testing within the next year. These unilateral decisions have created an atmosphere of resentment within the department and the teachers will be seeing the academic vice-president next week. I will contact you after that meeting to inform you of the outcome.

21. As a way of fostering community relations and of providing work experience for its art students, Metro College held some Saturday morning art classes for young children in the area. Below is the release form the parents were asked to sign before enrolling their children. Revise it, keeping in mind that the parents have varied cultural and educational backgrounds.

Release Form for Children's Art Classes

In consideration of the aforementioned child being permitted to participate in the aforementioned program, I, as parent/guardian of the said child, do hereby release and forever discharge and agree to save harmless and indemnify in full Metro College and all of its respective agents, officials, servants, and representatives, from and against any and all kinds of actions, causes of actions, claims, liabilities, costs and expenses, and demands, in respect to death, injury, loss, or damage, occurring just prior to, during, or subsequent to any part of the aforementioned program and whether on the premises of the Metro College or otherwise, to the person or property of the said child, howsoever caused, and arising out of the said child being permitted to attend or in any way take part in the program as a participant.

_____

Signature of parent/guardian   Date

By submitting this application, I acknowledge having read, understood, and agreed to the waiver release indemnification.

22. a) A manager drafted the following short message to his workers as part of a New Year's edition of the company newsletter. Try to improve it by getting rid of the clichés and clutter and making some of the points more concrete. You may have to add some details.

b) Rewrite the message as an email note to staff.

Times are changing and things aren't what they used to be. No longer are North Americans on top of the world with regard to business. The challenge from foreign parts is not to be taken lightly. Indeed, in the near future it may pose a grave threat to the livelihoods of countless people.

At this point in time, we must all bear in mind that profits are earned. Nobody owes us a living. Life is not a bowl of cherries. When all is said and done, if we're going to become number one in our business, we've got to keep our nose to the grindstone. Needless to say, I'm not pointing a finger at individuals, but have as my intention to spur us all on to greater effort as a team on a regular basis. I'm of the opinion that those of us in the seat of power and those who are not must join hands in an all-out attempt to become top of the heap in our business. As we face the New Year let us respond to this challenge. Victory is within our grasp!

PEARSON
mycanadianbuscommlab

Visit www.mycanadianbuscommlab.ca for everything you need to help you succeed in the job you've always wanted! Tools and resources include the following:

- Composing Space and Writer's Toolkit
- Document Makeovers
- Grammar Exercises—and much more!

Routine and Good-News Correspondence

"In the travel business, as in any business where customer service is critical, the ability to communicate well is an essential skill. It has contributed to my own success, and it's a skill I look for when choosing managers for our offices."

—Rob Dexter, chairman and CEO, Maritime Travel

Rapid developments in information technology have given us new choices for communication. Email, with its speed and efficiency, has become the most frequently used medium for routine communications within an organization. Furthermore, there has been a dramatic increase in the amount of email sent outside the company, since the Internet is relatively inexpensive and allows us to communicate almost instantaneously on a global level. Despite the rapid acceptance of email in business communication, however, some situations require a paper-based document, such as a letter or memo.

Where formality, legal import, or confidentiality matters, a paper copy remains the currency in many organizations. Normally, memos go to insiders but letters often go to people outside the writer's organization. Although the formats differ, the principles of organizing are the same. For simplicity, the discussion here will refer mainly to letters, but the advice applies equally to memos. Since "time is money" in any business, it pays to be able to write both letters and memos efficiently.

Different cultures have different conventions for letter writing. Layout, phrasing, and punctuation may all vary. As international trade expands, don't make the mistake of assuming that the way you are used to seeing business letters is the only way that is acceptable, even in countries where the language is English. Although the advice in this chapter applies to North American custom, when communicating with people on different continents be flexible in your attitude and sometimes in your approach. Even in North America, the trend in many types of organization is toward informality, unless there are legal issues at stake.

Letters

In all cultures, appearance matters. Just as people's looks often influence how they are judged, so the look of your letter will influence its reception. The quality of the paper, the typeface (or font), and the layout can all improve the look of your letter. For most business letters you should use good-quality white or ivory paper. The typeface can vary from letter to letter but should be consistent within each.

Elements of a Business Letter

A business letter has a number of components in a standard order:

1. **Company letterhead or return address.** When writing a letter for an employer, use stationery with the company letterhead. For personal business letters, key in your address at the top of the letter. The examples in Figures 4-1 and 4-3 illustrate correct formats for both types of letter.

2. **Date.** Figures 4-1, 4-2, and 4-3 show the correct placement for the date according to the type of letter you are writing.

3. **Inside address.** This element includes the reader's name, title, and company, and the full company mailing address. If you don't know all the exact details, including correct spelling of the reader's name, contact the company's human resources department to get the information you need.

4. **Attention line.** An attention line is useful when you're dealing with a particular staff member or department. It directs the letter to the appropriate person but indicates that others may also deal with it. The attention line typically precedes the salutation but may also follow it.

5. **Salutation.** "Dear _____" is standard. Wherever possible, use the person's name and courtesy title (Dr., Professor, etc.). This personal approach will help to establish a rapport with your reader.

   Here are some useful guidelines for determining an appropriate salutation in particular contexts:

   ▪ If you use an attention line, the salutation is determined by the first line of the inside address, not by the attention line. For example, a letter addressed to "Kovak Ltd." with the attention line "Personnel Manager" requires a plural salutation.

   ▪ When you don't know the person's name, as in the previous situation, you have a choice:

     – In a formal letter, you may still use the traditional "Ladies and Gentlemen" for a plural salutation or "Dear Sir or Madam" for a singular salutation, although these seem increasingly old-fashioned and awkward. Another option is to use "To Whom It May Concern," often seen in letters of recommendation.

     – In the case of a singular salutation, you may give the person's title or status: "Dear Personnel Manager" or "Dear Customer."

     – When addressing a group, you may omit "Dear" and begin with "Sales Representatives," "Colleagues," "Members," or any other common identifier.

     – You may also use a heading instead of a salutation, for example RECALL NOTICE or NEW PRODUCT.

   ▪ For a person whose gender is unknown to you, you may simply use the first initial: "Dear L. Jonas." Although less common, you may also use *M.* to cover both genders.

   ▪ For a woman whose marital status or preferred form of address is unknown to you, use *Ms.*

   ▪ A way out of all these difficulties is to use the **simplified style**, which omits the salutation and the complimentary close (see the example in Figure 4-2). Since this approach is impersonal, save it for a business letter with a routine purpose. For a sensitive matter, take the trouble to search out the name of the person you are addressing.

Figure 4-1   Full-Block Style on Letterhead

HARRINGTON DESIGNS INTERNATIONAL

1499 Bayview Crescent   **Ph: 406-289-4356**
Thunder Bay ON K4B 2E1   **Fax: 406-289-4360**

January 12, 2011

Centennial Gift & Supply
429 North Avenue
Orillia ON K7L 8H3

Dear Ms. Fung

It is my pleasure to welcome you as a Harrington customer. We are committed to providing you with our quality products and service and appreciate being selected as a supplier to a fine company such as Centennial.

We have established a credit account for you with the following discount rates:

Monthly Purchases	Discount Rate
$ 500–$ 999	10%
$1 000–$1 999	15%
$2 000–$2 999	20%
$3 000–$3 999	25%
$4 000 and above	30%

I am enclosing an account confirmation form for your signature. Please return it to us as soon as possible so that we may activate your account before the February sale.

Sincerely

Robert Judson

Robert Judson
Credit Analyst

Attachment
c Client file

Figure 4-2   Simplified Style

United Couriers

1721 Freeman Crescent Nanaimo BC K8L 3H5

January 18, 2011

ABC Design Group
22 Cherry Lane
Fredericton NB E7B 2F8

PACKAGING PROCEDURES

As requested, we are enclosing our guidelines for preparing items for shipment with United Couriers. You will notice that fragile items require special protective packaging. We have designed and produced our own crates and liners for the convenience of our customers, and we highly recommend their use for items of special value. Should you decide to use our customized packaging, please use the enclosed order form.

Beth Heaton

Beth Heaton
Office Manager

Enc.: 2

Phone: 614-289-2312   **uc@nnmo.net**   **Fax: 614-289-2313**

Figure 4-3 Personal Business Letter

275 Golden Mile Road
Victoria BC K4V 9X2
January 24, 2011

Mr. Sanchez Romero
Sales Manager
Fort Industries
100 King Street
Calgary AB K2T 4B9

Dear Mr. Romero

I am enclosing a cheque for $174.98 in payment for the following items listed in your January flyer:

• #2940	Quartet Display Board	$119.99
• #3685	MSP Presentation Case	$ 54.99

As agreed, I will pick these items up at your Elbow Drive location when I am in Calgary on February 4.

Would you please include a copy of your Spring Sales catalogue with my order.

Sincerely

Kiri Subramariyan

Kiri Subramariyan

Enc.

Phone: 614-555-2312   **abc@nnmo.net**   **Fax: 614-555-2313**

6. **Subject line.**   A simple heading in capital letters, such as RETIREMENT PARTY FOR JAN WEIMS, although optional, can quickly convey the focus of the letter to a busy reader. It can either replace the salutation or be put below or above it.

    Make the subject line as specific as possible. Instead of a vague reference, such as BENEFITS, say something like CHANGES TO DENTAL INSURANCE PLAN.

7. **Body.**   The body should be placed in the middle of the page. To achieve this balance, vary spacing between the parts—namely between the letterhead, date, and reader's name. In the case of a personal business letter, you can vary the size of the top margin and the space between the date and the inside address.

    Since the body is the key part of the letter, the method of selecting and organizing the content will be discussed more fully later.

8. **Complimentary close.**   The simple ending, "Sincerely," or "Yours sincerely," is standard. Professional firms that want to be more formal sometimes use "Yours truly," or "Yours very truly." On the other hand, writers who know their reader well may prefer the less formal "Cordially," or "Regards."

9. **Signature and signature block.**   Allow three to five lines for your signature underneath the complimentary close. If your name isn't already part of the letterhead, key it in full below your signature. Add your title or the name of your position below your name. With someone you write to frequently, you may choose to sign only your first name, even though your full name is typed below.

10. **Reference initials.**   The typist's initials often appear at the bottom left of the page. Alternatively the sender's initials appear in capitals, followed by a colon and the typist's initials in lower case:

    MP:jc

    If you're creating your own correspondence, simply omit this notation altogether.

11. **Enclosures.**   If you're enclosing or attaching documents with your letter, they can be identified with a notation below the reference initials:

    Enclosures: 2
    Enc.
    Attachment: resumé

12. **Copies.**   If you're making duplicates of your letter, identify them with the notation "c" followed by the initials and last name of the recipients.

    c J. Bell
     A. Hadji

    Blind copies are sent with no notation on the original, so that only the recipient of the copy is aware of its existence. They are identified with the notation "bc" on the copy.

13. **Page headings.**   Additional pages in a multipage letter should be identified by a header that includes the name of the recipient, the date, and the page number:

    Shuli Chang
    March 13, 2011

Format

Although you may occasionally see other layouts, the full-block style has become standard because of its ease and simplicity. In the full-block style,

- every line begins at the left margin, including the date, complimentary close, and signature block;
- a new paragraph is formed by leaving an extra line rather than by indenting at the margin.

Punctuation

Within the body of a letter or memo, always use standard punctuation. With the other parts of a letter the trend is to use **open punctuation**:

- The return address and inside address have no punctuation either in or at the end of the lines.
- The salutation and complimentary close have no punctuation.

Envelopes

The *Canadian Addressing Guide* (Canada Post, 2004) outlines the most technologically efficient formats for addressing envelopes.

Each element is to be typed in upper case with no punctuation unless it is part of a name (for example, *St. John's*). Addresses should be aligned left. Postal codes should always appear on the same line as the city and province, in upper case, with one space between the first three elements and the final three. Two spaces should separate the province and the postal code.

A two-letter symbol for the province or territory should be used as follows:

Alberta	AB	Nunavut	NU
British Columbia	BC	Ontario	ON
Manitoba	MB	Prince Edward Island	PE
New Brunswick	NB	Quebec	QC
Newfoundland/Labrador	NL	Saskatchewan	SK
Northwest Territories	NT	Yukon	YT
Nova Scotia	NS		

The following examples demonstrate the correct formatting for a variety of typical addresses:

MS. W. OWEN
170 MAIN ST
MONCTON NB E1C 1B9

D. JONES
MARKETING MANAGER
FORREST DISTRIBUTING LTD
1603 BATHURST STREET
TORONTO ON M5P 3J2

MR. B. ROSS
4417 BROOKS ST NE
WASHINGTON DC 20019-4649
USA

Figure 4-4   Memo

TO: Arlene Novak

FROM: Susan Vukovich

RE: Spring Registration

DATE: March 1, 2011

Our course offerings for the spring semester have been published and will appear on our website and in a newspaper supplement next week.

Would you please notify all staff in the Applied Arts office that students will be registering as early as Monday, March 12.

I am enclosing 10 copies of our course bulletin, which will be helpful for students registering in person. Please give me a call if you have any questions about registration procedures.

Thanks for your help with this, Arlene.

SV:jm
Enc.: 10

For additional information on addressing standards and examples of addressing formats, consult the *Canadian Addressing Guide* online at www.fnesc.ca/Attachments/BCeSIS/PDF's/addressing_guide-e.pdf

Memos

Although email has become the most common medium for correspondence within a company, there are situations where a paper-based memo is desirable. Many businesses have company memo stationery for ease and uniformity in sending messages. If this is unavailable, simply type the memo headings as illustrated in Figure 4-4.

Memos have no salutation, complimentary close, or signature, although some writers sign their initials or name at the bottom to create a more personal tone.

Although memos are often written informally to familiar associates, don't be misled into thinking they don't matter. Since they often convey important information or ask for something to be done, they need to be as precise as letters. Like any form of correspondence, they can have a big impact—for good or ill. Make your memos work for you.

Email

When businesses initially began using email, it was typically perceived as being a fast, efficient medium for short notes and routine messages. However, with the rise of Internet commerce ("e-biz") and the increasing need for communicating on a global scale, electronic communication has taken on a more substantive role.

In today's business environment, email is commonly used as a marketing medium or to circulate drafts of reports that previously would have been sent as paper-based documents. Where a paper record was at one time essential, email communications constitute official records, making them an appropriate medium for longer and more complex records. Sending formal documents as email attachments is a common practice, allowing the recipient to open files without losing formatting and layout features that don't always translate well into email. For more complex formats, pdf and PostScript files provide a "snapshot" of fonts and images, ensuring that the original look of the document is retained.

As far back as 1999, a communications study conducted by Watson Wyatt (Sanchez, 1999) cited email as the most frequently used medium for employee communications, with 90 per cent of respondents using email on a routine basis. However, its relatively low effectiveness rating (55 per cent) illustrates the difficulties we have yet to overcome in using email efficiently. A common problem is the large number of emails, both business and personal, that employees receive every day. This high volume makes it difficult for people to take the time to adequately process and understand their email. One workplace study reveals that daily email overwhelms 60 per cent of executives, managers, and other workplace professionals (Abernathy, 1999). These statistics point out the need for responsible email use on two levels:

1. **Outgoing.**   Send email that is clear and concise and has an obvious purpose. Avoid using email that is irrelevant or inappropriate and may be annoying to the recipient.

2. **Incoming.**   Check your email regularly and be sure to respond promptly to any message requiring action on your part.

Whether you are using email, letters, or memos, the following tips will help you create efficient and effective business correspondence.

Guidelines for All Correspondence

1. **Keep to one topic.**   Do not, for instance, give a sales report and make a staffing request in the same memo. Rather, for each topic send a separate communication. The reader will more easily remember information relating to one topic and won't have to divert attention to a separate subject.

   An exception to this rule is correspondence supplying miscellaneous routine information. A department head, for example, may be asked to supply the boss with a monthly report containing different categories of information, but even in this case, the overall subject is really departmental performance.

2. **Be brief.**   The well-known KISS acronym for business writing—"Keep It Simple, Stupid!"—should be amended to "Keep It Short and Simple." Procter & Gamble, the successful soap empire, insists on one-page memos, and spends considerable time training new recruits to do them well. Even if the reader of your letter or memo is not as insistent on brevity, there is a subtle psychological barrier to turning a page. The moral is obvious: keep to one page if you can. If you can't, at least be as brief as possible.

3. **Make sure the information is complete.**   This advice might seem a tall order if a one-page memo or letter is the goal. How can one be complete and brief at the same time? It may take a little practice. To be complete means to include all the information

needed for a letter to achieve its purpose. If you are placing an order, you obviously need to include all the details that will permit the reader to fill it. If the supplier has to telephone or write to you about some aspect you have forgotten, your letter was incomplete.

Incompleteness is often a result of vagueness. If you write to a plant manager saying, "Mr. Biggs wants to meet some employees on his next visit," you likely will get a quick call asking which specific employees he wants to meet, why, and when he is planning to visit. The information would have been more complete if you had said, "During his June visit, Mr. Biggs wants to meet the shift supervisors and the employees on the Safety Committee to discuss the safety program. I'll let you know when he decides on the date." Remember that to be brief doesn't mean to omit details but to sift out those that don't matter.

Complete information means not just the facts but also some indication of why the information matters. You are trying to keep the reader from merely shrugging and saying, "So what?" In other words, if you want people to turn off their computer monitors at night or to come to a meeting, give the reason as well as the request. If you are announcing a new policy, show how it affects the reader.

4. **Keep the focus "you-centred."**   Since correspondence is between people, not machines (even if you use machines to write or send it), make it personal and centred on the reader. *You* and *your* are useful reminders to a reader that you are aware of the individual. Try to use these pronouns throughout the correspondence, and especially in the opening and closing sentences. Instead of saying, "I received the report today," say "Your report arrived today" or "Thank you for your report."

Even when you are not using the pronoun *you* or the reader's name, keep the message focused on the *reader's* interest rather than on the writer's.

✗ We require a signed contract before starting on the project.

✓ Your project will begin as soon as you sign the contract.

Using the reader's name in the body of the letter is useful occasionally to emphasize the personal touch, but don't overdo it. Once is enough in a letter, and make sure you use the reader's name only in connection with something positive.

✗ Mrs. Martini, your account is overdrawn.

✓ Mrs. Martini, we're extending your line of credit by $500.

5. **Be positive.**   Naturally you don't want to make the reader feel irritated or defensive. By substituting positive for negative phrases, you can help maintain a friendly, courteous tone. Avoid words that sound accusing or suggest blame.

✗ You neglected to give us the name of your bank, so we cannot deposit the funds yet.

✓ As soon as you send us the name of your bank, we can deposit the funds directly.

✗ We are not responsible for administering the project after June 30.

✓ We will be responsible for administering the project until June 30.

Similarly, avoid negative words and phrases:

blame, error, mistake, fault, careless

you failed to

you disregarded

surely you don't

you claim (or allege)

Structuring Correspondence: The Direct Approach

Size up your reader: Will he or she be receptive to what you have to say? If so, the primary rule is, "Get to the point quickly." The first sentence in a routine or good-news letter should contain the key information. You don't have to be a psychologist to realize that when people are eager for information or curious about something, they become impatient with unimportant preliminaries. A business letter can lose the reader's interest with a flat opening. As a general rule, emphasize the opening news by keeping it in a separate paragraph.

This organizational approach is variously called the "direct approach," the "top-down approach," or the "pyramid approach." Journalists use it to report the news, since people read what is at the beginning of news stories but often don't continue to the end, especially if they have to turn a page. And since the end of a news story contains the least important points, editors feel free to trim from the bottom to fit a given space without fear of distorting the story.

The basic pattern of a routine or good-news letter is easy to follow if you remember the "put it up front" principle:

1. Put the most important points first.
2. Give supporting details.
3. End with a goodwill statement.

A goodwill statement is really a final cordial touch—a sentence that expresses appreciation, offers extra help, or looks to future relationships. Such a finishing touch will strengthen the personal, courteous tone of a business letter. In a routine or good-news letter, rather than putting such a goodwill statement at the top, as novice writers tend to do, put it at the bottom.

✗ Thank you for your order. We at Laurentian Packaging are happy to do business with small companies such as yours and look forward to future orders. The corrugated cartons you ordered on April 4 were in stock in the Aries line, which has a reinforced bottom. The shipment of 1 500 should arrive in Brandon on April 15. We fulfilled your request and shipped them by train. They were sent this morning.

Thank you again for your business.

✓ The 1 500 corrugated cartons you ordered were shipped by train this morning. You should receive them in Brandon on April 15. They are in the new Aries line, which has a reinforced bottom.

At Laurentian Packaging we are happy to do business with developing companies such as yours and will promptly fill any of your future packaging needs.

Often the first sentence of a letter or memo is weakened by an unnecessary opening phrase. Here are some "throat clearers" that will never be missed:

✗ This letter is to tell you that . . .
✗ I would like to inform you that . . .
✗ With regard to your memo . . .
✗ Pursuant to your letter of May 20 . . .

Avoid this kind of clutter. Instead, start right in with the main point. On rare occasions, as a legal technicality, it may be useful to refer to the date of previous correspondence, but most of the time it's not. You needn't fear that you will seem too abrupt.

A Caution about Directness

Before using the direct approach, remember that directness is a Western, and especially a North American, value. In other cultures—in Japan, for example—to be direct is often thought to be rude. Even among European nations, differing degrees of directness are appropriate. For example, the Germans are usually more direct than the French. Within Asian cultures, Hong Kong Chinese, exposed to Western ways, are used to being more direct than are people in mainland China. The Japanese habitually favour an indirect approach, even for routine requests. When communicating with people from other cultures, therefore, first find out what level of directness is customary.

For most business correspondence in North America, however, the direct approach is best. Many different kinds of letters and memos fall into this category, with the most common being letters of request and replies to requests. Letters of thanks and congratulations can also be an important part of the job for managers who deal with many people.

Routine Requests

Placing an order, asking for information or credit, and making a routine claim are all situations that call for the direct approach. In each case, follow these steps:

- Make sure the request is explicit rather than merely implied.
- Supply all the details needed for the receiver to fill the request. In making an application for personal credit, for example, give details of your employment and your banking arrangements.
- If the request has several parts, itemize them using a list format. If there are many items, group them into categories.

Requesting Information

✳–⎡Explore
Letter 5: Request (Product Inquiry)

✳–⎡Explore
Memo 1: Requesting Info

When you want information from someone who will receive no direct benefit from supplying it—such as details of company policies or procedures—make sure the request is as brief as possible. A rambling list that seems to ask for the moon may end up getting nothing.

The following request for information about a prospective employee is vague about the requirements of the job. It's also unselective and repetitive.

✗ I am considering employing Arthur Seaburg in my company. I understand that he has worked for you in the past. Would you please give me information about his educational background, job responsibilities, work habits, ability to get along with others, organizational ability, health, initiative, reliability, and experience? He has named you as a source for a reference and we would appreciate it very much if you could supply the above information.

Compare it with this version:

✓ Would you please give me some information about Arthur Seaburg, who has applied for a job as a management trainee in our bottling company. He has worked in your office for the last two summers.

- Does he work well with people?
- Has he given evidence of organizational ability and initiative?
- Is he honest and reliable?

We would be grateful for any other information that would help us determine his suitability for the management trainee position.

Of course, your remarks will remain confidential.

The improved version is more direct in its organization. It omits the request for facts that should be obtained from the applicant himself—such as educational background and health. It also helps the reader by stating the type of job in question. The vertical list highlights for the reader the specific information needed.

Making a Claim

The direct approach may seem an odd choice for routine claims, since a claim can hardly be good news for the receiver. Yet successful businesses want customers to be satisfied, and most are interested in resolving reasonable complaints or difficulties. A letter that communicates the problem simply and directly gives the recipient the chance to resolve it with goodwill. When making a claim

 Explore
Letter 6: Making a Claim

Explore
Letter 7: Making a Claim

Explore
Letter 26: Persuasive Claim (Complaint)

1. **Don't beat around the bush.**   State right at the beginning the nature of your claim and the reason for it. You may also want to give some urgency to your claim by relating the consequences of the problem, for example, a loss of sales or a business activity that has had to be curtailed.

2. **Be explicit about what you expect the company to do.**   Don't exaggerate or indulge in emotional outbursts. A reasonable request that sticks to the facts is more likely to get a prompt, favourable response than one that makes accusations. An angry reader often resists settling claims.

How would you react to this letter?

✗ I had always wanted a computer and finally I spent a lot of money and got one. I bought it from you because friends had told me it was a good system. Now I realize that it is totally unreliable. I have had it only eight months and the DVD drive doesn't work. I want it fixed immediately. The warranty covers the repair but it doesn't cover the nuisance.

How do you expect people to buy your products if they don't work? I for one don't plan to buy them any more.

Wouldn't you react better to this version?

✓ Please replace the DVD drive in this computer. As you can see from the enclosed bill, it is only eight months old and still under warranty. Since this problem is preventing me from completing work at home on the weekends, I would appreciate it if you would repair and return the computer to me before May 15. Thank you.

Routine or Good-News Replies

Use the direct approach when responding with favourable or neutral information. If you have to temper the information with some facts that are not favourable, make sure you don't undermine your effort by being unnecessarily negative.

Explore
Letter 8: Positive

The following letter should be a good-news one, since it gives the customer a benefit he or she is not entitled to under the warranty. Yet the accusing tone and negative wording are likely to annoy the reader. Moreover, since it doesn't use the direct approach, the positive message loses its impact.

✕ Instructions were supplied with your new automatic coffee maker warning that the base should not be immersed in water. Our repair people tell us that the mechanism in your machine had rust spots, which indicated that you had got it wet. Since misuse is ordinarily not covered by warranty, we should charge you for the repairs. Nevertheless, we like to keep our customers satisfied, and therefore are replacing the damaged parts free of charge. You should remember in future, however, not to get water in the mechanism.

Your coffee maker was shipped to you this morning by Xpresspost.

The next reply is likely to produce a satisfied customer, even though he or she has to pay for part of the repair cost.

✓ Your repaired automatic coffee maker was shipped to you this morning by Xpresspost. It is in perfect working condition.

We have enclosed with the coffee maker a copy of the instructions, which show how to clean it without immersing the base. Rust spots on the interior mechanism were the cause of your problem, a condition ordinarily not covered by the warranty. We want to keep you a satisfied customer, however, and are therefore not billing you for labour, but only for parts.

Remember to keep the mechanism dry and your coffee maker should give you years of convenience—and good coffee.

Letters of Thanks or Congratulations

A note of appreciation can strengthen business relationships as well as personal ones. It needn't be lengthy, as long as it is genuine. This proviso is the key: you need to show that your thanks or congratulations are not an empty formality. If people have done things that benefit you, let them know precisely how. Give one or two details that show why you are grateful. If you are congratulating someone on an appointment or award, state why you think it is deserved or comment on how that person has benefited the company or community.

The following thank-you letter is perfunctory because it lacks concrete detail; it sounds like a form letter.

✕ Thank you for letting the class visit your plant. It was a very interesting experience for us and we appreciate your assistance.

Thank you again.

On the other hand, the next letter does not seem genuine because it exaggerates. It is too effusive—almost gushy—and therefore has the mark of insincerity, despite its claim.

✕ We want to express our sincere appreciation for our visit to your plant. It was the most exciting moment in the course, and the illustration of robotics was awesome. All of us in the class were really impressed by your unique talent as a manager. We are indeed grateful for your kindness in giving us this special treat.

Now for a letter that is direct as well as being sincere in its thanks. Notice how paring down the superlatives improves the effect.

✓ We appreciate the tour of your plant last week to see robotics in action.

The visit was a highlight of our course on technological innovation since it gave us a practical illustration of the theory we are studying. We were also impressed by the methods you used to introduce the robots.

Thank you for the opportunity of seeing how to manage technological change effectively.

Internet Issues

As discussed earlier in this chapter, email has assumed a major role in business communication, conveying information rapidly both within an organization on the company intranet and externally via the Internet. However, the benefits are accompanied by some potential liabilities. In order to capitalize on the benefits of email and avoid its pitfalls, keep in mind the following guidelines:

1. **Respect workplace rules on Internet use.**   Using company email to conduct private communication is costly for employers. It ties up company resources and results in decreased productivity, to the point where some businesses monitor Internet use by employees. If you are unsure of your employer's policy, make some inquiries, and be sure to observe any regulations on Internet use.

2. **Use simple formats.**   Browsers and email programs sometimes differ in the way they "read" certain features such as apostrophes and quotation marks, especially when these are copied from a word processing document. Smart quotes (" ") may appear as a question mark, diamond, or some other symbol. For this reason, avoid the use of "smart quotes" and use "straight quotes" instead.

3. **Use email attachments.**   Although attachments are an unnecessary complication in the case of short notes, they are an important aid to ensure that longer documents, or those with complex formatting, arrive in your reader's mailbox looking the way they should. In these cases, create the text in a word processing program and send it as an attachment to a brief email note. The receiver can then open and print the document in its original format.

4. **Create an email signature.**   Your email program contains a feature that enables you to create a signature block that will automatically appear at the bottom of all your messages. Signatures typically include your name, position, company name, and email address but can also include mailing addresses, phone numbers, websites, and even slogans.

5. **Keep Internet liability in mind.**   Electronic signatures are gaining legal ground, and you should assume that your email could be legally binding. For your own safety, treat email with the same care you would take with paper documents.

6. **Avoid content-free email.**   A frequent lament in today's office environment concerns the massive amount of email many people receive. One response to the high volume is to delete messages either with a quick glance or without reading them at all. Respect the time constraints of others by making sure your email has a clear purpose and succinct message.

7. **Use clear, specific subject lines.**   This helps the recipient to identify those messages that are particularly important and will prevent your message from being accidentally or hastily deleted.

Exercises

✓●—Practise
Exercise 3: Invitation to Visit Plant

✓●—Practise
Exercise 4: Reply to Request for Interview

✓●—Practise
Exercise 6: Follow-up to Trade Show Request

1. List the weaknesses in the following memo:

to R. Fletcher   May 13, 2011

from A. Dunn

Regarding the proposal for a touring promotional show sent to me on Tuesday, I read it yesterday. When you have corrected the problems I have found in it, I will gladly give it my support at the next divisional meeting, since it has merit. The financing section is sound, except that you failed to include the cost of gas. You should have estimated a cost per kilometre along with your leasing figures. I also think your marketing section lacks enough detail. Ruth, you should have added more facts.

Other than these problems, the proposal looks fine. By the way, when you do the estimates for the London office renovations, include a breakdown of costs for the Waterloo and Hamilton renovations. They will help us make comparisons.

Sincerely,

Allan

2. Rewrite the following letter, changing the format to full-block style with correct addressing format. Then change the letter to a memo, adding text as needed to create correct memo format. In both cases assume that you are using stationery with company letterhead.

January 10, 2011

Ms. Cecilia Wong

Manager, Human Resources, Simex Limited,

P.O. Box 25,

Sudbury, Ontario

P4B 5T9

Dear Cecilia:

Please add my name to the list for the March seminar on interviewing techniques at the Skyway Hotel.

If others from the company are planning to attend and need transportation, I will be taking my car and can pick up those people who live in my area. Ask them to get in touch with me.

Thanks for letting me know about the seminar.

Sincerely,

Jerry Dutka

3. Consider the order of this memo. How would you reorder it? Would you make any other changes?

To: A. C. Biggar, Administrative Assistant

From: K. Pivniki

Salaries

Last week Ann Timmins and I met to discuss employee salaries. As you know, you had asked us to review salaries among all support staff in our division and to recommend to you a correction for any inequities.

Ann and I reviewed salaries with the help of the benefits group's new computer program for assessing employee compensation. You had asked us to comment on the effectiveness of the program for company-wide application.

We found only one area where the salary range for support staff is inequitable. The library assistants are underpaid by comparison with other staff. We therefore recommend that the salary range for library assistants be increased by $2 000.

We also found that the computer program was a practical and efficient tool. You can be confident about using it for the whole company.

I hope this is satisfactory. If not, please call me.

4. Last Thursday, Alice Chiu, personnel director at Northern Bank, was the guest speaker at your business club's monthly lunch. The subject of her talk was "Employee Training Programs: The Challenges Ahead."

Since it was your turn to write a letter of thanks on behalf of the club, you quickly wrote the draft below. You now realize it is unsatisfactory in its organization, tone, and wording. List the problems.

Dear Ms. Chiu:

The speech that you delivered last week was something I had looked forward to for a long time, since I work in the personnel field. It was indeed an honour to have someone of your stature come to talk to us on such an interesting subject. Thank you again for your time and effort on our behalf.

5. Make these sentences more reader-centred:

   a) We know our construction crew is experienced and capable.

   b) It is the organization's policy to require partial payment before beginning the second stage of a large project such as this one.

   c) On May 10, we will deliver the complete report.

   d) Our research engineers have tested the product for 10 years to make sure it is safe.

   e) A subsidy is available from our office for companies hiring student trainees.

   f) We are in receipt of your brochure.

   g) Technical assistance with the new database program is available from three highly trained IT technicians.

   h) The office desk is available with a variety of optional attachments, according to individual preference.

6. Where possible, eliminate negative words or phrases, and create a more positive approach in the following sentences:

   a) You claim that we did not send a refund, but our records show it was sent by registered mail on July 12.

b) Since the office will be closed on Friday, don't forget to pick up your parking permits before 5 o'clock on Thursday.

c) The Accounting Department has informed me that 25 per cent of you have neglected to submit your expense reports for last month.

d) You incorrectly assume that we will be reducing the number of part-time technicians.

e) We do not assume responsibility for damage to cars left anywhere but in our underground parking garage.

7. In a message to students at the college where you work, you need to clarify some rules regarding the use of computers in the Student Centre:

> The lab is reserved for use by students registered in a full-time program. All registered students have Internet access as well as a college email account and 600 MB of space on the college server. No food or beverage is allowed in the lab and students are asked to leave workstations clean when they leave. The lab is open from 7:00 a.m. until 10:00 p.m. Monday through Friday and from 9:00 a.m. until 3:00 p.m. on the weekends. The latest versions of Microsoft Windows and Microsoft Office are installed on all computers in the lab.

Write up this message using a vertical list format for clarity and conciseness.

8. Indicate whether email, a letter, or a memo would be the most appropriate choice in the following situations:

a) A notice to all staff reminding them of new summer hours

b) A response to a customer who has complained about poor service

c) A request to a local supplier that future orders be sent by courier

d) A report to your manager about your recent health-related absences

e) A note of congratulations to a long-term employee who has recently received a 25-year pin

f) An invitation to clients to attend an office opening

g) A request to the board of directors for increased funding for your department

h) A message outlining new procedures for exiting the building during a fire alarm

i) An announcement to all staff regarding the new scent-free policy

j) A notice to all clients informing them of price increases

9. As the administrative manager at Apex Food Services Ltd., you want information about Smith Microwave Ovens. You need microwaves for 10 sites where Apex has new contracts, and you hope you can get a discount for purchasing in quantity. You also want to find out about the different models and their features as well as the kind of guarantee the supplier offers.

Write a complete letter of inquiry to Select Equipment Co. The address is 12 Queen Street, Hawkesbury, Ontario, K1B 1L2.

10. On November 10, you phoned Confederation Hotel to make tentative arrangements for the annual sales awards lunch for your company, Novatech Systems. Subject to your later confirmation, you reserved the Dominion Room for Friday, January 10 for a three-hour period starting at noon. You also arranged for a buffet lunch for 30 people at a cost of $25 each. The cost is to include 15 bottles of wine. You now realize that you will also need a lectern, a laptop with Internet access, and a screen.

In a letter to the manager of the hotel, John Stubbs, confirm the arrangements and ask for the additional equipment.

11. You have just learned that Helen Thomas, the energetic assistant buyer for National Fashion Stores, has been promoted to chief buyer. She is now in a position to make important buying decisions.

    As the sales manager of Elegance Manufacturing, you have dealt with Ms. Thomas before in selling your line of women's sportswear. You get along well with her and think that, since she is efficient, she will be good at her new job.

    Write her a letter of congratulations.

12. You are heading up a fundraising drive to furnish a new children's wing in your local community hospital. You want to send a letter of thanks to all contributors.

    The drive has reached its target of $100 000, and the children's wing will have its new acquisitions (furniture, toys, and play equipment) by spring. Compose the letter.

13. A year ago you bought a cellphone at Biltmore Wireless for $179. The text messaging display failed after eight months and you returned it to Biltmore for repair. Now the display has failed again and the cellphone is just out of warranty. You want it either repaired free of charge or replaced since the problem seems to be ongoing.

    Write a letter to Biltmore explaining the situation and making your request.

14. As head of customer service at Biltmore, you have received the request for free repairs made in Exercise 13. You have decided to agree to the request. Write a letter that will inform the customer of your decision and increase customer goodwill toward Biltmore.

15. You are in charge of customer relations at Northway's Resort Hotel. The hotel specializes in vacation packages for families. It advertises free tennis, swimming, and windsurfing.

    The O'Connor family (parents and two children) came for a week in July and paid a bill of $3 000. However, Mr. O'Connor has written asking for a partial refund since the tennis courts were being repaired and were out of play for four of the seven days. He says the family's main reason for choosing Northway's was the tennis facility.

    You think Mr. O'Connor's claim is a fair one and decide to send a $500 refund. Write the accompanying letter.

16. Your job as assistant to the registrar of your college is to write a letter to new students giving them information about the following:

    a) Food services on or near the campus

    b) Sports facilities and activities

    c) Campus social activities

    Write the letter as it would appear on your school letterhead.

mycanadianbuscommlab

Visit www.mycanadianbuscommlab.ca for everything you need to help you succeed in the job you've always wanted! Tools and resources include the following:

• Composing Space and Writer's Toolkit
• Document Makeovers
• Grammar Exercises—and much more!

Bad-News Correspondence

Learning Outcomes

This chapter of *Impact* will help you to

1. use both the direct and the indirect structures for communicating bad news;

2. apply guidelines for using the indirect approach effectively;

3. respond to an unsuccessful job applicant;

4. decline an invitation;

5. turn down a claim;

6. refuse a credit application;

7. understand the limited role of email in communicating bad news.

"I believe strong and effective leadership is what differentiates successful organizations. An effective leader must have confidence, compassion, conviction, and most importantly the ability to communicate those attributes."

—John See, president and CEO, TD Waterhouse

It's always harder to say "no" than "yes," and harder still to say "no" in writing. Nobody likes sending a letter that causes disappointment or anger. In the twenty-first century, receivers of bad news are unlikely to follow the example of those ancient Greeks who killed the messenger, but they may still resent the writer. In business there's no easy escape; from time to time you will have to refuse a request, turn down an idea or a person, or send a written reprimand or negative evaluation. The challenge is to send a message that gives the unpleasant facts but doesn't create hostility between you and the receiver.

Structural Options

You have two main options for structuring bad news. As in so many other instances, let your decision be guided by the context, especially your expectations about the reader. Whatever structure you choose, the tone of your message matters. Expressing yourself in a way that shows sensitivity and courtesy can take some of the sting out of bad news.

The Direct Approach

If you know the reader well, or if the reader is impatient for a response to a query, you may be better to stick with a direct approach. You should probably also be direct if the bad news is expected or not very important. For example, the direct approach would be appropriate for letting a colleague know that a routine report will be completed late or for telling a boss the details of a known problem. The trend in North America is toward more directness for bad news.

The direct order for bad news is similar to that for good news (see Chapter 4), except that it tries to soften the message by offering the reader a helpful alternative. Here is a list of the steps to take when using the direct approach:

1. **State the bad news simply and directly.**

2. **Give the reasons.**

3. **Give an alternative, if possible.**

4. **Close with a goodwill statement.**   Don't refer back to the bad news. You don't want to keep reminding the reader of the source of any displeasure.

Watch
Perils of Pauline: Writing Bad News

Explore
Memo 7: Negative News—Direct Approach

Explore
Email 10: Negative News—Direct Approach

Here's an example:

> Dear Mr. Moore:
>
> The reference you are looking for doesn't seem to have originated with our company.
>
> In looking through our record of corporate speeches on the effect of free trade on agriculture, we haven't come across anything similar to the remarks you mentioned. When I asked Mr. Lockhart, he had no recollection of anyone in the company having made that type of analogy.
>
> However, we have conducted a quick Internet search and have found a number of sites that may well give you the information you are seeking. The Agriculture and Agri-Food Canada website at www.agr.gc.ca/itpd-dpci/ag-ac/4969-eng.htm is probably a good starting point for your search.
>
> We hope you find this information helpful.

The Indirect Approach

 Explore
Letter 19: Negative News—Indirect Approach

 Explore
Memo 8: Negative News—Indirect Approach

 Explore
Email 11: Negative News—Indirect Approach

If you don't know the reader well, or if the bad news is unexpected or could cause a negative emotional reaction, consider the advantages of the indirect approach. It has this order:

1. **Begin with a neutral or pleasant opening statement related to the subject.**   This is the buffer that gets the letter started on an agreeable note.

2. **Discuss the circumstances leading to the bad news.**

3. **State the bad news as positively as possible.**   Occasionally, if you have paved the way clearly, you may be able to imply the bad news without actually stating it.

    Suppose, for example, you want to turn down a request to develop a new trade show in Vancouver. You could imply a refusal by saying: "We have decided to concentrate our efforts on establishing ourselves in the American market for the next three years and not to develop new shows in Canada during this period." However, if you do merely *imply* a refusal, be careful that the reader knows clearly that the answer is "no."

4. **Give a helpful suggestion or alternative, if one exists.**

5. **Close with a goodwill statement.**   Think of human nature. People usually react better to bad news if they are prepared for it. Unpleasant facts will encounter less resistance if they seem to follow logically from an explanation. By contrast, reasons after the bad news are more likely to be interpreted as excuses. Since the indirect approach is the path of least resistance, you will find it more appropriate for your trickiest writing tasks—when you are faced with the possibility of angering or upsetting a reader.

When using the indirect approach remember these tips:

1. **Don't mislead the reader with an opening that's too positive.**   You don't want a buildup to lead to a letdown.

2. **Do keep the reasons or explanation as short as possible.**   The reader shouldn't have to wade through a lot of detail to get to the key information.

3. **Do make sure the reader is clear about the bad news,** especially if you don't state it but only imply it. A misinterpreted message is a failed message.

4. **Do avoid negative words and phrasing** if there are positive ways to give the message. (See page 68 for a list of undesirable negatives.)

5. **Don't end with a statement that is artificially upbeat** when you know the receiver will be deeply disappointed by the communication. You may seem like a Pollyanna—someone who is relentlessly cheery even in inappropriate circumstances. One possibility here is to refer to future business or service, an approach that is both positive and sincere.

Here is a letter that uses the indirect approach to turning down a request for funding. Notice how the writer creates a reasonable and helpful atmosphere.

✓ Every year in February our Donations Committee meets to discuss deserving appeals for funding, such as your request for support of the Montrose Revue.

Your proposal arrived in March, after we had already made our selections for this year. Our budget for charities is now fully committed and we are therefore unable to help you at this time. If you plan to make the show an annual event, we will certainly add your proposal to the list for consideration next year. Please let us know before January 31.

In the meantime, I wish you every success with this year's revue and congratulate you on your initiative.

If the following letter had been sent instead, its harsh negativism would likely have created antagonism toward the writer or the writer's firm. The blunt refusal in the opening sentence would have made the reader less receptive to the explanation.

✗ We regret that we are unable to give financial support to your proposal. We have many requests for funds and have already committed our budget for charitable giving for this year. Unfortunately we have to reject many ventures such as yours, since we have only so much to distribute.

We wish you success with your venture.

The final goodwill statement at the end rings false, since the tone of the rest of the letter is so writer-centred and impersonal. It has the mark of a form letter—and a poorly constructed one.

Turning Down a Job Applicant

Most companies these days have far more applicants for jobs than they can possibly hire. Some are inundated every spring with application letters from students, and it is increasingly common for employers to answer only those applicants they want to interview. Some companies will state this approach in their ad; others simply do not respond, which is discourteous. A company should be concerned with its public image, and treating job applicants poorly can give a business a bad name. Besides, an applicant who one year is turned down may another year be an important prospective customer or client.

Personalizing the Message

If you are in charge of responding to job applicants and you haven't the resources or time to reply individually to a flood of applications, devise one or several form letters.

If you have taken more of the applicant's time by having an interview or requesting references, you should write a personal letter. Whichever route you follow, try to avoid rejecting the individual as a person. Focus more on the reasons for the company's selection.

Compare the order, tone, and wording of the following two letters. Both of them could be form letters, but the second has a more reasonable and reader-centred tone as well as an indirect structure.

✱ Explore
Email 14: Rejecting a Job Applicant

✔ Practise
Exercise 9: Direct Approach to Bad News

✕   We are sorry that we must refuse you employment at Wisharts. We had many applicants seeking employment with us this year, no doubt because of Wisharts' growing success and reputation. Obviously we could accept only a few for the Accounting Department, and after careful consideration of all applicants, we have decided not to offer you a position.

We wish you success with other employers.

✓   Thank you for taking the time to apply for an accounting position at Wisharts.

Since we received more than 200 applications for the 3 positions available, we have had to disappoint many well-qualified candidates. We based our initial selection for interviews not only on academic background but also on work experience. The applicants finally chosen for the positions have at least three years of relevant employment. Although we cannot offer you a position at this time, our decision is no reflection on your potential to do well in accounting.

We appreciate your interest in Wisharts and wish you success in your accounting career. If in future an appropriate opening comes up, we would be happy to consider another application from you.

Being Truthful

If you would never consider the applicant for a job, do not suggest that you would. By falsely raising hopes, you will only produce more bitterness down the line. The last sentence in the preceding letter could easily have been omitted for an applicant who is unlikely to be considered seriously. A good substitute would be to suggest alternative employment routes. On the other hand, if the applicant is someone you might employ another time, it's a good idea to say somewhere that this rejection is only for the job or jobs available at the time.

Declining an Invitation

Practise

Exercise 5: Indirect Approach to Bad News

Business people are often invited to join organizations, give speeches, or sit on boards or committees. If you have to refuse such an invitation, at least do it graciously:

- **Show that you appreciate the invitation.**
- **Acknowledge the importance of the organization or event.**
- **Give specific reasons for your refusal.**
- **Suggest an alternative, if you can, or leave the door open for another time.**

Remember that the more concrete you are, the more you will appear to have taken the invitation seriously. If you keep to generalities, your refusal will run the risk of offending. You may not always be able to give as specific an alternative as the following writer does, but at least you should try to soften the refusal with some positive remarks.

I have always admired the work that the John Howard Society does in helping prisoners and am honoured to be asked to speak at your annual dinner. However, on checking my calendar, I realize that unfortunately I will be in Alberta that week attending the Canadian Bar Association convention.

If you would like someone else to talk on the role of Canadian business in prisoner rehabilitation, you may want to try Henry Albright, director of personnel for Consolidated Industries, who had considerable success in hiring former inmates when he was the plant manager in Kingston. He is an experienced speaker.

I'm sorry that I won't be with you on April 9, but I'll continue to follow with interest the work of the John Howard Society.

Rejecting a Claim

Some claims are more reasonable than others and some people are more honest. Yet no matter how outrageous you think a claim is, or how skeptical you are of the details, you should respond with courtesy and tact. Customers are not always right, but they're always prospective customers. Of course, if someone is a persistent pest and you don't want the business, be as frank as you like, as long as you are not rude.

Most people who take the trouble to make a claim believe they have a strong case. They want satisfaction, or at least expect an explanation. You must present the refusal in such a way that, even if they are not happy with your answer, they at least know the exact reasons for it and do not doubt your honesty. The dos and don'ts of refusing claims are an extension of the basic guideline for all business writing: put yourself in the reader's shoes. Consider the claimant's position and respond in a way that will make sense to the person reading your reply. Specifically,

✻ **Explore**
Letter 21: Refusing a Claim

✻ **Explore**
Email 12: Refusing a Claim

1. **Do begin with a statement you can both agree on.**   You might try an opening such as "You are right to expect top quality from New Wave products." Or "Your clear and straightforward statement of the problem with the photocopier deserves a clear and straightforward answer."

2. **Do review the facts.**   Be objective and unemotional in your tone so that your subsequent refusal seems a logical conclusion to your analysis. Don't be long-winded, but provide enough detail to make the reason for refusal obvious.

3. **Don't accuse or lecture the claimant.**   A rejection letter is one instance where passive verbs may be more effective than active ones. Instead of saying, "You dented the gearbox," soften the tone with "The gearbox was dented." Avoid phrases such as

   - you failed (neglected, disregarded)
   - you claim (insinuate, imply)
   - contrary to what you say
   - we take issue with

4. **Don't belittle the claimant.**   Avoid phrases such as "surely you must know," "it should be obvious," and "if you had read the instructions."

5. **Don't use company policy as an excuse.**   Other people don't care about company policy. They want a reasonable explanation—just as young people want more than a "because I said so" answer from a parent or teacher.

6. **Don't offer elaborate apologies for refusing.**   A simple "I'm sorry" will do if the circumstances warrant an apology. However, an apology is often not needed and it is better to avoid one.

7. **Don't pass the buck,** saying it's not your responsibility or your department's responsibility. If it truly isn't your job to respond, give the claim to someone whose job it is.

8. **Do close in a friendly, positive way.**   You have some options for closing, depending on the circumstances:

   a) After refusing the claim, you might offer a counterproposal, which shows that you are trying to be helpful even if you can't do exactly what the claimant wants. You might, for example, offer to repair a part even if you can't replace the whole. Or you might suggest a substitute for the product or service—or even some information about where to get help with the difficulty. (This last approach is not passing the buck if the solution lies outside your company's responsibility.)

b) You might indicate that if the claimant has additional information available you'll be happy to review the case. This, of course, is useful when the claimant has not included an invoice or has omitted some important evidence. Naturally you would not want to use this closing indiscriminately, inviting every claimant to try again.

c) Often you can end with a remark pointing out the benefits for the claimant of using another of your products or services. You need to be tactful here, so that your letter doesn't seem like a sales pitch rather than a response to a claim.

Whatever close you use, be positive. Don't suggest that the reader may be dissatisfied ("I'm afraid you may be unhappy with this decision"). Neither should you plead with the claimant ("Please try to understand our position" or "I trust you will agree with this explanation"). By doing so you imply that the claimant may not understand or agree—a negative way to end. If you have responded to the claim in a reasonable, helpful, and courteous way, you should let the case rest.

Now for two examples of claim refusals that work:

✓ One of our aims at Domestic Appliances is to provide homemakers with time-saving kitchen equipment at a reasonable price. The inexpensive blender you bought two years ago has proven to be one of our most popular products. I'm sorry it has not given the satisfaction to you it has to so many others.

When you bought the blender, the description on the label and in the instruction manual stated that it was not designed for crushing ice.

We have checked your blender and found it in good working order. It will continue to give you excellent results with normal use. We stand by our money-back guarantee of our products, but since the blender has now had two years' use and is working as it should, we are unable to give a refund.

For crushing ice, may I suggest our Blendomix II. This food processor will save you time and do a superb job on tough foods as well as crushing ice. I'm enclosing a discount slip that will allow you 10 per cent off the regular price of the Blendomix II at any of our retail outlets.

We are pleased to have you as a customer and are confident that our products will give you many years of reliable service.

✓ I can appreciate your need for a reliable lawn mower, especially with your large lawn.

Our mechanics have been able to identify the problem with your machine. The blade cover was pressing on the blade, preventing it from turning properly. A dent on the cover indicates that something was dropped on it. Since our one-year warranty does not cover damage to the machine, we must charge you for the new blade cover. When we replaced the cover, however, we also cleaned and oiled your machine—free of charge. With proper care, your Turfmaster should give you many years of efficient and easy mowing.

Refusing Credit

Granting credit to a person is easy. A direct letter of acceptance is usually all that is needed. Refusing credit is more difficult. In fact, it is a more sensitive task than refusing a claim because it is a more personal matter. The most frequent reasons for not granting credit are the character and/or financial position of the applicant—both sensitive areas. It is a letter-writing challenge to produce a tactful refusal that retains the goodwill of the person refused.

The general tactics are the same as for other "bad-news" letters:

1. **Begin with a "buffer"**—a neutral or positive statement related to the credit application. Try to tie it into the explanation that follows. For example, if the refusal has to do with the relatively few assets (against liabilities) of the applicant's new business, you might start with, "Your application for credit indicates that your new business is progressing well. We are interested in helping new businesses keep on a sound financial footing." This opening could then easily connect to a second paragraph explaining that the applicant might wish to reapply when the company's assets have increased.

   If you must send a refusal in a form letter because of the numbers you have to deal with, you may have to stick with the trite "Thank you for your application for credit" kind of opening. But even here, try to be a bit more specific by including the name of your company or the help you can give to the applicant: "We are grateful for your interest in opening an account with Harcraft Hardware and want to help you obtain quality building supplies."

2. **Explain the circumstances leading to the refusal.** One good approach is to state the conditions under which you grant credit. Your refusal to someone who does not meet these conditions then seems to follow logically. For example, you might say, "One of the conditions of granting credit is that a person has been employed for at least a year," or "We find that credit works best with companies that have a strong asset-to-liability ratio."

3. **Refuse tactfully.** In some cases, such as when the reasons relate to character rather than finances, it may be better to refuse by implication rather than by explicit statement. If applicants have been dishonest or have left a trail of bad debts, they know it. A hint that you know is all they really need. A statement such as "once your credit rating is firmly established" can suggest the reason for the refusal without overtly questioning the integrity of the applicant.

4. **Finish with a positive, friendly statement.** No one likes to be turned down, but you will leave a better impression if you can point to a more positive relationship. You might suggest a future credit acceptance, point out the benefits of cash buying, or indicate some other way in which you could be of help.

✕ We regret to inform you that your application has been denied. Our review of your financial situation indicates that you do not meet the conditions we require to grant credit to small businesses. Unfortunately we cannot lower our requirements because of the past problems we have had with poor credit risks.

✓ We appreciate the interest you have shown in our merchandise through your application for credit.

As a manager, you will understand that to run our own company effectively we have had to establish certain conditions for granting credit. One is that the assets of a small business should be at least twice its liabilities. At the rate your business is growing, it will soon meet this condition. When it does, we will be pleased to review your application.

In the meantime you can enjoy our 5 per cent discount for cash sales. We look forward to giving you prompt, efficient service.

Internet Issues

Despite its ease of use and its efficiency, email has its limitations. For sensitive issues, email usually is not the best choice of medium for delivering bad-news messages. In a situation where you wish to notify a large number of people of bad news that is not cat-astrophic—for example, the failure to meet a United Way target—email may be the most efficient solution. However, for more personal matters such as a disciplinary issue or a refusal, avoid using email. There are several reasons for this:

1. **Bad news requires a personal medium.** Although conveying bad news is a difficult task, always try to do it in person in an effort to break the news gently and discuss its impact with the recipient.

2. **The privacy of email cannot be guaranteed.** Most of us have encountered prob-lems with email, for example, a message sent to the wrong address or a delivery fail-ure. It's also easy for someone to forward your email message, so you need to be aware that anyone with an email account could see what you've said. The rule of thumb is that you should think of your email as a postcard that can be read by many readers on the way to its destination.

3. **The legal and ethical implications of email use pose a risk.** Sending confidential or sensitive messages electronically can create an ethical dilemma if others see them. The transmission of confidential or sensitive messages electronically has been the subject of grievances and legal challenges. Even the potential for breaching an individ-ual's right to privacy makes it advisable to find an alternative for delivering this type of message.

Exercises

1. Revise the following sentences, making them more positive and less accusatory or demeaning to the reader:

   a) Since you did not include the receipt, we cannot give you a refund.

   b) Surely you don't think we can act on a complaint two years after the purchase?

   c) We suspect that you dropped the laptop and damaged the components.

   d) You haven't survived in business the required six months, and therefore we cannot give you credit.

   e) It's too risky for us to give someone like you credit since, frankly, your credit rating leaves much to be desired.

   f) Mr. Elliot, you haven't supplied a full and honest explanation, and we need the explanation if you want us to replace the machine.

   g) The basis of your complaint is a misreading of Section 2 of our policy statement.

   h) Any good entrepreneur would know, Mr. Taylor, that a sound financial footing is necessary for a business to prosper.

   i) Your failure to follow the operating instructions caused the breakdown of the machine.

2. List the weaknesses in the following refusal of credit:

   We are sorry that we cannot grant your application for credit. Our company policy is to extend credit only to those people who have been employed for a year. You fail to meet this requirement.

   We trust you will understand our position and are sorry we cannot oblige you at this time. In any case, we hope you will continue to shop at our store on a cash basis.

3. List the strengths in the following refusal of credit:

   We appreciate your continued interest in using Harwood products in your construction business, as shown by your application for credit.

   In this tough economy, one of the ways we keep ourselves on a sound financial footing is to require that a business be in operation for two years before we grant credit. Although your references confirm your good reputation, your business hasn't yet reached this position. Your record of growth suggests that you soon will, and we look forward to reviewing your application again at that time. In the meantime, we promise you prompt and reliable service with your cash orders and enclose a flyer about our spring discounts for cash sales.

4. Indicate whether you would use a direct or indirect structure in the following situations:

   a) Telling a fellow employee that you will have the information she requested a week later than promised

   b) Turning down a request for a contribution to a local charity

   c) Informing a customer that the repairs to his DVD player are no longer covered by warranty

   d) Notifying your boss that the spare parts room in your factory requires reorganizing

e) Refusing a request from a community organization to act as master of ceremonies at an upcoming retirement dinner

5. Indicate whether each of the following statements is true or false:

a) Bad-news messages should always begin with a buffer.

b) Email is a good way of communicating bad news because it does so quickly and efficiently.

c) You can effectively turn down a claim simply by quoting company policy.

d) Sometimes you can just imply a refusal without actually saying "no."

e) Good-news messages are usually easier to write than messages that deliver bad news.

f) Form letters are impersonal and should never be used when replying to a request or an application.

g) The best way of turning down a request for money is to say "no" in the first paragraph so that the refusal is completely clear.

h) You should always end a letter of refusal by suggesting that the writer should try again another time.

i) There are certain instances when using the passive voice in a bad-news letter is effective and practical.

j) Although a direct approach is sometimes appropriate in communicating bad news, an indirect approach is more effective in most cases.

6. A local environmental group has written to your company asking for a financial contribution. Which of the following two letters of refusal is better? Why?

a) We must refuse your request for a donation at this time, since we restrict our support to organizations that provide assistance to people in need. Please contact us again next year, as by that time our policy may have changed.

b) The work of Greenmakers has been very beneficial to our community, and our organization follows your endeavours closely.

We adopted a policy in January to allow our staff to select one local charity that we would support for the year, and the choice for 2011 is Beckstead House.

If you wish to have Greenmakers listed as a possibility for our 2012 fundraising, please notify me and I will ensure that your group is included for consideration.

7. For the last two years, you have been helping young children learn to play hockey. The president of the local hockey association, Arthur Hughes, has written you a letter, asking you to coach the peewee team this year. As a post-secondary student, you have already decided you will need to devote more time to academic work in order to raise your marks for graduate school. You haven't the time to do the coaching job this year.

However, your roommate has mentioned an interest in coaching the team and is a good hockey player.

Write two letters to Mr. Hughes declining the job. Use the direct approach in one and the indirect approach in the other. You may add details if needed. In pairs or small groups, evaluate each other's letters. Which approach is easiest to write? From the reader's perspective, which seems best?

8. In front of the class and with a partner, take turns role-playing for one or more of the following "bad-news" assignments. Alternatively, work in groups of three with the third person being the observer and commentator afterward. (These assignments may also be adapted for written responses.)

   a) You are in charge of a student entertainment show in which a big-name musical group will be performing. On the day of the show, you discover that through a miscalculation you have sold 25 more tickets than there are seats in the auditorium. Fire regulations prevent your adding more seats or allowing standing room. You hope that some "no-shows" will take care of the problem, but 10 minutes before the show begins nine angry ticket holders approach you with nowhere to sit.

   Your task is to

   - give the bad news that you can't find room;
   - give a refund and tickets to attend another performance later in the week;
   - try to pacify your nine angry ticket holders and persuade them to leave peacefully.

   b) After interviewing four people for a summer painting business owned by Paul Purdy, you have hired the people the company needs. You chose those who either had painting experience or had done a lot of physical work. The fourth applicant had neither. Now you must let that applicant, Sharon Brown, know your decision. She will realize that the three you have hired are male and may suspect that your decision is sexist.

9. An out-of-town friend has asked you to see his son, Paul Dubois, a young college graduate who wants a job in sales. As the sales manager of Lancer Foods you agree to talk to Paul about his plans, knowing that a junior sales position will soon become available.

   During the interview, it becomes clear that, although Paul has a pleasant, outgoing personality, he has no sales experience. More importantly, he has no record of work or other experience to indicate that he is hard-working and reliable.

   Since Paul is going home the next day, you promise to write to him within two weeks. When you discuss the job opening with your personnel manager, you find that other applicants are more qualified.

   Write a letter of refusal to Paul.

10. A neighbour and owner of Garden Master Franchises, Herbert Carter, has applied for credit to buy garden equipment from your company, ABC Industries. As credit manager of ABC, you discover that Carter has a record of late payment of his bills and that his business appears to be financially shaky.

    Write a letter to Carter in which you refuse his application for credit.

11. You are the owner of The Donut Shop and you have received a letter from Bill McIntyre, director of the Frontenac County Softball League. He has asked you to sponsor the boys' midget team in the amount of $1 000. Your promotional budget is already allocated for this year. Since you already sponsor a girls' softball team, you are not likely to sponsor another team in the next few years.

    Write a letter of refusal to McIntyre. You will be including with it 100 coupons for a free doughnut to be distributed to the boys in the league.

Persuasive Writing

"Effective communication is incredibly important in any leadership position. So many times you are selling others on an idea, a service, a product, or yourself. Through communication you can arouse their emotions and convince them to take action."

—Gregg Hanson, former president and CEO, Wawanesa Mutual Insurance Company

You would probably be surprised if you stopped to count the number of times during the day when you are trying to influence others to do something or when others are trying to influence you. A typical student might ask a friend to lend some lecture notes, pick up an extra coffee at the cafeteria, get tickets for the hockey game, or go on a date. The same student working in an office might ask a fellow worker to handle a difficult customer, check over a letter or report, or help straighten out a bookkeeping error. These are small favours, unlikely to need much persuasion or meet with much resistance. However, when you want people to do things they have no interest in doing or don't want to do, you need greater powers of persuasion. In business writing, a persuasive letter or memo requires special strategies. It must appeal to a reader or readers in such a way that they make up their minds to act.

Persuasion is not an easy job. There is no surefire way of doing it. Psychologists, politicians, marketers, and advertisers have spent millions researching the subject. Although they still can't tell what will always work, they have discovered some approaches that work better than others. Annette Shelby (1986) has developed a useful classification of current theories of persuasion. In planning persuasive communication, you have three basic influences to consider: your own credibility, the motivation of the receiver, and the structure and content of the message itself.

Credibility of the Persuader

To persuade successfully, you should first consider how credible you are. Here are some contributors to credibility:

1. **Position power.** If you are the boss or hold an important position, you clearly have built-in credibility since the position itself confers a certain clout or authority. However, using the credibility of your position to persuade is different from coercion—using your position to enforce your point of view. In most cases you will want to use the former power.

This chapter of *Impact* will help you to

1. analyze the roles of sender and receiver in persuasive communication tasks;
2. use different types of appeal in persuasive writing;
3. apply a Rogerian approach to structuring an argument;
4. understand basic patterns for persuasion;
5. write effective letters of request;
6. understand and apply the AIDA sales letter sequence;
7. learn the correct sequence for writing collection letters;
8. understand the uses and limitations of email in persuasive writing.

Watch
BCVL: Ethical Communication

2. **Expertise.**   People will often heed the suggestions of a subordinate who has specialized knowledge that they don't possess. What special knowledge do you have?

3. **Trust.**   Are you considered trustworthy and fair-minded, especially on the subject under discussion? If you are perceived to have a hidden agenda or a vested interest in what you are advocating, your credibility will be diminished.

4. **Similarity.**   Most people have a tendency to believe someone with similar outlooks and attitudes. What do you have in common with the receiver? What bonds of similarity can you point to—hometown, background, clubs, special interests?

If your credibility is low, consider getting the support of someone who is more credible than you are to strengthen your case. In business, this might be a respected senior executive or an acknowledged expert in the field.

Motivation of the Receiver

It's a truism that to get people to do something they must want to do it. Remember the old saying "A man convinced against his will is of the same opinion still." It's true for both sexes. But how do you get a person to want to act? What is it that provides motivation? There are no definite answers to these questions, but Abraham Maslow (1987), the well-known organizational behaviourist, provides one useful guide. He suggests that there is a hierarchy of needs that individuals strive to fulfill. Only when they have satisfied basic or "deficiency" needs do they move on to higher ones. Figure 6-1 indicates the five different levels of needs.

Figure 6-1   Maslow's Hierarchy of Needs

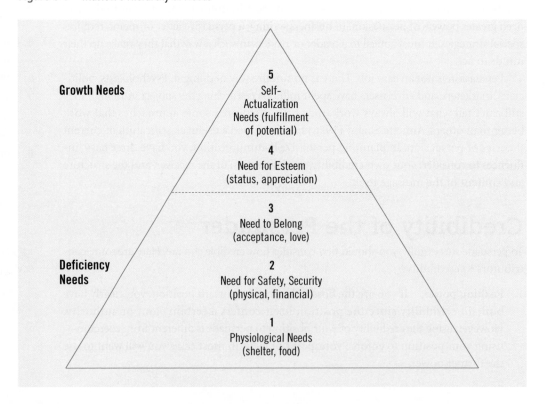

Maslow's ranking of needs is disputable. Poverty-stricken artists are often less concerned with food and security than with self-fulfillment. However, his insistence that people react according to individual needs is undoubtedly correct. Even with business managers at the same level and in the same type of job, one manager may be concerned about costs, another about prestige, and another about group harmony.

When planning persuasive communication, therefore, spend some time determining the precise need of your receiver. In sales training, this step is often referred to as "qualifying" the potential customer, finding out through questions and discussion what need the customer wants filled so that the later sales pitch can work to satisfy it. In your persuasive communication, you should similarly tailor your message to the receiver's perceived need.

The research findings of Wheeless, Barraclough, and Stewart (1983) complement Maslow's hierarchy of needs and suggest these strategies for persuasion:

- To persuade someone motivated by survival and safety needs, preview the consequences of following or not following the advice. Advertisements for insurance or road safety often take this approach.

- To persuade someone with a need to belong, stress group identity. Most beer and pop ads are examples of this strategy.

- To persuade someone with a desire for self-fulfillment, stress values and social obligations. Fundraising drives often exemplify this approach.

Message Options

Your message can be shaped by appeals based on reason, emotion, authority, and evidence.

◉ Watch

Perils of Pauline: Writing Persuasive Messages

Appeal to Reason

Managers try to act on reason. They often reach their decisions after analysis, whether they use techniques learned in business courses or the judgment of experience. When you want to influence people in business, therefore, it's appropriate to present your case in a reasonable way and to appeal to the receiver's desire to be reasonable. Logic—or even the appearance of logic—is convincing.

HANDLING OPPOSITION

When you are talking to the converted—that is, suggesting something that fits with the receiver's viewpoint—you can get a quick response by reinforcing only one side of the case. If you are facing someone with an opposing point of view, however, you will seem more balanced and fair-minded if you present a two-sided argument.

The psychologist Carl Rogers (1995) maintains that people are more likely to change a point of view when they don't feel threatened. The most effective approach with opposition, therefore, is to demonstrate not a combative attitude but understanding.

For written arguments, a practical application of this strategy is first to describe the opposite point of view in a non-evaluative way. When you have shown that you appreciate the reader's position, the reader will be more willing to listen to yours. With a Rogerian argument you are less concerned about "winning" than about gaining support.

You can structure such an argument in two ways, as Figure 6-2 shows:

1. **Begin with a concession statement.**   In a paragraph or two summarize the opposing position clearly and objectively. Then proceed to your side of the case, showing how

Figure 6-2   A Rogerian Approach to Argument

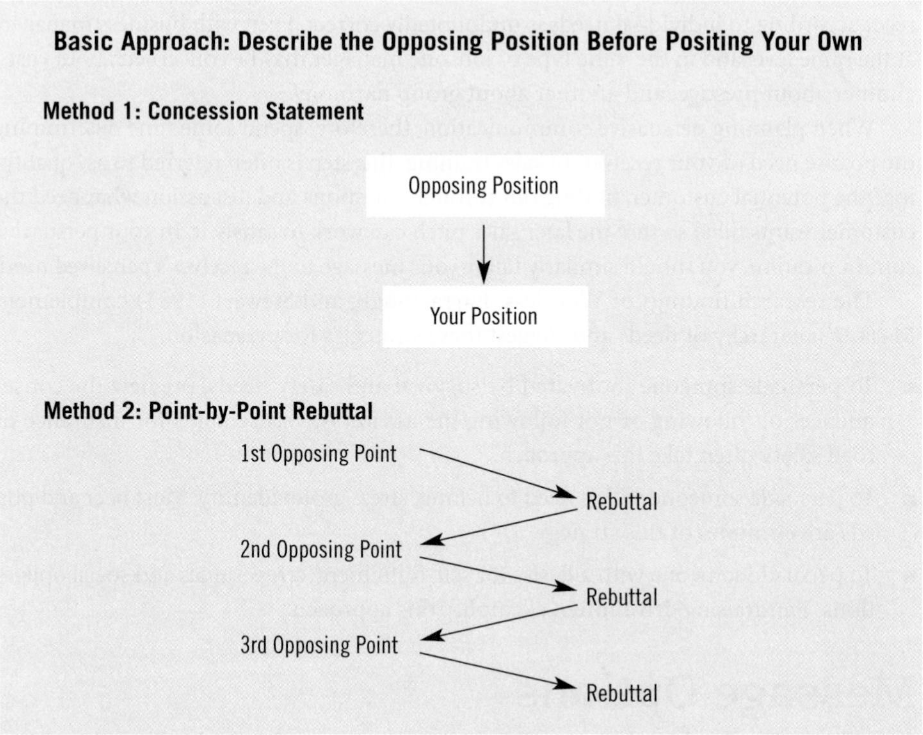

Basic Approach: Describe the Opposing Position Before Positing Your Own

Method 1: Concession Statement

Opposing Position

↓

Your Position

Method 2: Point-by-Point Rebuttal

1st Opposing Point

Rebuttal

2nd Opposing Point

Rebuttal

3rd Opposing Point

Rebuttal

it overrides the preceding argument. For example, if you want to support the advantages of North American free trade, begin with the reasons others give for not supporting the concept.

2. **Use a zigzag structure.**   Begin with one of the opposing points, then counter it. Move to the next opposing point, and counter it. And so on. As a supporter of free trade, you could use this structure to present and counter three popular arguments against free trade.

Here are two examples of Method 1, a concession statement:

We understand your wish to return home as quickly as possible for the Christmas holidays. However, the college-wide exam schedule makes it impossible for us to alter the date of your accounting exam.

Your request to hold an all-staff convention in early August is a creative and thoughtful attempt to solve the difficulties we have been experiencing. I think we should discuss this idea again when we look at next year's budget, but time constraints will not allow us to consider this as an option in 2011.

Note the importance of a transitional word or phrase ("however" in the first example and "but" in the second example) to move smoothly from the opposing position to your position.

Method 2, point-by-point rebuttal, requires the same transitional elements. Here is an example:

In your response to the planned reduction in library hours, you state that our proposed hours of 8:30 a.m. to 6:00 p.m. will deprive clients of the opportunity to use the library after work hours. However, our statistics show that library use peaks at 5:00 p.m. and that only 5 per cent of user time occurs after 6:00 p.m.

You have also expressed concern that our municipal funding will decrease if our hours of service are reduced, yet a council motion on July 30 guarantees continued funding at the present level.

Your final point about possible reductions in staff has also been of concern to us, although we have arrived at a new staffing plan that reduces only one part-time position by 10 hours a week.

Appeal to Emotion

Even with "hard-nosed" decision makers, reason will not win the day in all circumstances. Sometimes it takes an added appeal to move people—an appeal to emotion.

Take cigarettes, for example. Most smokers are convinced—that is, they rationally agree—that cigarettes are bad for their health and that smoking is a silly habit. But are they persuaded to stop smoking? Obviously not.

Advertisers know that no matter how objective we try to be in our judgments, emotion has a way of creeping in. Advertising copy often capitalizes on this fact by appealing to one or more basic emotions: pride, fear, envy, or the desire to be loved, happy, or respected. The promotion of consumer products, whether liquor, cars, or fragrance, usually has a strong emotional appeal. In other kinds of persuasive business correspondence, the play on emotion is usually subordinate to reason and more subtle.

An emotional appeal does not work with someone who is strongly opposed. Nor is its effect very long-lasting. It is most useful as a way of tipping the balance for someone who already has good rational arguments. When you choose to play on emotions, be moderate in your appeal.

Examples of an appeal to emotion are

You deserve the best in viewing comfort.

Make the planet safe for your children by contributing to "Blue Skies" today.

Join thousands of discriminating buyers and experience the superior resolution of a Trueline printer.

Appeal to Authority

If your credibility is low, this appeal is especially useful. By using the testimony or support of someone the receiver trusts or respects, you can bolster your own case. Here are examples:

The executive board has given full support to our proposed restructuring.

Marvin Hanley, a specialist in total quality management and president of Netcom Systems International, is convinced that we should conduct an operational review before January.

Appeal to Evidence

Using statistics and other verifiable evidence will also help gain support when personal credibility is low. Be sure to use current sources wherever possible, since new evidence is always more persuasive than trotting out old and possibly outdated information. Consider the following examples:

The level of job satisfaction among our staff has clearly decreased. The staff survey we conducted in September shows a 40 per cent increase in applications for lateral transfer.

Our argument in favour of a new line is supported by a poll conducted in June by Market Analysts Inc.

Of course, the appeals described above are not mutually exclusive. You can combine more than one in any persuasive communication.

Basic Patterns for Persuasion

✳ Explore

Email 16: Persuasive (Using AIDA)

For most persuasive letters, the reader is more likely to be indifferent than hostile to what you have to say. Yet since indifference is an obstacle—a form of passive resistance—you will need to overcome it if you are going to persuade the reader to read on, let alone to adopt your suggestion. The basic order for a persuasive letter helps overcome this resistance:

1. **Get the reader's attention.**   This opening attention-getter should be brief—at most a short paragraph of three sentences.

2. **Introduce the proposal or product and persuade the reader of the benefit.**   Build interest by showing how the proposal or product fills a specific need. Anticipate any objections and answer them.

3. **Indicate the action the reader must take.**   Link the act to the benefit.

As with other kinds of business correspondence, persuasive writing must be "you-centred" if it is to work. Even though the subject of the communication may be a product or another organization's needs, the appeal must be directed at the reader.

Persuasive writing has many different uses, but it nearly always works best if it takes an indirect approach. Many writers mistakenly state the request at the outset, thinking this will save the reader's time. Admittedly, a routine or straightforward request to a receptive reader can and often should be direct. A request requiring persuasive power, however, needs reader preparation.

The most common kinds of persuasive writing in business are letters of request, sales letters, and collection letters. Each follows the basic persuasive pattern, although some, such as the sales letter, modify it considerably.

Letters of Request

As active members of society, business people are often asked to give unpaid help to an organization or cause or to identify others who will do so. Written pleas for donations or time, requests to give speeches or lectures at no charge, invitations to serve on the boards or committees of charities, calls for help with political campaigns—these are all forms of persuasive communication.

A request for unpaid help can often appeal to a person's social conscience, to a sense of obligation to the community, or to a desire to make a contribution. The good feeling and self-respect that come from doing valuable service can be reason enough for responding favourably. The writer's job is to make clear that the service is valuable.

Readers may also be moved by other indirect benefits to themselves or their businesses—the chance to meet potential customers, to promote their own interests or viewpoints, to obtain a position of leadership, or simply to enjoy a diversion from routine responsibilities at work. Whatever appeal or appeals you use—and often you can use more than one—be sure to give the reader good reasons for accepting rather than suggesting reasons for refusing. The letter below provides an easy out for the reader. It also mistakenly states the request directly:

✕ I have been authorized to ask you to join the Concerned Citizens Committee, which is planning a fundraising fair for London residents with physical challenges. We hope to raise enough money to purchase a bus for people with special needs. They vitally need our support, and we think our efforts will be improved by having people with business experience involved.

We know you are a busy man, Mr. Kraft, but hope that you will find the time to join our committee. Please let me know your answer as soon as possible.

By contrast, this next letter uses the indirect order for persuasion and is more concrete in outlining the request and the benefits. It tries to make the reader want to accept and suggests a specific action for the reader to follow.

✓ Many London residents who are physically challenged sit at home day after day, alone and isolated because it is difficult to go out. The Concerned Citizens Committee wants to correct this unhappy situation by providing a specially equipped bus for persons with physical challenges.

To raise money for the bus, we are planning a spring fair. Will you join our committee of community leaders and help make the fair a success? Your experience in business would be a great asset in organizing the event. We plan to meet for only two hours every other Tuesday evening until the May event.

Would you email me at jfox@telnet.ca or call me at 519-923-5150 within the next week to say that you will join us? It will mean a great deal to physically challenged members of our community.

Sales Letters

Since sales letters bring in millions of dollars, a great deal of money has been spent researching how best to do them. Sales letters tend to be longer than other kinds of letters because they include many specific facts. The concrete details about a product are what heighten a buyer's desire to have it. However, sales letters clearly do not just ramble on; every part is carefully crafted. Good ones have a flow and vitality that hold the reader's attention from beginning to end.

Many sales letters are form letters, sent out in the hundreds or thousands to people who haven't asked for them. Unsolicited sales letters require more skill than any other kind of letter because they must stir uninterested readers to action. Professional writers are well paid to keep us from throwing out "junk mail." Even though the percentage of returns is small, unsolicited letters are effective sales weapons. So, of course, are solicited letters. Written after a request for information, they are an easier task because they are responding to a demonstrated interest. Nevertheless, they must still meet the challenge of turning an interest into a sale.

Whether they are composed individually or as a form letter, all sales letters need careful planning. You should attempt to write one only after you have done some serious thinking about the product (or the service or idea) and its market. At the very least, you should have answers to the following questions:

■ What is the product or service? How does it work? What does it provide?

■ What are the outstanding features that make it different from its competitors?

■ What is the price and how does it compare with the price of competing products or services?

✱ Explore
Letter 24: Sales (Using AIDA)

✱ Explore
Letter 25: Persuasive

✱ Explore
Email 15: Sales

✓ Practise
Exercise 7: Selling a Service

■ What warranty or guarantee does it have?

■ What is the profile of the intended buyer? Here's where market research helps. Analyzing the demographics (age, sex, income, area, and type of residence as well as lifestyle) of the target market will help you identify the buyer's perceived need.

■ How will the intended buyer benefit from the product or service? Is it better, faster, more efficient, more economical, more user friendly?

After you have analyzed the product and the market, determine what your central **selling point** will be. There may be several outstanding features to choose from and you will probably want to mention all these features in the sales letter, but one central selling point should dominate. This point becomes the theme of your sales letter—the focus that holds all the other details together.

Sales Letter Sequence

A sales letter follows the indirect order of other persuasive letters, but the formula is more precise (see Figure 6-3). Its sequence can be remembered by the acronym AIDA: *attention, interest, desire, action.*

CAPTURE ATTENTION

A sales letter must capture the reader's attention immediately or it won't be read. Here are some strategies for "hooking" your reader:

■ **A startling or thought-provoking fact.**   "One out of every four adults will develop a back problem"; "If you had invested in Fairview Estates 10 years ago, your property would now be worth at least three times what you paid for it."

■ **A stimulus to the imagination.**   A description with concrete, sensuous details works well, especially with a product that has romantic appeal, such as a sailboat: "Picture yourself at the tiller on a sunny July day, sailing over the crystal waters of Georgian Bay." Remember that *sensuous* refers to all the senses.

■ **An anecdote or narrative.**   Many products can be introduced effectively by a story: "When Mrs. Miller bought her Nulite sewing machine 20 years ago, little did she know it would still be sewing her grandchildren's clothes today."

■ **A bargain.**   Few people can resist finding out the details of a bargain. Many will be caught by the possibility of a good deal, such as the come-on "Now you can get three magazines for the price of one."

■ **An offer.**   Like a bargain, an offer presents a direct benefit and can draw the reader through the rest of the letter to find out the details: "Here's a way to cut your shopping time in half."

■ **A question.**   "Would you like to cut your heating bills by a third?" "Should Canadians be worried about our environment?" If you use a question to capture attention, make sure the reader will not want to answer negatively. If the answer is a quick "no," the reader will not bother to read on.

■ **Visual attention-getters.**   Images are especially useful for emotional appeals, since they are concrete. For example, showing a picture of an appealing child who is disadvantaged in some way is an effective introduction to a request for funds to combat the problem.

Figure 6-3   Sales Letter

THE HOUSEGUARDS

20 Cawlish Road
Toronto ON M4T 1B2

January 18, 2011

Dear Neighbour

Attention ⎰ Do your pets or plants keep you from enjoying a good holiday? Are you worried about the garden or vandalism while you are away?

Interest ⎰ **THE HOUSEGUARDS** can help you. We are a group of college students in the neighbourhood who look after properties while residents are away. We'll be pleased to look after your house, care for your pets, and do your chores.

Desire ⎰ We can
  • water your plants or lawn
  • cut your grass
  • feed and exercise your pets
  • pick up your mail

If you like, we can even set automatic timers on your lights and adjust the locations regularly to discourage prowlers.

Our services are reliable, bonded, and reasonably priced. We come with good references from your neighbours.

Action ⎰ Call **THE HOUSEGUARDS** today at 416-928-4159. We'll visit you promptly and give you a free estimate of our services. Let **THE HOUSEGUARDS** help make your getaway carefree!

Sincerely

Ron Thayer

Ron Thayer
President

Phone: (416) 928-4159   **houseguards@bos.net**   **Fax: (416) 928-4160**

A word of caution: make sure that any attention-getting opener is related to the central selling point of the product. It's no help having a catchy beginning if it doesn't lead into the sales pitch.

CREATE INTEREST

This is the "hook." Identify the reader's needs and what you can do to help. Think about the question "How will the product make a difference to the reader?" When you introduce the product, immediately identify its benefits. Here are examples:

> The Voyageur Business Travellers Insurance Plan will rid you of the high cost—and accompanying anxieties—of sickness or injury in foreign countries.

> or

> The expert copywriters at Adbanks will cut your advertising costs and allow your staff to devote their time and energy to product development.

BUILD DESIRE

This step extends the effort to gain the reader's interest. You are increasing the sales pitch, trying to make the reader not just appreciate the product but want it.

Details sell, and the more concrete they are the better. Showing the product in action has more effect than an inert description. Try to describe the product as if the reader were actually using it. Instead of saying, "This comfortable Reilly chair has a cushioned leather seat. It can swivel as well as recline," you might describe the chair as if the reader were in it:

> Sink into the soft leather of the cushioned seat. Lie back and catch forty winks. Or swivel around to watch your favourite TV program. Either way, you'll feel comfortable and relaxed in a Reilly chair.

Remember that the more sensuous your descriptive detail—the more the reader has a sense of seeing, touching, hearing, tasting, or smelling—the more the product will come alive, whether it is a camera or a can opener. Don't pile on the adjectives, however. A few, chosen to convey the central selling point, are better than a lot. If your central selling point is luxury, you are better to repeat the word *luxury* or *luxurious* than to spray the text with a range of less-appropriate adjectives.

In building desire, you can appeal to emotion or to logic, but you are trying to move the reader to ask, "And how can I get this?" Beyond concrete description, you can offer additional evidence or incentives, such as the following:

- **Statistics.**   "More than 1 000 000 students have enjoyed the benefits of our scholarship plan in the last five years"; "Independent research shows that cars with Rust-Away last an average of five years longer."

- **Testimonials.**   The credibility of the person doing the persuading can affect reader reaction. For this reason many sales letters use testimonials from people who are generally considered trustworthy, such as doctors and scientists. Even though their credentials are not scientific, sports and entertainment celebrities are often hired to endorse products. Buyers assume that since they are experts in one area they are believable in another—questionable logic perhaps, but often effective.

- **A good deal.**   When a bargain is not the central selling point, offering one can often provide an incentive to buy. The offer of a free bonus or a home trial with a money-back guarantee can sometimes tip the balance of reader desire. Even if you are selling an idea or service rather than a product, you can show how it will save money.

URGE YOUR READER TO TAKE ACTION

Here's where you ask for the order. It's crucial at this point to include all the information the reader needs. Do it concisely, however. A brief paragraph of one or two sentences will make it seem simple for the reader to act.

- **Stress promptness.**   The longer readers delay, the less likely they are to order. Say something like "Send in your order today" or "We'll mail you the prospectus as soon as we hear from you." Keep the directions simple. Enclose a self-addressed envelope or order form and be sure to give telephone, fax, and email information.

- **Be positive but avoid super-hype.**   Speak confidently. Instead of a phrase such as "I hope . . . ," give direct instructions that assume the prospect will act. On the other hand, don't harangue your reader with a lot of "Act now! Don't delay getting this fabulous bargain!" exclamations. Although sales letters for some products habitually seem to shout, many readers are turned off by this tactic. A calm but positive tone is usually a better bet than supercharged hyperbole.

A Note about Price

If cost effectiveness is the central selling point, you should emphasize it from the beginning. If it is an added feature, you can include it in the "interest" section. If price is not a selling point at all, discuss it at the end of the sales pitch, just before you give the details on how to buy. One way of deemphasizing the cost is to link it to benefits. You can make it the subordinate part of a sentence in which the main part mentions the reward: "For only $72 you can have 24 issues—two years of entertaining reading."

If you simply want to use the sales letter as a chance to get in the door, you may want to eliminate the mention of price altogether. The action step you want in that case is a request for a brochure or an appointment. This approach is often used when the price of getting something will initially seem high. The disadvantage is that the reader has a potential objection that remains unaddressed, but that trade-off may be better than the risk of losing a prospect because of high price.

Collection Letters

If you are in a business that has many transactions with customers or clients, you will likely be faced with the problem of unpaid bills.

Although chasing money is distasteful to many people, it's a job that cannot be ignored or done in a half-hearted way if the business is to stay profitable. Successful bill-collecting is a matter of three Ps: promptness, patience, and perseverance. It requires promptness in going after the debtor at regular intervals, patience in remaining courteous, and perseverance in not letting the debtor off the hook.

The collection process usually takes the form of a series of letters making increasingly insistent demands on the reader to pay the bill. If you are in a company with a lot of debtors, it is probably best to design a series of form letters that can be personalized using the Merge feature of your word processing software. As with any other form of customer or client correspondence, the more individualized the letter, the more likely it is to be effective.

The collection series usually consists of three to five letters sent over a period of one to four months after payment is first due. Whether all or some of the letters are sent depends largely on the character and record of the debtor. In deciding what kind of letter will be most effective, therefore, the first step is to assess the debtor: Is the individual or company a good credit risk or a poor one?

A good credit risk

- usually pays on time; or
- sometimes forgets but pays promptly when reminded; or
- makes arrangements to pay in instalments when he or she cannot pay immediately.

A poor credit risk

- has a record of unpaid bills elsewhere; or
- is habitually late in paying; or
- pays only when threatened with legal action.

By trying to figure out in advance the type of person you are dealing with and the likely reason for the unpaid bill, you can adapt the letter to the situation, increasing the chance of recovery and decreasing the likelihood of hard feelings.

General Guidelines

Three guidelines apply to all good collection letters: be polite, stick to the facts, and follow through on what you say.

BE POLITE

When the other side in a dispute is clearly at fault, it's easy to be hostile. A good collection letter remains polite, even when it is severe and stringent in its demands. Remember that the aim of most collection efforts is not to impose some penalty but to get the debtor to pay. If the customer or client is someone whose business you want to retain, it's doubly important to keep the relationship as free from animosity as possible. Here is the kind of language to avoid, and some alternatives to it:

✗ If you were dissatisfied, you should have returned the saw during the 10-day trial period.

✓ Our 10-day trial allowed you to test the saw and return it for a full refund if you wished.

✗ Since you have failed to pay your bill, you are being charged interest at a rate of 26.9 per cent per annum.

✓ Until the bill is paid, interest will be charged at a rate of 26.9 per cent per annum. [This is an instance where the passive verb works better than the active, since "you have failed" is accusatory.]

STICK TO THE FACTS

Give precise dates for when you expect payment and give exact figures of the amount owing. Don't exaggerate or indulge in emotional overkill:

✗ You are forever forgetting to pay your bills.

✗ Clearly, nobody can rely on you.

✓ Please remit your payment of $329.85 by April 15 in order to avoid an additional credit charge.

FOLLOW THROUGH ON WHAT YOU SAY

Be honest about your intentions and then stick to your guns. If you say that you are willing to negotiate terms for payment, be sure that you will do so. If you threaten to take legal action by a certain date, when the time comes act without delay. If your threats are seen as idle, they will be disregarded.

Collection Letter Sequence

The most common sequence of letters in a collection series is a reminder followed when necessary by an inquiry, a positive appeal, a negative appeal, and an ultimatum.

STEP 1: REMINDER

This is usually the first letter sent, unless the debtor has a record of late payment. Many people, especially individual consumers, will simply have forgotten or been too busy doing other things. A reminder is often enough to get quick payment. Even for habitually late payers, a reminder can serve notice that interest charges are building:

> This is a reminder that the $840 final payment for your new carpets was due on April 30. To avoid a buildup of interest charges, please slip your payment into the enclosed envelope and drop it in the mail.

> Thank you for doing business with Fenwick Carpets.

For reminder notices, some businesses simply send a copy of the original invoice with a stamp or sticker saying "Reminder," "Overdue," or "Second Notice" in a conspicuous spot.

STEP 2: INQUIRY

The purpose here is to obtain immediate payment or, alternatively, to get an explanation that will allow you to work out a plan for future payment. This approach works well for customers who fully intend to pay but who have a temporary cash shortage. By asking for the reason for nonpayment (and implying or explicitly offering to negotiate terms for payment), you have a good chance of getting a response, if not fast payment. If the customer's record is good enough to justify paying by instalments, you can at least get the process started:

> Although we have sent you two reminder notices, we still have not received payment of your account in the amount of $840, outstanding since April 30. Interest charges are accumulating. Since you are a trusted customer, we wonder what has happened.

> We would appreciate immediate payment or at least an explanation for your delay. If you inform us of your circumstances, we may be able to work out a mutually satisfactory plan for payment.

> We await your prompt response.

In asking for an explanation, be careful not to provide ready-made excuses for the customer, such as suggesting possible dissatisfaction with goods or services.

STEP 3: POSITIVE APPEAL

This appeal may take several forms, but essentially it appeals to the customer's better qualities or gives positive reasons for paying the bill. The emphasis in this and other appeals should be on the benefit to the customer rather than to the company. Depending on the customer, the central message may appeal to one or more attitudes or emotions:

- **Fair play.**   Here you can point out what you have done for the customer and suggest that it is the customer's turn to balance the equation. Most people think of themselves as fair and honest, and many will react positively to a call for fair play:

Last July we sent you a shipment of lumber to help you meet your cottage-building needs. Now we in turn ask you for payment of your bill for $1 410, which was overdue as of August 30. We have already sent you two reminders and a request for an explanation.

We value your business and will continue to strive to give you prompt and efficient service. We anticipate your prompt payment of the outstanding balance of $1 410.

- **Pride in reputation.**   People in the public eye or in positions of leadership are usually especially conscious of maintaining a good reputation. Many are justifiably proud of their good name and do not want to be known for anything discreditable. These people will likely respond well to a letter that appeals to their pride:

We are sure you value your reputation as a successful small business owner and want to retain the respect of the business community by paying your bills promptly.

or

Through sound management, your company has acquired a good credit rating in the business community. In order to keep this rating and the respect that accompanies it, please pay your bill promptly.

- **Practical self-interest.**   In this appeal you simply show how prompt payment will directly benefit the reader—usually by preventing extra expense, whether high interest charges or legal costs. This is obviously less an appeal to emotion than an appeal to reason. You are counting on the reader seeing the benefit of making payment and avoiding more problems.

If we receive your payment on or before July 31, you will avoid the additional expense of 26.9 per cent interest on overdue accounts.

or

We believe that you will want to avoid the expense of legal action by making a payment of $550 by May 10.

STEP 4: NEGATIVE APPEAL

People who are normally good credit risks are more likely to be frightened of the consequences of nonpayment than are poor risks. People with a history of defaults often try to get away with it again. A negative appeal emphasizes the consequences of nonpayment, such as loss of reputation, inability to get credit with other businesses, or costly court action. Take care that your tone is direct and matter of fact in laying out the consequences; let the threatened consequences rather than abusive or inflammatory remarks do the work:

Since we have received no payment or explanation from you since the due date of April 30, our next step will be an application for garnishment of your wages. To avoid this embarrassment please settle your account by July 15.

or

We are sure you realize the damage to reputation and credit rating that a court case will entail, as well as the extra cost in time and money. You can avoid these consequences by promptly settling your account.

You can emphasize the urgency of your request by sending it as registered mail. You can also get someone in a higher position in your company to sign it.

STEP 5: ULTIMATUM

This letter of last resort is a straightforward warning to pay or be prepared for the consequences—either the intervention of a collection agency or immediate legal action. If you think the customer will fight the case, it's a good idea to mention your previous notices and appeals. You should also give the precise date on which you will take further action if the bill is not paid:

> On February 15, we delivered four new chairs to your office. An invoice in the amount of $2 542.95 was mailed on February 28. Despite four requests since that time, we have received neither the money nor an explanation from you. We have no option now but to take direct action.
>
> If we do not receive payment of $2 695.53 (the current balance, including interest) by July 31, we will instruct our lawyers, McBinn and Naylor, to start legal proceedings.

For small bills, the cost to you or your company of legal proceedings makes a final ultimatum of this sort impractical. Your only hope in these cases is to make the other appeals strong enough that the customer tries to pay the debt to you before paying any other creditors. If you are supplying a continuing service or product that can be stopped, such as fuel delivery or cleaning services, you can effectively paint a picture of the pleasure or convenience that the customer will now lose—or could retain—by paying the bill.

In any case, despite some bad apples, most customers and clients want to pay their bills and want the comfortable feeling of a transaction satisfactorily completed. Unless you have evidence to the contrary, you are best to be positive before being negative in handling collections. You will more likely get your money—and keep a customer.

 # Internet Issues

Increasingly, sales pitches are sent by email, often in response to an Internet inquiry or search on a related topic. For corresponding with an acquaintance or co-worker, email requests are standard. However, as the examples in this chapter illustrate, many persuasive messages work best in a paper-based medium. Let's look at the three types of persuasive writing discussed in this chapter to determine how well suited they are to an electronic medium.

Letters of request are more suited to an electronic medium than are sales letters or collection letters. Using email for a request, especially if you know your reader, is fast and efficient. If important details such as date, time, and place are included in your message, you will want to send a follow-up letter to ensure that your reader has a permanent and portable record of the information.

Sales letters sent as email are in danger of being hastily deleted as "spam." Most Internet users have become highly sensitized to spamming and regard unsolicited advertising as invasive. Although paper-based sales letters might be seen in the same light, it is likely that your message will receive a better reception if it is opened and read at the reader's leisure. A full mailbox doesn't lend itself to the thoughtful perusal of a sales pitch.

Collection letters should be paper-based to ensure that you have a clear record of any communication you have with the client. Although email can be used as a record, paper documentation is more reliable. In addition, the sensitive nature of this type of message and the lack of security of many email systems make traditional mail the preferred medium for collection letters.

Exercises

1. Clip an advertisement that contains at least three paragraphs of text and make three photocopies of it. In groups of three, discuss the dominant motivator and the type of appeal used in each advertisement.

   Then think of a way in which the advertisement could stress a different motivator and use a different type of appeal.

2. In small groups or as a class, consider the type of appeal you would choose in each of the following situations:

   a) As the new accountant for your small company, you think buying new accounting software would help you be more efficient and would create a better internal control system. Your boss is known to be a penny-pincher and does not yet trust your ability. How will you persuade your manager to invest in the software?

   b) As a way of increasing sales, the vice-president of your company has divided the sales force into four regional groups, with a promise of cash rewards to those groups that reach their new sales targets for the next six months and a special prize to the group that achieves its target first. As a regional sales manager, you plan to write a memo to subordinates urging them to strive for specific monthly targets. How will you motivate them?

   c) As the new assistant director of outpatient services for your town's hospital, you want to hire a consultant to create new databases for your department. You have in mind an acquaintance who played a similar role at a much larger general hospital. The director you report to has been very supportive in general. You know, however, that she is skeptical about consultants, having had several bad experiences with them. How will you convince her to hire your acquaintance?

3. A colleague has drafted the following letter appealing to fellow employees to join the company's United Way Campaign Committee. He is unhappy with the letter and has asked you to revise it.

   a) List the weaknesses in the letter.

   b) Rewrite the letter.

   > Dear Fellow Employee:
   >
   > Will you become a part of our company's United Way Campaign Committee? I know people are involved in a great many activities these days, but I hope you can spare the time in the next few months to help this valuable cause. The United Way is an important part of our community and has done an excellent job for many years. Our company is trying to do its share by asking our employees to donate. Please let me know soon if you can become involved.

4. The following sentences are all excerpts from sales letters. Revise them, making them concrete, positive, and active. Try to put the reader into the action.

   a) The interactive tutorials make it unnecessary to train office personnel in the use of this program.

   b) A return trip to London can be had for $625 during the special early-bird sale, but the sale ends April 30.

   c) With this wire whisk, there need be no more lumps in sauces but instead the sauces will be smooth.

    d) Free bonus: a ballpoint pen goes with every order, as long as the order isn't under $10.

    e) The cost of this self-cleaning machine is more than that of a conventional one, but it eliminates clogging and a lot of cleaning downtime.

    f) This computer workstation looks good and suits most office decors.

5. Assess a persuasive letter or sales letter you have received recently. Note its strengths and weaknesses. Revise any weak parts.

6. Assess the specific weaknesses in the following sales letter according to the guidelines discussed in this chapter. Then revise it.

> It's never too late! Just because you missed the Boxing Day sale doesn't mean you need to miss this bargain!
>
> We are offering our ultra-slim Soundforce MP3 player to select buyers. It weighs just 54 grams and features 16 GB of memory, a built-in speaker, and up to 40 hours of battery life.
>
> The price is only $149.95, as you can see from the order form below. Amazing value! Beat your friends to it and buy now! Don't delay!

7. As sales manager for Whitestone Education, you feel that all your sales reps should be supplied with laptops to demonstrate products on their road trips. The laptops would allow potential clients to see your products "live and in colour" and would permit sales reps to demonstrate software products and instructor resources. You think a digital display is far more effective than the standard catalogue.

   Whitestone employs 10 sales reps and the cost of a laptop is $499.

   The controller of your company, Martin Tight, needs to approve the expenditure. He is known to be very cost conscious, but he can be persuaded by sound reasoning.

   Write a proposal to Martin Tight. You may add any details you need.

8. As a summer assistant at your university's Career Centre, you have been asked by the director to write a letter to be sent to fellow students in the fall. You are asking for volunteers to work as career-planning assistants in the centre.

   The director gives you the following fact sheet on which to base your letter. Organizing and rewording the facts as you see fit, write a persuasive appeal.

   Position: Volunteer Career-Planning Assistant

   Hours: four hours per week during the academic session

   Qualifications: no experience needed—training provided

   Responsibilities:
   - direct students to Career Centre resources
   - critique student job-application forms
   - plan career talks
   - assist in career workshops

   Benefits:
   - learn effective job-search techniques
   - develop leadership skills
   - get work experience

   Information and application forms available at information desk, Career Centre, Room 01202. Deadline: September 30.

9. You are heading the United Way Campaign in your factory. Although the contribution rate has been good in the past (85 per cent), you hope fellow employees will increase their donations this year since the need for United Way services has increased dramatically in your city. Moreover, you know that many people have used or will use a United Way service at some point. You have heard objections that administrative costs for the United Way are too high, but you have discovered that 90 per cent of donations go directly to client services.

   Write a letter to all employees and enclose a payroll deduction form. You may add any realistic details that will help create an effective letter.

10. Select an advertisement from a current magazine or newspaper.

    a) Ascertain the market for the advertised product or service, the image or selling point projected by the advertisement, and the special features mentioned.

    b) Write a sales letter based on the advertisement. Use the AIDA formula discussed in this chapter. (Include the advertisement when presenting your letter.)

11. Last fall you began a winter snow-shovelling service. You offered customers a choice of a fixed cost of $300 to cover all snow removal throughout the winter or an hourly rate of $15. You hired students to do the clearing, and you provided equipment and handled the sales and paperwork.

    Jennifer Harvey agreed to the fixed cost of $300 and paid $50 in advance. The winter had an unusually light snowfall and your employees were only required to spend a total of 10 hours at the Harvey property. Mrs. Harvey has written to you and enclosed a cheque for $150, saying that this will cover the work done. You don't agree.

    Since Mrs. Harvey is out of the house a lot and doesn't return your calls, write her a letter asking for the account balance in a way that will not antagonize her. (Remember that the Harveys' neighbours are customers and potential customers.)

12. You have decided to set up a small catering business, operating from your house. You will specialize in casseroles and desserts for people who want to entertain without fuss. In testing your recipes on friends, you have discovered that two favourite casseroles are Beef Supreme (beef with hot peppers and mushrooms in a wine sauce) and Almond Duck (duck with almonds and wild rice in a subtle orange sauce). Your raspberry trifle and chocolate-mint cheesecake are dessert hits. You think you will attract most of your customers through personal contact and word of mouth, but you want to send an initial promotional letter to friends and neighbours. Included with it will be a separate menu and price list.

    Write the body of the letter.

13. You are the owner of an accounting office that shares a driveway and parking lot with Handy Cleaners. Since the parking lot needs repairs, you talked to Sam Mavis, the owner of Handy Cleaners, who agreed to share the cost of resurfacing, estimated by All-Weather Paving to be $4 000. You arranged for the resurfacing.

    When the job was completed, you paid the bill and sent a copy of the invoice to Sam Mavis, asking him to send you a cheque for $2 000. Two months have passed and he has not paid. You have tried without success to reach him by phone (he does not work in the store) and have left messages with his employees. Write a step-one collection letter to Mr. Mavis.

14. A customer of your sportswear store, Mrs. Elsa Wilkes, bought $500 worth of clothing on June 15, and three months later she still has not paid her bill. Until this point she has been a reliable customer, paying her account on time. You have already sent her two reminder notes and have received no payment.

Write the next letter in the collection series, as suggested in this chapter.

PEARSON
mycanadianbuscommlab

Visit www.mycanadianbuscommlab.ca for everything you need to help you succeed in the job you've always wanted! Tools and resources include the following:

- Composing Space and Writer's Toolkit
- Document Makeovers
- Grammar Exercises—and much more!

Informal Reports

Learning Outcomes

This chapter of *Impact* will help you to

1. understand the differences between informational and analytical reports;
2. effectively analyze the subject, audience, and purpose of your report;
3. decide when to use direct or indirect order in a report;
4. use different methods of organizing the body of a report;
5. develop strategies for overcoming writer's block;
6. maintain objectivity in your writing;
7. develop effective editing techniques;
8. create and format headings and vertical lists;
9. design effective charts and tables;
10. recognize the emerging role of electronic reports.

"Effective communication is the foundation of great leadership. Without it, plans, strategies, and dreams remain handcuffed to the boardroom table."

—Fred Jaques, former president and CEO, Dare Foods

"Clear and direct communication has never been more important. Today's business executives have less time to analyze the information they receive and yet there is more risk inherent in the decisions they are making with it."

—Bev Park, president and chief operating officer, Couverdon Real Estate

Whether they are formal or informal, good business reports have a common quality: objectivity. The very word *report* suggests a vehicle not for opinion but for cool-headed reflection based on facts. In writing a report, you will be providing material on which other managers will rely to make decisions. They will want information and advice they can trust.

They will also want a report that is easy to understand. Since managers have many demands on their time, they don't want to waste it sifting through an unnecessary clutter of details. Your job is to select and present the material in such a way that they can quickly grasp the essential features.

Informal reports are much more common than formal ones. They are usually shorter than formal reports, often only two or three pages, and they are more conversational, often using personal pronouns and contractions. (To recall the difference between an informal and formal tone, refer to Chapter 2.)

An informal report also has a less "ornate" physical structure than a longer formal report. It is often written as a letter or memo, with the content divided into sections and subsections with headings.

Determining the Purpose

There are two main kinds of informal reporting, and the one you use will depend on your purpose in writing:

1. **The informational report.** This simply gives the facts of a situation, often on a regular schedule, for example, a monthly sales report. Some companies have printed forms for regularly scheduled reports, and the writer has only to complete the necessary information in specified categories. The details recorded on forms like these tend

to be routine. As a consequence, the reader or readers may not really pay attention to the report, even though they are interested in having the information on record. Such a report may be filed rather than read.

A way to prevent regular informational reports from becoming mere bureaucratic busywork is to change the emphasis from the routine to the exceptional. Exception reporting is a way of highlighting the information readers ought to pay attention to. It reports on the significant changes from the routine—the achievements and the trouble spots.

2. **The analytical report.**   In both large and small businesses, this is the more common kind of report and the more challenging to write. It is a problem-solving report, analyzing a situation and recommending a certain course of action. The primary reason for such a report is to help others make a decision; the writer wants to convince the reader of the appropriateness of the analysis and the resulting recommendations or conclusions. Moreover, since presenting ideas or solutions is a harder task than presenting facts, the writer of an analytical report needs to take greater stock of the anticipated reader response in deciding how to organize the report.

Planning the Report

To make sure that a report is effective, you need to set aside a block of time for planning. Then when you sit down to write, you will have a firm idea of where you are heading and how you are going to get there.

Chapter 2 discussed the kind of assessment you should always make of the reader and the reason for writing. Remember that it's important to determine at the outset exactly what type of person you are addressing: consider the reader's position, knowledge, concerns, and possible objections or biases. In the same way, you should decide the precise reason or reasons for writing the report, including the results you hope to obtain from it. If you spend some time on this assessment, you will find it easier to organize and focus your material. In turn, you will find the report easier to write.

The next step is to work out in exact terms the subject of your study. In defining your subject, think of building a fence around a topic. What exactly are the boundaries of your discussion? What will be included and what will be left out? By being as exact as possible, you will create from the start a clear picture of the territory you are covering and make it easier to organize your analysis. For example, "A Study of Cars" is too vague, whereas "A Cost-Benefit Analysis of Three Options for Company Cars" is more precise. The subject might not be the eventual title of the report; the title might in the end be "A Recommendation to Buy X as a Company Car." Nevertheless, defining the subject clearly will help keep the proportions of the study manageable and identify for potential readers the exact nature of the report.

You don't want to spend time on areas of marginal importance or on details that the reader won't care about. For example, if you are asked to write a report on the kind of car the company should lease for its sales force, you will be wasting time—yours and the reader's—if you examine every kind of car available, from sports cars to luxury sedans. It is better to establish in advance the kind or price of vehicle worth considering seriously and then to analyze in detail the two or three most suitable options. You might also determine beforehand whether to consider buying as well as leasing.

Ordinarily a short report does not require a great deal of research. It is usually written by a person with expertise on the subject. Although the writer may have to gather some facts beyond his or her immediate knowledge, generally the information is the kind that can be collected with two or three telephone calls or a quick Web search. If you do have to do extensive research for an informal report, the next chapter offers some advice.

Choosing the Best Order

Two considerations will determine the best order for a report:

1. **What is the most important information?** For an analytical report, the most important information is likely to be the conclusions drawn from the investigation or the recommendations for solving a problem. For an informational report, it may merely be a summative statement that generalizes from the facts or draws attention to the most important ones. In any case, construct a hierarchy of information or ideas; decide what matters most and what matters least. The information or ideas you select as being most important will become your key points.

2. **What is the reader's likely reaction?** You can assume that readers of informational reports want to receive the information, even if it is routine. Similarly, most analytical reports are written at the request of a reader who will be interested in the conclusions or recommendations. In rare cases, however, the reader may be predisposed to reject your conclusions because of a personal bias or conflicting interests. A manager who dislikes change or easily feels threatened can be negative by habit. Predicting reader response is an important step in deciding how to organize your report.

Direct and Indirect Organization

1. **Direct order.** When the reader will be pleased or interested, put the key points before your explanation of how you reached them. This is the best order for most business reports. For a short report, try following this sequence:

Purpose

↓

Key Points (conclusions or recommendations)

↓

Discussion of Findings

Unlike an essay, a report needs no final, summary paragraph. As with a newspaper report, the vital information is at the beginning and the least important details are at the end. (Make an exception if you are sending a short report to an outsider in letter form, in which case you can end with a goodwill close.)

2. **Indirect order.** For those rarer occasions when the reader of an analytical report will be displeased or skeptical, follow the path of least resistance. Build gradually toward the conclusions or recommendations by following this sequence:

Purpose

↓

Discussion of Findings

↓

Key Points (conclusions or recommendations)

Now let's discuss what goes into each section.

Elements of the Report

Purpose

Open with a short statement of purpose. At its simplest this may be a sentence that says, "This report examines paper use in our office and recommends ways to reduce it." Or it can link purpose with recommendations: "This report on paper waste in our office recommends a smart-card system to control printing costs." This statement can be worded differently if the subject line or title clearly reveals the aim of the report. If the method of obtaining information is important—if the recommendations are based on a survey, for example—you can include the method in the introductory statement.

Key Points

Most short reports have either conclusions or recommendations, depending on whether they are informational or analytical. In a short direct-order report, you can usually introduce these points in a concise paragraph linking them to the statement of purpose. If there are a number of recommendations or conclusions, list them with the most important first. You may also want to summarize the main findings that support the conclusions or recommendations. Sometimes you can indicate the main recommendation of a short report in the title, for example, "Recommendation to Install Skylight in Reception Area." In this case, merely summarize the findings leading to the recommendation.

You may find it easiest to write this section last, after you have completed the detailed discussion. It will then be obvious which points should be inserted after the statement of purpose.

Discussion of Findings

Here you show how the facts lead to the conclusions or recommendations. This is the most extensive part of the report and may have several headings. It can be organized in various ways, depending on the subject. The most common methods of organizing the body of the report are as follows:

ORDER OF IMPORTANCE

Here you simply follow the direct approach again. For example, if you have determined the different causes or effects of a problem, start with the most important one and give the details. For each point or finding, make a new section and heading. If the focus of your report is a list of recommendations, you can make each one the subject of a section.

CLASSIFICATION OR DIVISION

This method of organizing divides a topic into classes or component parts. Here are some examples:

- A report on the environmental damage to fish in a certain body of water could classify findings according to the different types of fish.
- A study of the recreational habits of people in an area might classify the target population according to age groups, income groups, or types of occupation. Alternatively it could be organized according to types of recreation.
- A marketing study for a new appliance might be divided according to the traditional four Ps: product, promotion, price, and place.

When classifying or dividing the subject

■ **Do incorporate all relevant information** within the categories you have devised.

■ **Don't let information overlap categories.**   For example, a classification of stores shouldn't have small stores and department stores as two of the categories, since it's possible to be a small department store.

■ **Don't put vastly different amounts of information in each of the categories.**   If one category has most of the information and the remainder have little, you should try to create different categories or to merge some of the small ones.

CHRONOLOGICAL ORDER

This arrangement groups information according to time periods. It can be an effective way to report on trends, for example, the health problems of babies over the last 50 years or house construction needs for the next 20 years. It can also be the obvious choice for reporting a sequence of events or actions.

Take care that you don't choose this order just because it's easiest to arrange. Save it for situations where the sequence itself matters or a time frame makes the information easier to understand.

SPATIAL ORDER

Here the division is according to geography or location. This would be an appropriate order for reporting on individual branch offices or for analyzing buying trends in various regions.

COMPARISON

The best way to compare the merits of two or more options is to create an alternating arrangement. Use the criteria for judging them as the basis for division; then compare the alternatives within each section. For example, suppose you are investigating cars for a company fleet and comparing the two most likely cars on the basis of purchase price, maintenance record, and gas consumption. You can organize your findings this way:

Point-by-point comparison:

1. Purchase price
   a) Car X
   b) Car Y
2. Maintenance record
   a) Car X
   b) Car Y
3. Gas consumption
   a) Car X
   b) Car Y

Another way to organize comparisons is by parallel arrangement in which the various options are examined fully one by one.

Block comparison:

1. Car X
   ■ purchase price

- maintenance record

- gas consumption

2. Car Y

   - purchase price

   - maintenance record

   - gas consumption

This arrangement is not as effective, however, since the reader has to skip back and forth to determine relative merits. Use it only when the things being compared are so diverse that it is impossible to establish common criteria.

Writing the Report

Overcoming Writer's Block

Some reluctant writers will do anything rather than put pen to paper. They put off the fateful moment with inventive delaying tactics. One such ploy is to do yet another round of research and to build up such an array of facts that more study is needed. Of course such unnecessary analysis only leads to further writing paralysis.

If you recognize yourself in this description, take note that there's a better way. The cause of your reluctance to write is probably not laziness so much as fear that you won't do a good enough job. If this is the case, remember that few successful writers get their results by just sitting down and producing polished copy. Rather, they know how to rewrite, revise, and edit. You can follow their example by not aiming for perfection in the first draft. As soon as you have decided how to organize the material in the report, try to get it all down on the page as quickly as possible. Computers are a help. Don't worry about typing errors. Since it's easy to change what you have written—to add, delete, or move whole sections around—you will feel less constrained if you assume that your first draft is imperfect.

Here are two other methods experienced writers have found useful in preventing or overcoming writer's block:

1. **Dictating.**   Some people find that they can overcome writing paralysis by dictating the first draft orally. Speaking doesn't seem as formidable as writing. This method works best if you have already devised an outline for your report and have mostly to fill in the details of sections. You should be prepared to do some heavy editing of the transcribed draft.

2. **Free writing.**   Start with the part of the report you understand best or find easiest to explain and put your thoughts down as they come, regardless of order. Keep writing continuously without hesitating and correcting as you go. You might even begin simply by saying "The point I want to make is . . ." and continue from there. The aim is to get the writing juices flowing. If you don't stop until your thoughts run out, you may be surprised at the amount of material you've written. This method requires more revision than most, but at least you have something on the page to work from.

Whatever method you use, ignore your grammar and spelling as you write; simply keep working until you've got all the ideas and information down. When you have a draft in front of you, you will be over the major hurdle.

Writing Objectively

The opening sentence of this chapter states that reports should be objective. A report that is free of personal prejudice and subjective opinion will surely have more influence than one that is not. Yet it's not easy to be objective, particularly if you have a special interest in your proposals or recommendations. Here are some guidelines that will help keep your reports as unbiased as possible:

1. **Identify your assumptions.**   If you have assumed that some aspects of a given topic are not worth discussing in the report, say so. If you have chosen to limit the topic, give the reason. For example, you may have decided to limit your study of possible company cars to two-door models, based on the assumption that the drivers would rarely have more than one passenger.

    By identifying your assumption, you demonstrate your thoroughness—you have considered all possibilities and have fixed upon the most appropriate ones.

2. **Substantiate your opinions.**   Your conclusions and recommendations should follow from the facts. Personal opinion can have weight if the person expressing it is an authority on the subject, but in most cases opinion needs the support of evidence or explanation. Don't imply what you cannot prove. In using statistics, show the level of uncertainty for any calculated values if you can. If your findings aren't foolproof, show where the uncertainty lies.

3. **Avoid subjective language.**   Words such as *awesome* or *terrible* have an overcharged, emotional tone. Instead of saying, "Ergon Products experienced fantastic growth in sales last quarter," let the facts speak for themselves: "Ergon Products had a 30 per cent sales increase during the fourth quarter."

4. **Be specific.**   As discussed in Chapter 3, concrete language is livelier than abstract language. It can also be clearer. Although you needn't give specific details for every idea or fact you include in a report, you should try to be exact when referring to people, places, times, and amounts—especially when you think the information might be disputed:

✕ After the press contacted plant personnel, it was reported that some of the storage equipment was faulty.

✓ After *Globe* reporter June Fisher called Harry Brown last Friday, she reported that two storage tanks had cracks.

✕ Plant management was involved in the safety discussion process.

✓ Jim Peters, the plant manager, and Helen Falt, the assistant manager, came to three meetings of the Employee Safety Committee.

Be especially careful with ambiguous phrases or words that can have more than one meaning. Terms such as *windfall profit* or *downsizing* can have various interpretations, depending on the reader.

Editing the Report

When you have finished the first draft, it's time to take a break and forget about it for a while. Go to a movie or to the gym for a workout. Not only do you deserve a reward, but you will edit more effectively if you come back to the job refreshed. When you leave enough time before editing to forget what you've said, you'll be better able to assess the draft. You'll quickly spot the weaknesses and confusing parts in your report when you go through it as a relatively detached reader rather than as a harried writer.

The crucial guideline for editing is to put yourself in the reader's shoes. Just as you anticipate the reader's attitudes and expectations when you plan the report, so in editing you should check to see if you've adequately responded to them.

Experienced writers are sometimes able to edit different aspects of their writing at the same time, but if you are not experienced, your revisions will be more effective if you work through your report several times. The best place to begin is with the organization of your material. First ask yourself these questions:

1. **Is the report properly focused?** Will the reader be able to state the central message in a sentence or two? Does the choice and arrangement of detail point to this message?

2. **Is the report complete?** Has it addressed the reader's concerns? Will the reader have unanswered questions? Have I presented all the evidence and put it in a form that is easy to follow? If I have not been able to provide some important details, have I explained why?

3. **Do the conclusions and recommendations fit logically with the findings?** Are the links between them explicit? Have I considered all the evidence fairly? Would the reader be able to reach a different conclusion from the same evidence? In other words, do my conclusions seem objective or do they reflect a personal bias?

4. **Are there any inconsistencies, contradictions, or ambiguities in what I have said?** Could the reader misinterpret any part?

Once you've addressed these higher-order issues, you can turn to the surface structure of your report—to the grammar, punctuation, spelling, and style.

Most people find that editing onscreen is more difficult than editing on paper. The risk of missing errors seems to increase when you scroll through text on a monitor. For this reason, it's usually a good idea to print a hard copy for your final proofread, as this will increase the likelihood that you'll catch all errors and typos. Don't trust computer spell checkers or grammar checkers to catch them all.

Consider the kinds of mistakes you have made in past writing and do a special check for these. If your special weakness is joining sentences with commas, for example, run through the report looking only for these faulty splices.

The advice in the Appendix of this book will help you spot grammatical errors and use punctuation accurately. Chapter 3 will help you improve your style. Underlying all your stylistic editing should be the three basic precepts of effective writing: be clear, be concise, be forceful.

Creating Visual Impact

Although you may not judge a book by its cover, you are probably influenced by appearance. The same is true for a report. If it appeals to the eye, the reader will be more inclined to read it. Since you will want your reports not only to be picked up but also to be read through, they should have visual impact. Here are some ways to achieve the desired effect.

White Space

Don't cram your writing all together; leave spaces between sections and subsections. A densely covered page seems more formidable than one with spaces. Leave wide margins as a way of framing the text. If you want to give part of the report special emphasis, leave extra space around it, so that the white space sets off the black of the text. You can also use a different typeface or indent the text in that part of the report to make it stand out.

Headings

MAKE HEADINGS TELL THE STORY

Each section and subsection of a report should have a heading. Try to make headings "high information"—as descriptive and specific as possible—especially in your discussion of findings. They should tell the story of the report so that a reader glancing through it will recognize the important points. In fact, descriptive headings often reflect key points. Notice the difference between the following sets of headings for a short report comparing brands of office carpeting:

Low-information headings:

a) Durability

b) Cost

c) Colour Choice

High-information descriptive headings:

a) Brand X Is Most Durable

b) Brand Z Is Least Expensive

c) Brands X and Y Have Preferred Colours

It's not always possible to make every heading reflect a key point. Occasionally a heading that simply tells the nature of the content will serve well. For example, if you must have a separate section explaining how you conducted your research, it may be appropriate to call it simply "Method." On the whole, though, the more descriptive the headings, the easier the report will be to read and remember. Descriptive headings are a decided advantage.

KEEP HEADINGS SHORT

Although complete sentences are often useful for headings, keep them short.

✕ In the Future, Laptops Will Show a Substantial Decrease in Price

✓ Laptop Prices Will Drop

MAKE HEADINGS PARALLEL

Since headings act as signposts, they should all be written in the same grammatical form. The following headings are not parallel because they switch from one type of grammatical structure to another:

✕ ▪ Location

▪ Ordering Supplies

▪ Hiring Staff

The correct parallel structure is

✓ ▪ Location

▪ Supplies

▪ Staff

or, if more information is required

✓ ■ Five-Year Lease Has Been Signed

  ■ Supplies for First Quarter Have Arrived

  ■ Staffing Has Been Finalized

USE A NUMBERING SYSTEM

It's helpful, although not essential in a short report, to put numbers before the headings. Numbering lets readers easily refer to sections and it also shows the relative importance of sections and subsections. You can choose from several numbering systems. Two common ones use a combination of numerals and letters:

I	A
A	1
1	a
a	i
b	ii
2	b
B	2
II	B

Increasingly, technical reports are using a decimal system:

1.

  1.1

    1.11

    1.12

  1.2

2.

Whichever system you choose, be sure to use equivalent symbols for sections of equivalent importance.

FORMAT HEADINGS CONSISTENTLY

If you look at a well-edited textbook or published report, you will notice that headings have different typefaces, depending on whether they introduce chapters, sections, or subsections. The varying positions of the headings also indicate their relative importance, although some reports keep all headings at the left margin. There is no single preferred system for formatting headings, but it's important to be consistent. Figure 7-1 shows one of the more common systems.

Vertical Lists

As well as having visual impact, lists allow for quick comprehension. They emphasize that you are making a number of points and help distinguish one point from another. Whenever you can simplify material by using a list, do so. As a rule of thumb, try listing three or more consecutive items or ideas. Conversely, if a list becomes too long—say, beyond six or seven items—try grouping some of the items to make a smaller list. If you

Figure 7-1   Heading Formats

FIRST-DEGREE HEADINGS
Centred. Bold. All caps. Text is below.

Second-Degree Headings
At margin. Bold. Title case, with first letter of each word capitalized. Capitalize conjunctions except for *and*, *but*, *for*, *or*, *nor.* Do not capitalize prepositions (for example, *of*, *to*, *with*) or articles (*a*, *an*, *the*). Text is below.

Third-degree headings. At margin. Bold. Sentence case, with first letter of first word capitalized. Followed by a period. Text follows on the same line.

Fourth-degree headings are italicized and indented with no punctuation, as they form part of the sentence.

will be referring to any items in a list later in the report, number the items. If not, you can simply introduce each item with a dash (–) or a bullet (•).

Here are a few tips to consider when you are creating headings:

- Capitals have more impact than lowercase letters, but text in all caps is hard to read because there are no ascending letters (for example, "d" or "h") or descending letters ("j" or "y").
- Boldface is more emphatic than italics.
- Underlining is no longer used since it cuts through descending letters, making the text difficult to read. And if material is posted to a website, readers are likely to assume that underlined text is a hyperlink.
- Text in italics is harder to read than conventional typescript. Reserve italics for short headings rather than large blocks of print.
- Frequent changes of typeface create a cluttered look. Keep to two at most.
- Sans serif fonts with no extensions on the letters, such as Arial, are recommended for titles and headings.

Use **parallel phrasing** for all items in a list. Notice the difference in readability between the first list describing problems with some machinery and the two revised versions, which have parallel phrasing:

✗ Non-parallel:
- breakdowns frequent
- you will find service is slow
- costly spare parts

✓ Parallel (point form):
- frequent breakdowns
- slow service
- costly spare parts

✓ Parallel (sentence form):

■ Breakdowns are frequent.

■ Service is slow.

■ Spare parts are costly.

Illustrations

❋ Explore

Informal Report 5: Using the Right Graph

✓• Practise

Exercise 12: Building Better Charts

Charts, graphs, diagrams, tables, and other illustrations clarify information and reinforce points. Computer programs are available that will help create these graphic elements for you. Whatever help you use, design them so that they are simple and uncluttered. Provide a title unless the text immediately before the illustration gives its purpose. If the details aren't self-explanatory, clearly label each part or axis. In a report on scientific or technical matters, where quantitative precision is vital, include error bars (±) if you can.

When the information is important, integrate the illustrations with your text; when it is supplemental, put it in an appendix. All visuals should be numbered and referred to within the body of the text, for example, "Figure 1" or "Table 3." The term *figure* includes all illustrations except tables. Explain in the text the main point of any illustration, so that the reader will know why it is included.

Charts and graphs have greater visual impact than tables and are often preferable. Different kinds suit different purposes:

1. **A line chart or graph** (Figure 7-2) is the simplest way to show changes over a period of time, for example, trends in sales or fluctuations in the real estate market. In devising a graph, be sure to use a scale that will distribute the data points over the total area. Put quantities on the vertical axis and time values on the horizontal axis. Try to shape the dimensions of the graph to give an accurate visual impression of the extent of change.

Figure 7-2   Line Chart

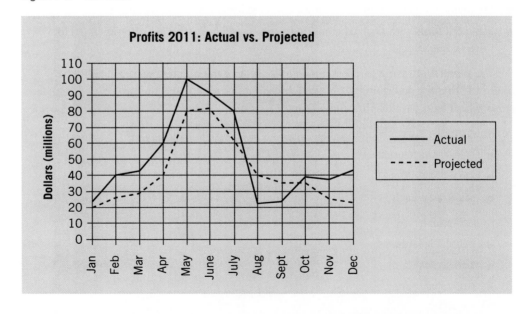

Figure 7-3   Bar Chart

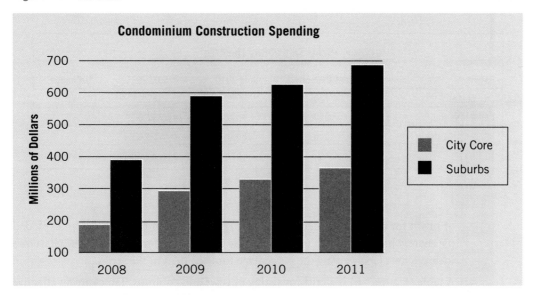

2. **A bar chart** (Figure 7-3) is best for comparing facts at a fixed point in time, such as the comparative training costs of several divisions within a company. The bars can be horizontal or vertical (also called a column chart), depending on the range of data. Bars can also be segmented (stacked) to show different parts of the whole. As with a line chart, a bar chart should use a scale that allows the data to spread over most of the total area.

3. **A pie chart** (Figure 7-4) emphasizes proportions. It draws attention to the relative size of parts that make up a whole—for example, the percentage of sales or the share

Figure 7-4   Pie Chart

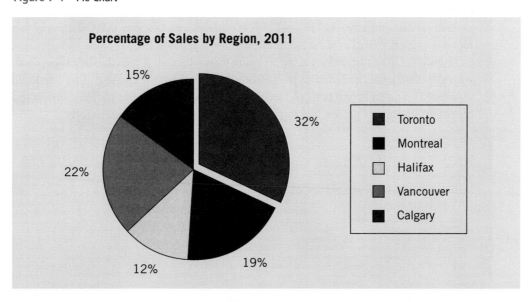

Figure 7-5   Table

Seats Sold at City Theatres			
Facility	Seat Capacity	Sold 2010	Sold 2011	% Change
City Centre	720	60%	62%	+2
Centennial Hall	950	45%	47%	+2
Princess Theatre	550	64%	63%	−1
Tri-Plex	1 000	28%	33%	+5

of profit for each department in a store. The example in Figure 7-4 is an exploded pie chart, which separates a particular value from the pie for emphasis. The chart also includes data labels giving the percentage for each item in the series.

4. **A table** (Figure 7-5) is a grid consisting of rows and columns. Tables are an effective way of organizing and presenting different types of information that might include a combination of text, numbers, and graphics. Stock reports, mortgage rates, and student demographics are often illustrated in tables.

Reports can use other kinds of illustrations, from flow charts to pictographs to cartoons. Some reports use traditional charts and graphs creatively, changing the shapes to suit the topic. For example, a pie chart in the shape of a light bulb could be used to show an electrical company's sales information.

Whatever type of illustration you choose, be careful not to distort the data you are communicating. Charts and graphs can easily mislead by the spread of distances or shapes. For example, a graph may exaggerate a trend by truncating the data—that is, by showing only the part of the scale when there was great change and leaving out the time when there was little. It can also underplay a change by spreading the distance between points. Notice the different effects of the graphs in Figure 7-6, despite the fact that they are based on identical data.

Since illustrations can "lie" just as much as statistics can, take care that the material you represent visually gives as accurate an impression as possible.

Figure 7-7 is a short, informal report using memo format. It uses the direct approach, with the conclusion included in the introductory paragraph. The use of bulleted and numbered lists, a table, and first- and second-level headings structures the information and highlights important points, making the report easy to read and understand.

Figure 7-6   Distorting Data

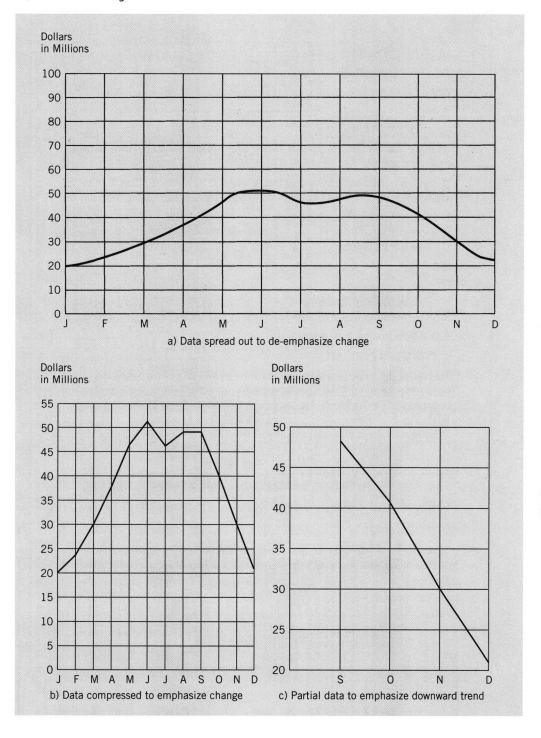

a) Data spread out to de-emphasize change

b) Data compressed to emphasize change

c) Partial data to emphasize downward trend

Figure 7-7   Short Informal Report (Direct Approach)

✳–Explore

Informal Report 1: Failure Analysis

✳–Explore

Informal Report 2: Personal Activity
Report—Sales Call

✳–Explore

Informal Report 3: Problem Solving

TO: Ron Miller

FROM: John Stone

DATE: December 5, 2011

SUBJECT: **Recommended Location for New Office**

As you requested, I have investigated several locations for our new office, including sub-
urban and midtown sites. The space at 10 Civic Square in Mississauga is, I think, the best
available location.

My search was based on the assumption that we wanted to lease about 1 500 sq. ft. in an
existing office building. The main criteria for selecting the Civic Square location were:

a) Cost
b) Accessibility
c) Quality of the building

With the help of Gil Gordon of Royal Realtors, I narrowed the initial possibilities down to
two:

* 10 Civic Square in Mississauga
* 451 Price Street West in midtown Toronto

Both of these meet our basic requirements.

1. MISSISSAUGA COSTS LESS

The low cost of leasing space in Mississauga as compared with midtown Toronto is a
major reason for selecting that area. The net rental cost is $50/sq. ft. in Mississauga as
compared with $100 in Toronto. Operating costs (maintenance, taxes, insurance) are simi-
lar ($10/sq. ft. in Mississauga as compared with $12 in Toronto), but parking for 10 cars
is considerably less in Mississauga ($360 per car as compared with $600 in Toronto).

Annual Leasing Costs

	Net Rent	Operating Costs	Annual Parking	Total Cost
Civic Square	$ 75 000	$15 000	$3 600	$ 93 600
Price Street	$150 000	$18 000	$6 000	$174 500

Since a long-term lease is better than a short-term one, the four-year lease available for
10 Civic Square, as compared with the three-year lease at Price Street, is a significant
benefit.

2. MISSISSAUGA IS MORE ACCESSIBLE

Since our present location is in the west end of Toronto, many of our employees live in that area. Other things being equal, it is sensible to choose a new location in the west rather than the east or north end of town. Moreover, since many employees are living even farther west in the suburbs, owing to the cheaper housing, Mississauga is a reasonable area in which to locate.

a. **Public Transportation.**   Being close to good transportation is important for employees without cars. Since the Price Street location is within a three-minute walk of the St. George subway station on the Bloor Street line, it is easier to reach by public transportation. However, Civic Square has good bus service, making it an acceptable alternative.

b. **Car Transportation.**   Both locations are on major roads and have ample parking facilities. Civic Square has easier access than Price Street to major highways—the Queen Elizabeth Way and Highway 401. It is also closer to the airport, a further advantage to some of our sales people and clients. Driving from Toronto to Mississauga in the morning and back to Toronto at night would be faster than the reverse route because of the much lighter traffic.

3. CIVIC SQUARE BUILDING IS SUPERIOR

The attached pictures give some indication of the superior quality of the Civic Square building.

a. **Office Space.**   The space available in both buildings is suitable for our offices, with good lighting and air conditioning. Both would need some changes in the partitioning walls as well as new carpeting. Civic Square has vertical blinds on all windows.

   The space we require (1 500 sq. ft.) would take up

   • one-half of the eighth floor at 10 Civic Square
   • one-third of the tenth floor at 451 Price Street

b. **Quality of the Building.**   The 15-storey Civic Square building is the more attractive and well-appointed of the two possibilities. It is only five years old and in excellent shape. The lobby is spacious and well decorated, the four elevators are fast, and the washrooms are large and clean.

   The 20-storey Price Street building is larger and older, having been constructed 30 years ago. Although it is clean and has a large front lobby, it leaves an impression of relative dinginess. The lobby and halls are dark and the floor tiles are worn in spots. The four elevators are slower than at Civic Square and are less well maintained.

All of these factors make the Civic Square location in Mississauga a logical choice for the new office.

Internet Issues

Although paper-based reports are still common, sending and publishing reports electronically is on the increase. With rapid developments in digital media, electronic reports are a quick and inexpensive way for companies to make information available to clients, investors, and the general public.

There are a number of different methods of sending or publishing a report electronically:

Email programs are not always able to read those formatting features created in another program, with the result that documents such as reports can end up looking very muddled. You can avoid this problem by sending a short email message and attaching your report as a word processing or pdf file.

Intranets, electronic networks within a single organization, make it possible for employees to "publish" their reports in an electronic environment. If you are writing an online report, make sure to use a screen design that will enable your readers to skim the content and quickly find the information they need.

Web-based reports are an emerging feature on company websites, which often contain links to informational or annual reports. These are often uploaded to the site as pdf files so that the look and design of the original is retained, but the Web is also an excellent medium for graphics, colour, and animation—impressive and effective public relations tools.

Here are some guidelines for writing online reports:

1. **Use features of page layout and typography that are easy to skim.**   Headings, vertical lists, bold fonts, short paragraphs, and borders all help your readers pick out important pieces of information and find what they're looking for.

2. **Remember that online readers often don't scroll down through a long page of text.** They usually skim through it, rather than stopping to analyze as they do with paper documents. Therefore, write in a minimalist style with short paragraphs and clear, concise points to keep your reader from clicking away to something else. And instead of putting everything on a single, text-heavy page, use links and image maps to take readers to additional information.

Exercises

1. Decide whether you would choose the direct approach or the indirect approach for reports in each of the following situations:

   a) You are halfway through a landscaping job at a summer resort, and the absent owner calls you to request that you send him a brief report on what you have done.

   b) After a lot of employee complaints, you have persuaded a reluctant boss to let you look into the matter of staggered work hours. You find that staggered hours would improve employee performance and morale, and you are going to recommend them.

   c) Your boss has asked you to investigate factory safety procedures and suggest ways to improve them.

   d) The sales manager has asked you to compare two possible choices for company cars for the sales force. You know he favours one, but you think the other is more suitable.

   e) You think your company's handling of customer relations could be improved, and you have some simple, inexpensive suggestions. You decide to write an informal report and send it to the customer relations manager.

2. You have been asked to investigate photocopiers for your office and prepare an informal report for your boss. You discover that the Beta brand costs no more than the CopyKing but produces faster copies. The copiers take up the same space. On checking further, you learn that both copiers are reliable. CopyKing appears to have a slightly better service record than Beta because the response time to requests for service is faster.

   Assess the following headings for your report. Are they effective and clear? How could you improve them? Consider weaknesses in the division and order of the sections as well as in the actual phrasing of the headings.

   1. Beta
      a) Cost
      b) Space Requirements
      c) Speed of the Machine
      d) Reliability
      e) Service Record

   2. CopyKing
      a) Cost
      b) Space Requirements
      c) Speed of the Machine
      d) Reliability
      e) Service Record

3. Since the office you work in is too crowded, the manager has asked you to assess the physical environment of an open-plan office occupying an entire floor in an old, downtown building.

   You discover that, although the space is big enough, it is very noisy because it has no carpets or soundproof tiles. Lighting is poor in some areas. In winter, the building is sometimes too hot and sometimes too cold. In summer, the air-conditioning is inadequate. Since your manager has said that she doesn't want to spend a lot of money renovating, you conclude that the office is unsuitable.

a) Write the subject headings and key points for the report.

b) Write descriptive, high-information headings for the detailed discussion of your findings.

c) Write a complete informal report (add details if you like).

4. Determine what sort of illustration would be most suitable to display the following kinds of information. Create an illustration for one or two of them. (Establish with your instructor whether you can invent the data.)

a) The number of full-time and part-time students in the last five years at your institution

b) The number of defence dollars contributed to NATO by each of its partners last year

c) A comparison of features, costs, and mileage for the three best-selling pickup trucks in Canada

d) The number of students enrolled in (i) colleges and (ii) universities in each of the provinces and territories in the last year

e) Stock prices of three leading oil companies over the last four months

f) Unemployment and inflation rates in Canada, the United States, Britain, and Japan during the last three years

g) A breakdown of expenditures of four leading charities

h) A comparison of the number of employees in the four largest auto repair shops in your city

5. Rewrite the following paragraph, using descriptive headings and lists.

Our buyers have now completed their monthly visit to branch stores across the province. Their buying decisions and suggestions reflect their observations about sales trends. They noticed that children's wear is selling well in all stores. They will have to restock playwear—specifically overalls and T-shirts—faster than anticipated. Clothes for children in all-cotton materials are more popular than they have been for the last five years, and buyers have ordered more heavy cotton clothes for fall. Sales for our line of cotton children's wear are up 10 per cent this year. Of course, cotton clothes for adults, both men and women, continue to be popular in these summer months. In the women's fashion section, summer skirts and dresses have lower sales than at this time last year, probably because of cooler weather. The buyers want to immediately discount these summer items by 30 per cent in order to move them before our fall line comes in. They have also decided to increase our order of the Leslie line of lingerie. This luxury line is moving faster than the others. In menswear, overall sales figures are on target, and buyers plan to continue our normal volume of purchasing. Wool sweaters continue to outsell acrylic sweaters. The only shift in our buying patterns will be an increase in pants in natural fabric instead of polyester.

6. Clients made the following comments to a travel agency after a charter flight and package tour to a southern holiday resort. In small groups, organize this feedback

into a clear outline that includes all comments without overlap. Put the outline on a flip-chart sheet or transparency. Compare your outline with those of other groups.

- Rooms were not ready when tour group arrived.
- Baggage was misplaced by airline.
- Dining room had lineups.
- Hotel food was excellent.
- Tennis courts needed new nets.
- Swimming pool had no lifeguard.
- Rooms were small.
- Tennis instructor was excellent.
- Hotel-run tours of the area were overbooked.
- Checkout procedures were inconvenient and slow.
- Dinner menu had too few choices.
- Hotel manager made us feel welcome.
- Airline served no meal on the five-hour flight.
- Flights were delayed for more than four hours each way.
- Some dining staff were inattentive or unfriendly.
- Tour guide was well informed and helpful.
- Swimming pool should have some adults-only hours.
- Hotel floor show was very entertaining.
- Group tennis instruction was overpriced.
- Most exercise bicycles didn't work properly.
- Spa package was well worth the extra price.
- Golf course was uninteresting and in poor shape.

7. The registrar, David Cole, wants to make your college as accessible as possible to people in wheelchairs and scooters. You have been asked to write him an informal informational report on the college's facilities for students with physical challenges. You are to consider such factors as

- parking spaces close to buildings
- exterior ramps
- elevators to upper floors
- space for wheelchairs and scooters in classrooms, cafeterias, and the library
- accessible washroom facilities
- emergency exit procedures

Write the report.

8. Helen Layton, director of Student Services at your college, wants to find out about the quality of student life. Since she has come to know you during your time at the college, she asks you to write her a short informal report in which you assess one of the following: food services, health services, athletics, social activities, or any other area you want to discuss. She says you do not need to do any formal research but should

simply base your assessment on your own experiences or those of your friends. Write the report.

9. You have been appointed assistant to the president of Dominion Merchandise. One of your first jobs is to advise your boss, Dominic Rosato, about gifts for the sales team. They should be under $200 each and will be presented at the annual dinner. You are to choose two or three possible gifts that would appeal to a variety of men and women of different ages and then write an informal report to Mr. Rosato in which you compare them and recommend which to buy. Write the report.

10. Your employer, Tiny Tim Ltd., a large and successful manufacturer of children's furniture, donates money to many charitable causes. The company has decided that, rather than giving small amounts to many charities, it will give half of its donations budget each year to a single charity with which it will become more closely identified. As a young management trainee with the company, you have been asked to select three worthy charities in the field of health, to describe their needs and the relative merit each might have as the special company charity, and to recommend one of them.

    Write an informal report to John de Wit, head of the Donations Committee.

11. As part of its community relations effort, the company you work for, Harkness Insurance, plans to participate in the community's "Let's Be Beautiful" campaign. The company wants to sponsor some low-cost visual improvements to aspects or areas of the community. The director of Public Relations, Ann Medhurst, has asked you to investigate and recommend some suitable projects, with the total cost not exceeding $25 000.

    Write her an informal report in which you describe two potential projects, giving some estimate of the time and cost required for each.

12. Oriole Food Products has recognized that profits for its Tastee Treat line are declining. The vice-president of Marketing, Al Fisk, has asked you for advice from the Sales Department.

    Departmental figures indicate that Tastee Treat sales have shown no increase for the last three years and that last year sales declined by 5 per cent. Trends in market share have remained constant for five years; sales declines are not the result of increased competition. A recent analysis by the Sales Department also shows that 70 per cent of Tastee Treat buyers are at least 50 years old.

    At a Sales Department meeting you have called to discuss the sales decline, several people suggest that the product could be repositioned for a wider market. Since it is a milk-based product, it could also appeal to younger women who want a high-calcium diet.

    Someone also suggests that the product could be altered slightly to include vitamin D, which helps the body absorb calcium. The addition would cost little but would increase the product appeal to health-conscious younger women.

    There is general agreement that the packaging could also be changed to give the product a more upbeat image.

    You and your department anticipate an increase in sales as a result of these changes. You also think that an aggressive advertising campaign will be required to generate awareness of the product among younger women.

Just as the meeting is about to finish, one member of your department suggests a promotional link with the annual Women's National Marathon. You think this suggestion has potential and is worth exploring.

Here is your task:

a) In small groups, create and organize headings for the report you must write for Al Fisk.

b) Either write the report individually or make a group presentation to the class.

13. You are the administrative assistant at the new Kingston branch office of Tech Edge Consulting. You report directly to the branch manager, Betty Miller, who in turn reports to the manager of the head office in Ottawa, Elizabeth Mercedes.

Tech Edge Consulting is a national firm, and the Kingston branch was established four weeks ago. It is now time for a progress report to be sent to Elizabeth Mercedes, and Betty Miller asks you to write it.

✳ Explore
Informal Report 4: Progress Report

To date you and other members of the Kingston office staff have devoted most of your time to the routine chores involved in opening a new office. You rented a suite of three offices and a reception area in the Falcon Arms building at 900 Princess Street. The rent is $3 000 per month.

You also ordered and recently received a shipment of office furniture consisting of the following: six desks at $1 500 each; six swivel chairs at $650 each; computer equipment totalling $15 000; five metal file cabinets at $200 each; four bookcases at $225 each; miscellaneous items (stationery, supplies, etc.) in the amount of $1 500.

During the second week of operation you and Ms. Miller interviewed a number of applicants for the position of secretary/receptionist. Your initial advertisement in the *Town-Standard* cost $375. You received 78 applications for the position. You then created a short list of 12 applicants, each of whom you interviewed. Four applicants were then recalled for second interviews. You subsequently hired Denise Ehring, a college graduate with several years of related experience. Her salary is $3 500 a month. This is the specified rate of pay for secretary/receptionist positions. The salary for an administrative assistant is $4 800 a month; branch managers receive $5 500 a month.

In order to create a high profile in the Kingston community, you placed ads in both the *Town-Standard* and *Community Bulletin* announcing your new location. The costs were $375 and $250, respectively.

A real bonus for the company was a feature story in the *Town-Standard* about Ms. Miller and her status as a manager with a large national corporation. This has attracted a lot of attention to the new branch office, and you decide to attach a copy of the article for Elizabeth Mercedes.

During your third week of operation, Betty Miller visited Queen's University and interviewed several members of the faculty from the School of Business. The purpose of these interviews was to attract people with outstanding credentials to do some consulting work for the company on a contract basis. Ms. Miller has obtained a commitment from three faculty members who are interested: Dr. W. W. Thomas, a marketing consultant; Dr. Jennifer Leamington, a specialist in human resources; and Dr. Eric Silva, a labour relations consultant. Ms. Miller also has the names of certain members of the business community with outstanding qualifications in total quality management and organizational behaviour. She is in the process of calling on them now at their places of work in order to create a more extensive list of experts she might employ in the future.

During your fourth week of operation, Betty Miller visited the Kingston Chamber of Commerce and began compiling a list of possible clients for Tech Edge. She has received an expression of interest from one client, Charles Manning of Godfrey Associates, who wants help with a project deadline in April. Betty Miller is currently confirming details of the contract with Mr. Manning, and several other local businesses have expressed interest in your consulting services.

Costs for your first month of operation include telephone, $205; Internet, $55; cleaning, $78; security, $95; and hydro, $175.

Include this information in a short informal progress report that you will send to Elizabeth Mercedes.

Formal Reports and Proposals

"It's hard, if not impossible, to get ahead in business these days without communication skill. By profession I'm an accountant, but writing and speaking have been key ingredients in my success. To make your case effectively, your message must be clear, it must be memorable, it must be compelling."

— Bob Harding, chairman, Brookfield Asset Management

The distinctions between formal and informal reports are often blurred. Nevertheless, a formal report is usually written to someone in another company or organization. Occasionally it is written for a senior manager in the same company, or for someone with whom the writer has little regular contact. Usually it is longer than an informal report and requires more extensive research. Unless you are a consultant, you are unlikely to be asked to write a formal report often. However, when you are, a lot may be riding on it—including your reputation.

The purpose of this chapter is to show you how to write a formal report and how to put together the kind of proposal that often precedes it. As Figure 8-1 shows, many of the elements of formal reports are the same as those for informal reports. You need to pay the same attention to headings, lists, and illustrations, for example. Although much of the advice in the previous chapter could be duplicated in this one, the emphasis here will be on those areas where there's a difference.

The Four Rs of Planning

As emphasized earlier, the first step in planning any piece of correspondence is to think about the reason for writing and about the receiver. For a long, formal report you need to add two more Rs to your planning sheet: restrictions and research.

Assessing the Reason for Writing and the Receiver

As discussed in Chapter 2, formal reports are usually less personal than informal ones. They omit the contractions of personal conversation and tend to name fewer individuals. Traditionally, formal reports tried to give a sense of objectivity by omitting the personal *I* or *we*. As a result, passages were often convoluted and difficult to read. While pronoun-free reports are still the practice in some circles, business writers are increasingly using *I* or *we* in formal reports to produce clearer and more forceful writing. (In informal reports,

This chapter of *Impact* will help you to

1. understand the differences between informal and formal reports;
2. develop strategies for planning a formal report;
3. be an effective member of a collaborative communications team;
4. use appropriate sources to research your subject;
5. choose an appropriate structure for your report;
6. document your sources correctly;
7. develop effective techniques for presenting a report;
8. use and acknowledge Web sources;
9. write and present a proposal;
10. develop strategies for writing online reports.

Figure 8-1   Contrasting Features of Informal and Formal Reports

	Informal	**Formal**
Reader	often internal	often external or distant within organization
Length	• usually short • several sections	• usually long (three pages or more) • sections and subsections
Tone	• personal • contractions	• more impersonal • no contractions
Summary	integrated	on separate page
Introduction	no heading	can have one or more headings
Title	appears as subject line in memo heading	appears on separate title page
Transmittal page	optional	covering letter or memo
Contents page	none	useful if report is more than five pages

personal pronouns are not only tolerated but recommended.) However, avoid "I think" or "in my opinion" phrases when you can complete the thought without them:

✗ I found that the fittings were defective.

✓ The fittings were defective.

✗ In my view, the market value will rise in the spring.

✓ Market value will probably rise in the spring.

If you are part of a group, using *we* lends the collective weight of a group and seems more objective than the singular *I*. Regardless, it's better to use *I* or *we* than to resort to something impersonal like *the writer(s)* or *the author(s)*.

Determining Restrictions

What are the limitations on the resources that will be available to help you with the report?

1. **Finances.**   What is your budget? What expenses will be involved and is the budget adequate to cover them?

2. **Personnel.**   Will you have the services of a good typist or illustrator? Will outside help be required?

3. **Time.**   What is your deadline? Create a realistic timeline on a graph with the various stages of the report plotted on it at specific dates—so many days or weeks for research, organizing, writing, editing, and final production. The larger the task, the more important these self-imposed dates become. In allocating time, you may be wise to leave a margin of error for delays, whether from bureaucratic snags, research delays, or printing issues. Remember that things always take longer than you think, and plan accordingly.

👁 **Watch**
Perils of Pauline: Brainstorming Sessions

✳ **Explore**
Formal Report 2: Research Report

Deciding on Research

Before beginning your research, explore the subject itself to avoid taking too narrow a path and overlooking important alternatives. Good questions are an effective stimulus for seeing different perspectives on an issue. Here are some ways to start:

Figure 8-2   Tree Diagram

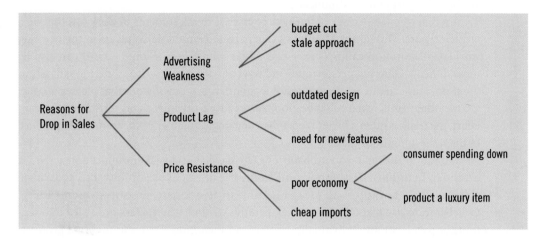

1. **Brainstorming.**   By yourself or with a colleague, blitz the subject. Jot down all the questions you can think of that relate to the topic, in whatever order they occur. Don't be negative or rule anything out at this point.

2. **Tree diagramming.**   Assume that the subject is the trunk and add as many large and small branches as you can to represent the different aspects of the subject (see Figure 8-2). Again, think of the branches as questions. Tree diagramming can be useful by itself or as a second stage of random brainstorming.

3. **The five Ws approach.**   In researching a story, journalists consider the Ws of reporting: Who? What? When? Where? Why? For your research planning, try asking the same five questions and add another: How? Use the basic questions to formulate other subquestions.

4. **The three Cs approach.**   A more thorough way to explore a topic is to ask questions about three areas:

   ■ **Components.**   How can the subject be divided? How many different ways are there to partition it?

   ■ **Change.**   What are the changed or changing elements of the subject? What are the causes or effects of certain actions? What trends are there?

   ■ **Context.**   What is the larger issue or field into which this subject fits? How have others dealt with the problems associated with the subject?

Once you have stretched your mind exploring the possibilities of a subject, move in the other direction. Think of limiting the subject and defining the precise focus of your study. Weigh the time and expense of the research against its importance to the report. Remember that it's better to explore a limited topic well than a broad one superficially.

Teamwork and Collaborative Communication

The days of sitting alone at a desk crafting a report or gathering information for a presentation are over. Exceptions surface mostly in government or multinational corporations. Today's high-tech business environment has created new expectations for quick

Watch
Perils of Pauline: Resolving Conflict

results and a rapid exchange of information, requiring the ability to collaborate on tasks and work as part of a communications team.

A recent trend, especially in business courses, is to ask students to work together on a written report. This approach mimics the increased emphasis on teams in the working world. Collaboration can make the task easier for all, but in some ways it can also be more difficult. Differing personalities and ways of working, as well as differing skill sets in the team, may cause tensions and result in an inferior piece of work that pleases no one. On the other hand, when collaboration creates a well-organized and conscientious team effort, the result is often a better report than any single member of the team could produce in the same amount of time.

Without realizing it, you probably engage in collaborative communication activities every day. In its most basic form, it might involve interactive situations such as asking a colleague how to express an idea or getting an associate to proofread your writing. Collaboration also takes the form of cooperative writing, where a task is divided into sections or parts that are individually written and then integrated into the final product. Perhaps the most complex type of collaboration is co-authoring, where participants actually create a piece of writing together.

When you are involved in situations that involve collaboration, there are a number of principles you need to observe to keep the process running smoothly:

1. **Build an effective team.**   You may have been involved in group presentations where one or two individuals did all the work and others benefited without making any significant contribution. Teamwork can be frustrating when participants don't work well together, but it can be very productive when proper protocols are established and observed. If possible, limit the size of the team to three or four members. Assign and assume responsibilities so that leadership roles and group interaction are clearly defined and understood. How can one avoid the traps and receive the benefits of collaboration? Plan early to weigh the differing skills and knowledge each member of the group can contribute:

    ■ Who should take overall charge of the schedule and logistics? You need a strong but fair leader for this task.

    ■ Who should complete the particular parts of the first draft? Establish from the outset the intended length of each part and the format to be used. Who should do the final edit? To keep the style uniform, one person is best for this task. To avoid disputes, the editor needs the authority to override any individual contributor who might be possessive about an idea or how to express it.

    Sometimes members are assigned to a group by the instructor, which makes it all the more important to work out from the start what each can contribute to the project. If the choice is yours, the temptation is to work only with like-minded individuals. The danger here is groupthink, with nobody challenging the prevailing view—which the instructor will likely do later, with penalties for gaps or simplistic thinking.

2. **Create schedules and meet deadlines.**   Although flexibility is always a good idea, make sure everyone on the team is aware of the final date for completing the project and then schedule each of the steps you will need to take in order to get there on time.

3. **Develop strategies for conflict management.**   A common complaint about collaborative writing is that the contributions among members of the group are uneven,

even though the marks for the writing are equal. One member of the group may in the end produce the lion's share of the work while another is a weak performer or may even seem a freeloader. There is no perfect solution to this problem except to realize that in collaborative writing, as with any sports team, it's better to focus on getting the job done well than on who does most.

If it's clear early on that someone is weak in the conceptual or drafting aspect of the assignment, give that person all the logistical tasks, such as arranging the meetings, assembling the drafts, and producing final copies of the report on time. Checking specific data or doing other research may also be a valuable contribution.

Feedback and evaluation are essential, but they should be constructive. If conflict becomes negative, it's important to divert it. Teach yourself to be a good listener (see Chapter 1) and an active participant. Accept constructive criticism and use it to make corrections and improvements, and make sure that any criticism you express is positive and diplomatic. Occasionally, to avoid gross unfairness, an instructor may ask each team member to rate the contribution of the others, but this approach can also undermine group harmony and the lessons in teamwork that collaborative writing is intended to foster.

If you feel unfairly treated in any particular piece of collaborative writing, see if you can learn from the experience and handle matters differently next time. In any case, remember that group assignments are a common feature of many organizations you may ultimately work for, so treat your collaborative project as essential training for the workplace, where your job may depend on your ability to be an effective team member.

4. **Observe gender and cultural differences.**   As in any communication, members of collaborative teams need to be sensitive to differences in style and approach among members. Some men might have learned to adopt a fairly assertive style, for example, while some women might be deferential and tentative in their approach. Be aware of these differences in yourself and others, and try to make allowances for them.

   Intercultural collaboration also requires an awareness of different perspectives and attitudes. If you're assigned to an international or intercultural writing team, remember that your way isn't the only way. Chapter 1 discusses some strategies for effective intercultural communication.

5. **Explore online collaboration.**   Collaboration is a form of networking, and electronic networking has become the norm in today's business environment. Commonplace examples are conference calls and email. Intranets allow people in different locations to work together on an ongoing basis. Networked computers make it possible to share files among a number of participants, so that everyone has simultaneous access to the same project-specific information. Computer-mediated environments make it possible to collaborate through teleconferences, Web conferences, and Webcasts. Take the time to explore the technology available to you, and make full use of the systems and facilities at your disposal. Learning to use your electronic environment will increase efficiency, avoid duplication, and save valuable time.

Finding Information

1. **Access information online.**   Increasingly, the Web is the first call for people seeking information. It's a quick and easy way to access a broad range of sites dealing with your subject, but it's not the most reliable source. Be judicious and remember that anyone

Watch
Research Video Tutorial: Evaluating Sources

can publish on the Web. Check the site to determine if it is hosted by a credible organization or institution, and make sure the information is frequently updated.

Newsgroups, discussion lists, and forums may also be useful, but the information in these posts is difficult to verify. Be especially wary of blogs, which are often personal journals or newsletters and may not have much validity as a research tool.

2. **Ask your librarian.**   Since research sources vary according to your subject, librarians can be a huge help. They are well-trained and knowledgeable and can often save you time by directing you to the sources most appropriate for your topic.

3. **Use the library catalogue.**   Most libraries today have computerized catalogues that are available from a remote location such as your home computer. Searchable by author, title, and subject, the catalogue will give you a list of relevant holdings and their location. If a particular source is unavailable at your library, you can probably obtain it through interlibrary loan.

4. **Search library databases.**   Most libraries now have access to extensive databases that allow you to quickly find needed information online. A librarian can help you determine which databases are the most relevant for your topic. CD-ROM indexes enable you to search by author, title, or key word, giving you a list of all articles on your subject with an abstract or summary and sometimes the full text.

5. **Consult internal sources.**   If you are doing a report on a particular company or organization, don't overlook the most accessible source of information—internal records and the employees themselves. Many an unsuspecting report writer has spent days searching for facts that are readily available in internal files. If the topic is one of continuing concern to the company, chances are that someone has looked at it, or an aspect of it, before. Some of the facts from an earlier investigation may be out of date, but it's likely that other information is timely and relevant.

Even when an earlier report doesn't exist, it is still sensible to find out if other people have worked on the topic. They are usually glad to discuss the issues. A short telephone or email inquiry may save you valuable research time or give you helpful suggestions for your exploration. Reinventing the wheel does nobody any good.

6. **Check the reliability of information.**   Establish whether any of the second-hand facts you get from your research will need verifying. Remember that a source with a special interest may exaggerate or gloss over certain information, often unconsciously. Even statistical data should undergo scrutiny. Any observer of election polls and campaigns knows that while statistics may not lie, they can certainly distort. If you have to get fresh data through a questionnaire or survey, make sure the results are as reliable and valid as possible. If you are not familiar with proper sampling techniques and have no knowledge of statistical reliability, consult someone who is competent in those areas. The cost of obtaining outside help may be less than the cost of losing your credibility through faulty data.

Arranging Information

1. **Use file cards.**   In doing lengthy research, many people find that file cards are an efficient way to record and keep track of details. Use a separate card for each different item of information you gather—whether the item is an opinion or an important statistic. You can then shuffle the cards according to the order you have chosen for the findings. Drafting the findings section of a report is much easier if the sequence

Figure 8-3   Point-Form Outline

Reasons for Drop in Sales

1. Advertising Weakness   A. Budget cut
                             B. Stale approach

2. Product Lag   A. Outdated design
                             B. Need for new features

3. Price Resistance   A. Poor economy
                                  i. Consumer spending down
                                  ii. Product a luxury item
                             B. Cheap imports

of information is already in front of you. If you prefer working on a computer, you can type the information and then cut and paste to order the data in the proper sequence.

   If you're gathering information from a published source, remember to include the bibliographical information on the card so that you don't have to spend time chasing down the reference later. Refer to "Documenting Your Sources" later in this chapter to determine which details you should record for a particular source.

2. **Create an outline.**   Some writers find that they work best by banging out a first draft as quickly as possible without worrying about details. In the case of a short informal report, you may not feel the need for an outline, but for lengthy formal reports an outline is almost a prerequisite for keeping yourself on track. The outline can be in point form (see Figure 8-3) or in full sentences. Numbering each section will help you keep in mind the relative value of each. Whichever numbering system you use for your outline, you can repeat it in the body of the report and in the table of contents.

Organizing Formal Reports

Although many variations are possible, a typical report structure is shown in Figure 8-4.

   Since you will begin your writing process with the main section, let's start by looking at various methods of structuring the body of your report.

Main Section

Although the sections will vary according to the subject, the basic principles of organization are the same as for informal reports.

   For readers who will be interested or pleased, use the direct approach. Here is the most common model:

✷ Explore
Formal Report 2: Research Report

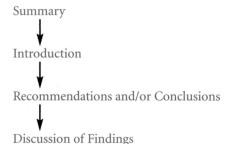

Summary

↓

Introduction

↓

Recommendations and/or Conclusions

↓

Discussion of Findings

Figure 8-4   Structure of a Formal Report

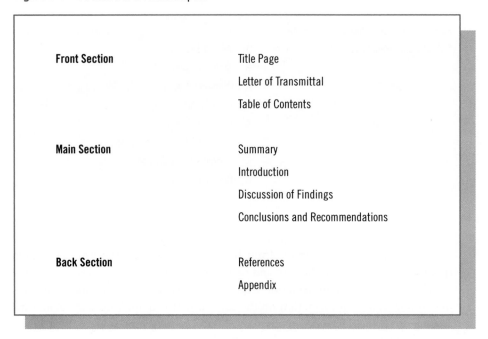

Front Section	Title Page
	Letter of Transmittal
	Table of Contents
Main Section	Summary
	Introduction
	Discussion of Findings
	Conclusions and Recommendations
Back Section	References
	Appendix

When readers will be displeased or skeptical, the indirect approach will lead them gradually toward the conclusions or recommendations:

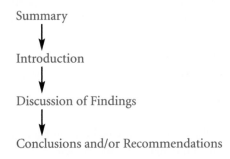

Summary

↓

Introduction

↓

Discussion of Findings

↓

Conclusions and/or Recommendations

The indirect approach is sometimes used in government and consulting circles even when the readers are interested. The trend is toward the direct approach, however, especially for busy readers.

The preceding suggestions are not an ironclad prescription for every report. You may want to change or add some sections. You may also have to adapt the following advice about what to put in each section. Let ease of understanding be the guide.

SUMMARY

A summary for a formal report—often called an executive summary—is really a condensation of the most important points. Unlike the introductory summary that begins most short informal reports, the summary for a formal report is put on a separate page with a heading. It's not an introduction to the report, but a synopsis—the report condensed. It's a convenience for the reader and may be the only part that senior management reads, but the report can make sense without it. For this reason, it's best to write the summary after you have completed the body of the report.

The summary doesn't have to give equal weight to all sections of the report. It often has only a brief account of the background or method, and may even omit them if they are unimportant. In a direct approach, the summary focuses on the conclusions or recommendations. On rare occasions, if the list of recommendations is lengthy, the title may be simply "Summary of Recommendations." In an indirect approach, where you're trying to gain acceptance for an idea or recommendation, the summary should focus on the statement of purpose and the method, since you want to influence the reader to accept your conclusions. Generally, in a summary it's best to follow the order of the report. That is, if the report takes the direct approach, so should the summary. Similarly, if the report has an indirect order, the summary should be indirect.

In the interest of brevity

- Use lists where possible.
- Omit examples, quotations, and other supporting details.
- Stick to the facts, avoiding unneeded references to the report itself. For example, instead of saying, "The Findings section reveals . . ." simply put a heading, "Findings," and list the facts.

Since there is a subtle psychological barrier to turning a page, especially for a reader who is extremely busy, try to keep the summary to a single sheet. If this seems an impossible task for a complicated or lengthy report, remember Winston Churchill's instruction to the First Lord of the Admiralty in the midst of the Second World War: "Pray state this day, on one side of a sheet of paper, how the Royal Navy is being adapted to meet the conditions of modern warfare" (Ogilvy, 1985, p. 35). Is your task more difficult than this one?

INTRODUCTION

This section may have a heading other than "Introduction," depending on the focus, and may have several subsections. It can include several or all of the following:

✴ Explore
Formal Report 4: Feasibility Report

- **Purpose.**   As in an informal report, a one-sentence explanation may be enough.
- **Background.**   Many report writers make the mistake of giving too much background. Include only the information needed to put the report in perspective. If explaining the reasons for the report, a total history is rarely needed. Focus on those conditions that have influenced the purpose and design of the report. If you do have to include a lot of material, you should probably have a separate section on background.
- **Scope.**   Here you define the topic precisely and reveal any assumptions you have made affecting the direction or boundaries of your investigation. If there are constraints or difficulties that limit the study in some way, say what they are. By doing so, you will help forestall any criticism that you didn't cover the area properly.
- **Method.**   If your findings are based on a questionnaire or survey of some sort, outline the steps you took. Reports with a heavy scientific emphasis often include an explanation of the technical processes used in the investigation. The process of information gathering is especially relevant when the data are "soft"—that is, open to dispute. Again, if the explanation is lengthy, consider making it a separate section.

DISCUSSION OF FINDINGS

This is the largest section in most formal reports. It discusses the details of your investigation, the facts on which you have based your conclusions or recommendations. It should

✴ Explore
Formal Report 4: Feasibility Report

be subdivided, with numbered and descriptive subheadings. (It may also be possible to give the section itself a more specific heading than "Discussion" or "Findings.")

In choosing the best arrangement for findings, remember that the most effective order is the one that most easily leads the reader to the conclusions or recommendations. As with informal reports, you can arrange findings by category or topic, by geographic or chronological order, or by order of importance.

How many subsections should a report have? It's a matter of judgment. Don't have so many that the section is more like a long shopping list than a discussion. On the other hand, don't have so few that there's a thicket of information in each one.

CONCLUSIONS AND/OR RECOMMENDATIONS

Explore
Formal Report 4: Feasibility Report

While some reports have both conclusions and recommendations, many have one or the other. Conclusions are the inferences you have made from your findings; recommendations are suggestions about what actions to take. A long, research-based report generally gives conclusions; a problem-solving report makes recommendations. Here are some tips for both types:

- If there are several recommendations or conclusions, format them as a list or in subsections.

- Normally, put the most important recommendation (or conclusion) first. If you face a skeptical or hostile reader, however, you might make an exception, and put the most controversial recommendation last, even if it is the major one.

- Number the recommendations or conclusions, making them easier to refer to. Numbers will also reinforce the fact that there is more than one. Otherwise, in later discussions the reader may focus on the most important or controversial point and forget that there are others.

- Be as specific as possible about how each recommendation should be carried out and who should be responsible. Some reports have an implementation subsection for each recommendation. Others have a specific action plan at the end of the report, outlining all the steps that should be taken.

- If implementation details are not feasible, consider including a recommendation to set up an implementation committee or task force. If your recommendations do include the details of implementation, suggest a follow-up mechanism so that managers or departments will get feedback on the results.

With the main section of the report in place, you are now ready to add the pages for the front and back sections.

Front Section

TITLE PAGE

Centre the information horizontally and vertically. Include the following:

- the title of the report, in bold type or in capital letters
- the name and title of the intended reader
- the name of the writer and the writer's title (or the name of the firm, if the report is by an outside consultant)
- the date

LETTER OF TRANSMITTAL

A letter of transmittal is a covering document in letter or memo form, depending on whether it's going to someone outside or inside the writer's organization. It provides the extra personal touch that formal reports generally lack. A covering letter is usually brief and follows this pattern:

- an opening statement, "transmitting" the report to the reader and stating its title or purpose (for example, "Here is the report you requested . . .")
- a brief outline of the major conclusions or recommendations
- a statement of thanks for any special help received from other employees
- a goodwill close that looks forward to future discussion or offers further assistance

Of course, a letter of transmittal can contain more or less than this model. Occasionally, a fairly extensive summary of the report in the covering letter will substitute for a summary at the beginning of the report. Sometimes, if the writer is an outside consultant hired for the job, the letter of transmittal expresses appreciation for the opportunity of working on the task. Whatever it says, however, the letter should have a personal, conversational tone, as the example in the formal report in Figure 8-5 illustrates.

TABLE OF CONTENTS

This is useful if the report is more than five pages. It follows the letter of transmittal and has no page number. It may be labelled "Table of Contents" or simply "Contents." List the sections of the report in a column on the left, using the same system of numbering used in the body of the report. If the report has subsections, list these as well, indenting them under the section headings. In a column on the right of the page, list the appropriate page numbers. If the report itself contains a number of figures and/or tables, list them under an appropriate heading—for example, "List of Illustrations."

Explore
Formal Report 4: Feasibility Report

Back Section

REFERENCES

If your report includes any facts or figures that are not general knowledge or part of the organization's internal operation, you should give the source of your information in a reference. A reference is unnecessary where the internal source is obvious, such as company sales figures or financial statements. For guidelines on formatting the references section of your report, see "Documenting Your Sources" below.

APPENDIX

This optional section appears at the end of a report and includes highly specialized or inessential information that is not an intrinsic part of the report but may be of interest to the reader. Tables, technical information, and other complicated or detailed supporting evidence are often put in appendixes so that the reader can quickly cover essential information in the report itself. If you do use an appendix, be sure to list it in the table of contents. If you use more than one, label them "Appendix A," "Appendix B," and so on.

Documenting Your Sources

Whenever you use another source you must acknowledge it, whether you have quoted directly from it, paraphrased it, or taken ideas from it. Style guides are published by various professional organizations, but the tendency in recent years has been to adopt the APA

Watch
Writing in Action Video:
Understanding Online Citations

method for references in business documents. For a complete discussion of the APA style, refer to the *Publication Manual of the American Psychological Association* (2010). The APA website at http://apastyle.org/also provides helpful tips and examples of the APA style of documentation.

In APA style, brief citations are given in parentheses within the text. A matching entry in a reference list at the end of the report gives full bibliographical information. Here are some guidelines and some examples of correct APA documentation:

In-Text Citations

Immediately following the "borrowed" information, give the author's last name and the date of publication:

The quarterly report shows improved returns for shareholders (Mallinson, 2011).

You may also mention the author in the text:

Mallinson's report (2011)shows improved returns for shareholders.

If you are referring to a specific location within the source material, your citation should include this information:

A recent study demonstrates the need for quality control standards in the industry (Parks, 2011, p. 49).

In a case where no author is named, give the first few words of the title. For articles, use quotation marks:

These economic effects made themselves felt within a month of the downsizing ("Study Results," 2011, p. 74).

For books or other publications published under a separate cover, use italics:

Impoverished writing ability among top-level managers is considered a problem in the international business community (*Business Style*, 2011).

For publications with a group or corporate author, give the name in full the first time and then abbreviate it in subsequent citations:

The Ontario Association of Chiefs of Police (2006) expressed support for the gun registry. . . . There is some evidence (OACP, 2006) for the fact that the registry has reduced the incidence of violent crime.

For online sources, use the same formatting principles as for print sources, giving the specific location within the source, if possible:

Employment statistics show a downward trend in age but an upward trend in educational background (Sanderson, 2006, para. 14).

Personal communications such as emails, letters, or telephone conversations are not included in the reference list but are cited in the text, giving initials and surname as well as the date:

The announcement, though unofficial, was made earlier that year (J. Saunders, personal communication, August 4, 2011).

For an entire website, rather than a specific Web page, no entry is required in the reference list. Give the site address in just the text:

Second-quarter results are available at the Enbridge website (http://www.enbridge.com/).

References

Complete information about the text citations appears in a reference list attached at the end of the report. The references are listed alphabetically by the author's last name. Entries are double-spaced and formatted with a hanging indent. Here are some examples of common items in a reference list:

BOOK

Buckley, P. J. (2002). *The changing global context of international business.* New York, NY: Palgrave Macmillan.

ELECTRONIC VERSION OF A PRINT BOOK

Field, J. (2003). *Social capital* [NetLibrary version]. Retrieved from http://www.netlibrary. com/Reader/

REFERENCE BOOK

Tasko, P. (Ed.). (2008). *The Canadian Press stylebook: A guide for writers and editors* (15th ed.). Toronto, ON: The Canadian Press.

ENTRY IN AN ONLINE REFERENCE WORK

Nikulin, M. S. (2001). Statistics. In M. Hazewinkel (Ed.), *Encyclopaedia of mathematics.* Retrieved from http://eom.springer.de/S/s087490.htm

JOURNAL ARTICLE WITH DOI

A digital object identifier (DOI) is an alphanumeric string assigned to provide a persistent link to articles published electronically. It typically appears on the first page of the electronic journal article, near the copyright notice.

Davis, J. H., Lee, M., & Ruhe, J. (2010). Trust: An intercultural comparison of consumer perceptions. *International Journal of Commerce and Management, 18*(2), 150–165. doi:10.1108/10569210895230

JOURNAL ARTICLE WITHOUT DOI

Sanyal, R. N., & Samanta, S. K. (2002). Corruption across countries: The cultural and economic factors. *Business & Professional Ethics Journal, 21*(1), 21–46.

NEWSPAPER ARTICLE

Hoffman, A. (2010, July 31). A Canadian key drives a Chinese success. *The Globe and Mail,* p. B4.

ONLINE NEWSPAPER ARTICLE

Cayo, D. (2010, July 30). Cap-and-trade faces many potential pitfalls. *The Vancouver Sun.* Retrieved from http://www.vancouversun.com

MAGAZINE ARTICLE

Wood, J. (2009, April 13). A fine rage: George Orwell's revolutions. *New Yorker, 13*(2), 54–63.

ONLINE MAGAZINE ARTICLE

Kirby, J. (2009, July 23). Will electric cars ignite a lithium boom? *Macleans.ca.* Retrieved from http://www.macleans.ca

BOOK REVIEW

Bell, D. (2010, July 31). Daddy Warburg. [Review of the book *High financier: The lives and time of Siegmund Warburg,* by N. Ferguson]. *The Globe and Mail,* p. F9.

Publishing a Report

✳—Explore

Formal Report 3: Research Report

After putting a lot of time and effort into a formal report, make sure that its appearance complements the content. The advice in Chapter 7 on creating visual impact in an informal report also applies to a formal report. Here are two added suggestions:

1. **Consider using coloured paper.**   If you are producing a long report, different colours of paper will help separate the sections visually. A conservative organization, however, may prefer uniform white paper (along with a uniform dark blue or grey suit on the writer). In this case, at least consider using a colour to highlight the summary page.

2. **Provide an attractive cover that will give your report a distinctive appearance and make it immediately identifiable.**   If the report is long, have it bound. You will have the confidence of knowing that the report looks well put together and will stay together if it is circulated. Figure 8-5 is an example of a formal report using a direct approach.

Presenting a Report

Sometimes report writers are asked to give a presentation to those who will be assessing the ideas expressed in the report. If you are in this position, remember that the presentation can never be a repeat of all that is in the report. Since speaking takes much longer than reading, the audience would be asleep before you were halfway through the material. Rather, think of your talk as another chance to emphasize the areas of most importance and to get some feedback. Chapter 9 discusses strategies for effective oral presentations, but you will find the following guidelines especially useful for the specialized task of presenting a report:

■ Determine whether the audience will already have read the report or whether they will receive copies after the presentation. If they have already read it, do a little sleuthing and try to determine their reaction in advance. You can then aim to address any objections or uncertainties and strengthen perceived weak areas.

   If the audience has not read the report, use the presentation to reinforce its key points. The talk will have more impact if it does not mechanically summarize the report but instead selectively emphasizes the most important or controversial areas. Usually the conclusions or recommendations should be the focus.

■ Be wary of giving out a copy of the report just before or during your talk. Members of an audience receiving such a handout will likely have their eyes on the text rather than on you and may miss much of what you are saying.

Figure 8-5   Formal Report

PEMBERTON'S CORPORATE PUBLICATIONS

Prepared for
Leonore Fielding
Vice-President of Operations
Pemberton Manufacturing

Prepared by
Sven Morgasen
Senior Research Consultant
Curtis Consulting Group

December 5, 2011

CURTIS CONSULTING GROUP

200 Avenue Road
Halifax Nova Scotia E4L 1B3

December 5, 2011

Ms. Leonore Fielding
Vice-President of Operations
Pemberton Manufacturing
Paris ON K4N 2T3

Dear Ms. Fielding

The attached report, which you requested on September 1, represents our findings regarding
the corporate publications at Pemberton Manufacturing.

Our report includes an assessment of current publications at Pemberton as well as an analysis of the current and future communication needs of your company.

The communications action plan outlined in our report reflects the results of our research
both within the company and in the national and international marketplace. We are especially grateful to the Pemberton staff, in particular the members of the Communications
Group, for their input.

I look forward to discussing our recommendations with you and will be happy to meet with you
and your staff regarding our report and its exciting implications for Pemberton.

Sincerely

Sven Morgasen

Sven Morgasen
Senior Research Consultant

TABLE OF CONTENTS

LIST OF FIGURES

Figure

EXECUTIVE SUMMARY

Recent changes at Pemberton and a new strategy for customer service have led to this review of current corporate publications. In this time of transition, effective publications will help Pemberton employees understand and support ongoing change. Good publications will also enhance the company's image and marketing effort.

As a result of our assessment, which included discussions with employee groups and major customers, we recommend five changes to the publications program:

1. Institute an electronic newsletter to be emailed to employees monthly. It will provide brief, timely information to employees and make feedback between management and employees easier to obtain.

2. Refocus the present print newsletter, *Newsline*, to emphasize discussion of policy issues. Rename it and reduce the number of issues to two a year from the current four.

3. Double the issues of the corporate magazine, *Salute*, to two a year, with the Marketing Department becoming more involved in planning and getting feedback from customers.

4. Enliven the annual report by increasing the use of visuals, upgrading the binding and cover design, and including comments from employees and customers.

5. Publish a version of the annual report on the Pemberton website to increase access to the global marketplace.

The Communications Group can begin to implement these recommendations immediately, if approved, for an estimated added cost in 2012 of $56 000 over the 2011 budget of $158 000.

iv

PEMBERTON PUBLICATIONS

INTRODUCTION

In its first year under new ownership and management, Pemberton Manufacturing has undergone major changes, including the adoption of a new strategy for customer service. As part of Pemberton's company-wide review, this report presents our assessment of corporate publications and recommends steps to increase their effectiveness in this period of change.

Our assessment included

- extensive discussions with the Communications Group;

- meetings with senior managers in all departments;

- ten focus groups, each with 15 to 20 employees. Individuals in the groups were selected to represent the various functions and levels at Pemberton. We chose to use focus groups rather than conduct a survey of all employees, since in the preceding month employees had completed a human resources questionnaire and would likely not have welcomed a second one so soon;

- ten interviews with Pemberton's major customers.

ASSESSMENT OF CURRENT PUBLICATIONS

Currently the Communications Group produces three publications:

1. ***Newsline.***   Pemberton's internal newsletter, published quarterly, covers a whole spectrum of topics, from employee news to industry matters. Our focus group discussions revealed that most employees read it and find it easy to understand. However, they find the news value is limited. Since it is published every third month, most news items have reached them through the grapevine before employees read them in *Newsline*.

    Our experience with other companies suggests that this type of publication is most useful for discussion of policies, issues, and ideas for which the "news" element is not as important. It is also suited for complex items, such as changes in employee pension

1

plan options. The ability of the Communications Group to write in simple, clear language is of great benefit in this type of publication.

The publishing cost for *Newsline* is currently $19 000 per issue.

2.   ***Salute.***   Published annually, this glossy, colour magazine for industry customers reviews new products and discusses industry issues. It has a high approval rating and serves a useful marketing as well as general public relations purpose. Customers say that the range of this publication gives Pemberton an edge over competitors. It is expensive—$35 000 to produce and deliver one issue of 3 000 copies—but readers want more than one issue a year.

3.   ***Pemberton Annual Report.***   Produced in two colours, the report performs a financial information function for investors. It also doubles as the Pemberton corporate brochure for people wanting general information about the company.

However, the impersonal focus, lack of visuals, and tabular presentation of data are conservative and leave a somewhat dated impression. The publication does not reflect Pemberton's new emphasis on customer service—on people serving people.

The annual report is relatively inexpensive to produce—$47 000 for 6 000 copies.

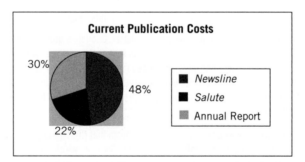

Figure 1

COMMUNICATION NEEDS FOR A CHANGING COMPANY

Internal Communications

Changes at Pemberton have created an increased need for timely internal communication. The focus groups with employees indicated that at all levels they want to be informed about new policies and planned changes. Without this communication, much productive time will be wasted on speculation and rumour.

As well, employees at all levels need to understand how the new customer service strategy translates into action. If they are to support it actively, they will need to know that management is responsive to their concerns and ideas. Although much internal communication with employees can and should take place informally through meetings and one-on-one discussions with others, written communications can also help. As the recent Infosystems study suggests, strong internal communications have a major impact on employee morale and productivity levels (Edson, 2010).

External Publications

Salute

External corporate publications can reinforce customer and investor perceptions of Pemberton's attention to customer service. Prior to 2010, the annual report was the single

Effect of *Salute* on Company Sales

Semiannual Sales

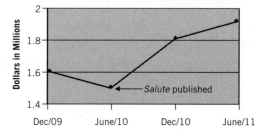

Figure 2

document distributed externally by Pemberton Manufacturing. In June 2010, management published the first edition of a new public relations magazine, *Salute*. The effect on sales was dramatic: an increase of 20 per cent in the first six months after publication.

The role of *Salute* in enhancing the profile of Pemberton products in the marketplace is clear; with the company's marketing effort increased, the magazine will assume a leadership role in developing new international markets.

Annual Report

Pemberton is acquiring a dominant position in the international marketplace, with the result that the company's annual report must be adapted to suit a new readership. The traditional format requires some updating to keep pace with current marketing trends; in addition, an online format will be a major asset in reaching a global market. Online reporting has resulted in increases of between 15 and 20 per cent in international sales (McLean, 2010; Stewart, 2010), an opportunity Pemberton can capitalize on in the next six months.

RECOMMENDATIONS

1. **Create an electronic newsletter.**   New information technologies are making it easier to send information quickly to many people and to enjoy the benefits of interactive communication. A monthly electronic newsletter would take advantage of Pemberton's highly computerized workplace, where all employees have access to company email.

    An electronic newsletter is useful for brief, timely items, not for lengthy multi-page discussions, which are harder to read online. It can also foster a two-way flow of communication with management. For example, it can ask for quick feedback on plans or respond to employee questions.

    Forty hours of staff time per month should be budgeted for the production of a monthly electronic newsletter, with an approximate annual cost of $15 000.

PEMBERTON PUBLICATIONS   **5**

2. **Refocus *Newsline*.**   With the new online newsletter, the print newsletter would not have to be produced as often. Two issues a year would likely meet the need for the kind of in-depth discussion of policies and issues that the print version is best suited to.

    The present cost of *Newsline* is $19 000 per issue or $76 000 per year. We anticipate an increase of approximately 10 per cent in printing costs, which would be offset by the savings realized by printing only two copies a year. This would result in a reduction of costs by approximately $34 000 annually.

3. **Double the number of issues of *Salute*.**   Concern for customer preferences as well as for costs suggests an initial experiment of two issues a year instead of one, with a re-evaluation of reader response after one year. Two issues would increase the present annual cost by $35 000.

    Since this publication provides an opportunity to market new products as well as enhance the company's image, the Marketing Department should be more involved in planning each issue as well as obtaining regular feedback from customers.

4. **Reformat the annual report.**   Three additions would help to produce a more dynamic, people-focused report reflective of Pemberton's customer-service strategy:

    - increased use of visuals, including photographs of plant operations;
    - interviews with Pemberton employees and customers to demonstrate the company's new customer service orientation;
    - upgrades of binding and cover design for a more professional look.

    These changes would increase the cost of the report by approximately $20 000.

5. **Publish a Web-based report.**   Pemberton's rapidly increasing global market requires the immediate transmission of information and suggests the need for an online report. The company website at www.pemberton.com is reporting in excess

of 3 500 hits per month, and publishing an annual report on the site is an obvious strategy for building global communications.

Pemberton's information technology staff have the expertise and the technology to do this; the estimated figure for staff time is approximately $20 000.

CONCLUSION

Overall, the estimated cost of implementing this communications action plan is $56 000 for the next year.

Publication	Current Cost	(–)	+	Projected Cost
Newsline: email edition			$15 000	$ 15 000
Newsline: print edition	$ 76 000	($34 000)		$ 42 000
Salute	$ 35 000		$35 000	$ 70 000
Annual Report: print edition	$ 47 000		$20 000	$ 67 000
Annual Report: online			$20 000	$ 20 000
Totals	**$158 000**	**($34 000)**	**$90 000**	**$214 000**

Figure 3

We have discussed our findings and recommendations with members of the Communications Group, who think they could make the changes within six months. Given the expertise of current staff and the state-of-the-art technology at Pemberton, the recommended changes would be unusually inexpensive to implement.

In addition, there would be no disruption to Pemberton's current organizational plan. The Communications Group could implement these changes with staff experiencing only minor changes in their job descriptions. There would be no layoffs and no new hires would be required. The stability at Pemberton would continue unimpeded and there would be no negative impact to employees or customers.

If management approves the proposed changes, Pemberton would realize almost immediate gains in productivity and sales at minimal cost.

PEMBERTON PUBLICATIONS   7

REFERENCES

Edson, M. (2010). Internal communications as an HR tool. *Corporate Concerns*, *65*, 1190–1195.

McLean, E. (2010). Online business reporting for the millennium. *Business Trends*, *49*, 129–143. Retrieved from http://www.businfo.org.html

Stewart, D. H. (2010). Electronic reporting and global trends. *Corporate World*, *73*, 248–279.

■ Make sure you use the opportunity for questions and discussion. If, for example, you have been allotted 40 minutes for the presentation, plan to leave 20 minutes for a spontaneous exchange. That way, lingering doubts in the audience will likely surface and you can respond to them. By forgetting to leave enough time for audience reaction, you run the risk of an objector raising an issue with others afterward, one which you could have addressed.

■ Visuals such as overheads, slide shows, or videos can be useful to summarize points or to give visual clarity to data scattered throughout the report. Remember to test in advance any technology you use so that you don't waste valuable time and encounter embarrassing problems during the presentation.

■ If you're pressed for time, it's better to ask the audience to hold their comments and questions until after you've finished. If the meeting is casual and you have lots of time, you might welcome queries as soon as they occur to the listener. Take care, however, not to let the questions run away with the presentation. If you sense the discussion is getting out of hand, ask that further discussion wait until you have finished.

■ Since it's always an advantage to have the last word, make sure you bring a question-and-answer session to a close with some conclusion that reinforces your main argument or key points.

Writing a Proposal

Explore
Proposal 3: Internal Proposal

Explore
Proposal 4: Quote (Short Letter)

Explore
Proposal 6: Sales Proposal

Explore
Proposal 8: Formal Proposal

Proposals can vary from an informal one-page memo to a boss to a massive document for a government department. An internal proposal might provide justification for a new expenditure or make a recommendation for a shift in policy. An external report can be used as a marketing tool and is often written in order to compete for new business or bid on a contract to provide services, equipment, or expertise.

Planning a Proposal

While proposals can be solicited or unsolicited, most are written in response to a formal or informal request. A request for proposal (RFP) outlines the specifications or requirements for the job. When a proposal is unsolicited the task is more difficult, since the reader will have to be convinced there is a need to act. In either case, however, begin planning by considering the following:

■ the reason for writing

■ the reader's needs and concerns

■ the competition

Think of the reason for writing not in your terms ("I want to get the job for the money"), but in the reader's terms: the proposal is a way of solving a problem for the reader or giving a benefit such as improved safety or increased productivity. Even if you don't mention the word *problem* in the proposal—and sometimes it's more tactful not to if the reader hasn't indicated one—thinking of the subject as a problem will help you focus your efforts on how best to approach it.

If you can choose your reader, select the person who will make the decision. Then try to determine what factors will influence the decision making. You may have to do some scouting to establish the reader's particular biases, attitudes, or special interests.

Organizing a Proposal

Use the direct approach. Begin with a clear overview of what you propose. If cost is an important consideration, the reader will want to know the bottom line right away. The intended completion date of your work may also be significant here.

✱─Explore
Proposal 2: Itemized Estimate
(Spreadsheet)

Follow with a discussion of the details. Determine what the reader needs to know to make a decision and then divide the discussion into several sections with appropriate headings. Here are the usual divisions:

1. **Method.**   First outline the method in nonspecialist terms. Then give a fuller account in which you are as specific as possible about the various aspects of the proposal and the way you would proceed. Include any technical information that specialists in the reader's organization might want to know. If the proposal is a response to a formal request, check that you have addressed all the specifications.

2. **Time frame.**   If time is important, be sure to mention the projected dates of completion for each stage. For a complicated project, it's helpful to provide a flow chart on which you plot timelines for the various stages. An example is shown in Figure 8-6.

3. **Cost.**   In a short proposal, the cost breakdown can be included in the discussion of method. In a long proposal, it may be simpler to have a separate section. Before putting down specific numbers, find out whether your total cost figure is an estimate or a competitive bid you will have to stick to. Then be as detailed as you can in listing costs without endangering yourself. Admit to any areas where you cannot yet give a fixed cost. Realism is safer than optimism.

    It may be practical, especially in a proposal for an outside organization, to break down costs according to the various stages in a project. This method is often easiest for the contractor to follow and budget for and will allow you some flexibility in allocating resources. By contrast, if you list the cost of each participant or function in the total proposal, you may face questioning or objection from the contractor.

4. **Qualifications.**   This section can focus on your qualifications and experience or on the credentials of the organization you represent. The heading should reflect the emphasis. If the credentials of those who will do the job are a primary issue, you could summarize the important points and then attach resumés. You should also consider providing references, including addresses and telephone numbers.

    Remember that previous work experience by you or your organization can be an important factor in the decision to accept your proposal.

5. **Benefits.**   This section highlights for the reader the benefits of acting on the proposal. If the benefits are intangible, they may not be immediately apparent to the reader. You should specify as precisely as possible the payoffs, both short term and long term.

    Formal proposals, like formal reports, include a title page, letter of transmittal, table of contents, and summary and may include illustrations, references, and appendixes. The example in Figure 8-6 is an external letter proposal written to a potential client seeking a contractor for major office renovations.

Figure 8-6   Proposal

THE IRVING GROUP

4953 Main Street
West Hamilton ON T4N 2T3   **(905) 525–3330**

July 12, 2011

Ms. Theresa Fuller
Manager
Fifeshire and Partners
291 Westdale Avenue
Hamilton ON T4N 1Y4

Dear Ms. Fuller

In response to the request for proposal delivered to us on June 24, The Irving Group is submitting our proposal for the renovation of your office suites at 2750 Bank Street.

Objective

Through design, furnishing, and decoration of your new offices, to create for Fifeshire and Partners an environment in harmony with the values and business objectives of the firm.

Proposed Schedule

Keeping to your budget of $450 000, we will take the following steps:

1.   Discuss with your Decorating Committee the firm's work patterns and needs, the committee's style and colour preferences, and the image the firm wants to project.

2.   Create alternative designs that meet your specifications and needs. These will include working drawings with sample materials and photographs.

3.   Create final plans after consultation with the committee. Committee members will be included in the selection of furniture and fabrics.

4.   Implement the designs, arranging for and overseeing the installation of all furnishings, including light fixtures, and the carpeting, painting, or wallcovering of all office areas.

FIFESHIRE AND PARTNERS   **2**

Cost

You will not be charged for our time, but only for the retail price of any purchases or services. Our payment is the difference between the wholesale or designer-discount price charged to us and the regular retail price.

Time Frame

If the construction of your offices proceeds as planned and we can begin this month, we think that you can be enjoying finished offices by the new year. Since the time between furniture order and furniture delivery is often about two months, the sooner the planning begins, the better.

A breakdown of the time frame for completing the various stages of the project follows:

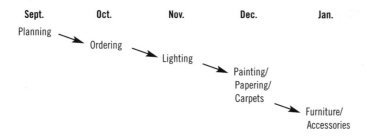

Our Qualifications for This Project

The Irving Group is experienced in office design and decorating. Our work has often been featured in national design and decorating magazines.

Senior Designer Mary Hunter was a prize winner in the Interior Design Program at Ryerson University. She recently carried out design and decorating work for several prestigious professional firms in the city, including,

• Lawlor, Bluestein, Foster
• D. H. Deacon and Partners
• Mills Thompson & Smith

She understands the business environment lawyers prefer.

FIFESHIRE AND PARTNERS   3

Why You Will Benefit from Our Work

- We will work from your needs, adapting tested design principles to create a unique environment that best suits Fifeshire and Partners.
- You will have undivided attention. Mary Hunter works on one project at a time. We pay attention to details.
- We are efficient. Since we do not charge for time, we all benefit from the speedy completion of the work.

As your RFP suggested, Mary Hunter and her team will meet with you at your new Bank Street location to tour the facility and discuss our proposal in detail. We will call you next week to confirm our next meeting.

Sincerely

Edward Fitzgerald

Edward Fitzgerald
Project Manager

Presenting a Proposal

Usually, a presentation is the second stage of selling a proposal and follows the acceptance of a written report. The presentation often serves as a mechanism for choosing a winner from a short list of proposers previously selected after a review of written proposals. For large proposals, you may be presenting as part of a team.

The guidelines for presenting a proposal are much the same as the guidelines given earlier for presenting a report. The difference is that in many cases you must sell yourself as well as your ideas, especially if you are an outside consultant.

It's important to be alert to the reactions of the audience, and especially the key decision-makers, if you know who they are. Use eye contact to spot any early signs of misunderstanding or disagreement. Be prepared to modify your presentation if that will help avoid opposition or strengthen your case.

As well, consider in advance those areas in your proposal where you can be flexible and those where you cannot. You do not want to look indecisive or malleable, yielding to any pressure. However, if you can show your willingness to adapt details without sacrificing the basic plan of your proposal, you will appear responsive to customer or client needs. Such responsiveness, along with an underlying conviction about the benefits of your proposal, will help signal that you are an easy person to work with.

✳ Explore
Proposal 7: Formal Proposal—
Cover Letter

✳ Explore
Proposal 8: Formal Proposal

✔ Practise
Exercise 15: Proposal Executive
Summary

 # Internet Issues

Researching Online

The Internet is a powerful research tool, and with it comes a whole new area of Internet liability. Remember to keep the following guidelines in mind when you are preparing your report:

1. **Acknowledge your sources.**   It is tempting to think that material on the Internet is public property, but this is not the case. As with paper reports, be diligent in documenting your sources. Methods for citing online sources are outlined earlier in this chapter.

2. **Verify the credibility of your sources.**   Anyone can publish on the Web, so be sure to check the credentials of your source. Look for the name of the company, organization, or publication hosting the site. And beware of blogs and postings to discussion lists and personal Web pages, as these can often give unsubstantiated and inaccurate information.

3. **Ensure that your sources are current.**   Web pages should be updated on a regular basis to keep the site contents up-to-date. To verify the currency of information published on the Web, check to see when the site was last updated, and avoid using material if it is too far out of date.

Writing for the Web

Corporate globalization has resulted in a major shift in business reporting. Although paper reports are still commonplace, they are often supplemented or replaced by electronic reports. Since electronic text takes longer to read, writing for electronic media makes its own set of demands on the writer. If you are publishing your report on the Web, you will want to keep the following guidelines in mind:

1. **Use a direct style.**   Presenting the most important information first will get your readers' attention and encourage them to scroll down or follow your links to additional information.

2. **Write scannable text.**   Since electronic text is more taxing for the reader, use bullets, lists, headings, and highlighting to make the text less dense and more readable.

3. **Make the report easy to navigate.**   Readers get impatient if they can't find their way around the site quickly. Make sure that your links work and that every page has an exit.

Exercises

1. Write a one-page summary of a business article that is at least four pages long. Your instructor may select an article for the class or allow you to choose your own from a newspaper or business magazine. Assume that the summary is for a boss who wants to know the main points.

   Remember to avoid referring to the article with such phrases as "the article says . . ." Instead, report on the points themselves.

2. Ajax Corporation is a conglomerate in the chemical field. Among its holdings are two plants, Northfield Aluminum and Belmont Processing, both of which produce aluminum sulphite, as shown below:

Comparison of Northfield and Belmont Processes

Item	Northfield	Belmont
aluminum sulphite production	intermittent batch process; considerable downtime	continuous process; no downtime
power consumption per tonne of aluminum sulphite	110 kWh	27 kWh
insoluble (deposits)	8–10%	1–2%
water content	9–15%	4–5%
colour	grey-brown	white
uses other than water purification	none	pharmaceutical

In small groups, create and organize headings for one of the following formal reports. Give specific, descriptive subheadings in the biggest section. You may provide any added information you need to do a good job.

a) Ajax is concerned about Northfield's poor profit picture as compared with Belmont's. It suspects that poor management is the problem but hasn't been closely involved with the operation. You are a consultant for Ajax, investigating and reporting on the problem, which you think is technical rather than managerial.

b) Domtech Corporation is another conglomerate in the chemical field, intent on expanding its holdings. Since it has heard that Ajax wants to sell some holdings, it has hired you to investigate and report on both plants.

c) Whitfield Industries is another conglomerate in the chemical field. It has heard that Northfield could be up for grabs and wants to buy it. As a consultant reporting to Whitfield, you have concluded that this would be a bad idea.

d) Ajax plans to close its Northfield operation while keeping the Belmont plant open. Your job is to explain the reasons for the decision in a technical report that will be made available to employees at Northfield along with the company's plans for relocation and severance.

e) You are the manager of operations for Northfield. Through discussions with local politicians, you discover that Northfield may qualify for a plant modernization grant but that Ajax would have to apply for it. Since Ajax will have to spend a lot of time negotiating such a grant and will have to make certain guarantees to the government, the president of Ajax asks you to write a formal report to him showing why the plant needs modernization.

3. Using the information supplied in Exercise 2 above, write a formal report for one of the five scenarios listed. Add information if needed.

4. Individually or in small groups, prepare and deliver a short oral presentation based on one of the reports prepared for the previous question. Have two or three members of the class play the role of the audience. Assume that they have not read the report and have some questions. The length of presentation will depend on the number of presenters—a maximum of four minutes per presenter, including any response to questions.

5. As a member of your college's Student Affairs Committee, you think it would be helpful if the college set up an information booth for the first month of the school year. The booth would be staffed five days a week by upper-level students, who would be paid $10 an hour. They would help new students find their way around the campus and inform them about student services such as sports facilities, health services, counselling, and tutoring. The booth would be located in the main mall, where there is a lot of student traffic.

   Since you think the information booth would make new students feel more at home, you want the administration to approve and finance the plan.

   a) Write a proposal to the dean of student affairs.

   b) Present your proposal to the class. Your presentation should be about three minutes in length.

6. Think of a way in which an activity you have participated in could be improved. The activity could be a paid or volunteer job, a sports team, a club, or a field placement. Write a proposal to the person in charge of that activity, suggesting why and how the change should be made. Assume that the person is open to suggestions.

7. Write the proposal outlined in Exercise 6 above, but this time assume that the reader is habitually cautious and nervous about change and may feel negative about your suggestions.

8. To help students earn money and gain work experience, the provincial government has agreed to fund several summer civic service or civic improvement projects designed to benefit a needy area or group in your community. The rules for the program state that the government will pay $10 per hour per student plus any material costs not exceeding $5 000. Students may propose a joint project with up to four other students.

   Write a proposal to Arthur Belmont, coordinator of the Student Summer Work Program. Be sure to state clearly the potential benefits of your proposal as well as giving a detailed breakdown of all costs.

9. Assume that your class is the committee that selects the best projects for the Student Summer Work Program described in Exercise 8 above.

   Make a brief oral presentation (under four minutes), in which you try to convince the committee of the merits of your proposal.

10. Form a three- or four-member collaborative team (either self-selected or appointed by your instructor). As a team, select one of the following categories:

    - mid-size cars
    - brands of beer

- tropical vacation spots
- ski resorts
- daily newspapers
- TV programs
- pop music

Following the guidelines for effective teamwork discussed in this chapter, complete each of these steps:

a) Each team member chooses or is assigned a specific example from the category chosen by the group. For instance, if you select ski resorts one member might choose Whistler, another Mont Tremblant, etc.

b) The team meets to define criteria that will form a basis for comparison. In the ski resort example, your criteria for comparison could include location, cost, snowfall, vertical drop, and lifts.

c) Each member drafts a two-page analysis and evaluation of his/her selection according to the criteria established in b) above.

d) Team members submit their drafts to the group for review, feedback, and revision.

e) The team meets to discuss the individual reports and arrive at a consensus regarding the merits and/or defects of each selection.

f) The team writes a collaborative report recommending one selection.

PEARSON
mycanadianbuscommlab

Visit www.mycanadianbuscommlab.ca for everything you need to help you succeed in the job you've always wanted! Tools and resources include the following:

- Composing Space and Writer's Toolkit
- Document Makeovers
- Grammar Exercises—and much more!

Presentations and Meetings

9

"Being able to communicate ideas in a way that gets right to the heart of an issue is an art everyone should learn. It's so fundamental to good leadership.

Throughout their careers, leaders need to hone their writing and speaking crafts, reworking and polishing them until they glow."

—Helen Handfield-Jones, president, Handfield Jones Inc.

"Communicating well means more than being correct, although that matters. It means understanding your readers or listeners and their needs and then being able to adapt your message to suit the person and the occasion."

—Rob Dexter, chairman and CEO, Maritime Travel

Oral Presentations

Although in our daily work we speak more often than we write, many of us have not overcome the fear of having to address a group. Yet the oral presentation is an important part of business communications, whether it is a speech or proposal to some external business organization or, as is more common, an outline of plans to a group of colleagues. The term *oral presentation* covers a variety of formal and informal speaking activities. For convenience, in this chapter the term *talk* will refer to informal presentations and the term *speech* will refer to formal addresses. Whatever the specific demands of your job, if you hope to climb up the managerial ladder it's important to master the skill of speaking in front of others.

The advantage of speaking rather than writing is that it permits immediate feedback. Listeners can comment or ask questions, and the speaker can respond to their nonverbal reactions and clarify any confusing points. On the other hand, the audience cannot go back over material. Speaking is therefore not a good channel for conveying a lot of detailed information. The message in an oral presentation has to be relatively simple if it is to have an impact on the audience. Since simple does not mean simple-minded, planning for an oral presentation is just as important as it is for a written document.

This chapter of *Impact* will help you to

1. plan for an oral presentation by analyzing the audience, purpose, and conditions;
2. organize the material for a presentation;
3. use audiovisual aids for maximum effect;
4. develop techniques for delivering a presentation effectively;
5. handle questions during and after a presentation;
6. introduce and thank a speaker;
7. plan and organize a successful meeting;
8. develop strategies for managing a meeting successfully;
9. understand the role of electronic networking.

Assessing the Reason and Receivers

⊙─Watch
BCVL: Giving an Oral Presentation

ARE YOU INFORMING OR PERSUADING?

While humour can add spice to any business presentation, the main aim is usually to inform or persuade. Although professional speakers may also aim to entertain in their speeches, business people rarely have the comedian's gift—or the need to be funny. If your purpose is to inform, you should emphasize facts. If it is to persuade, you may consider an appeal to emotion as well as to reason. Even if you are selling a straightforward business proposition, you may have to overcome resistance. As a first step in planning, consider the results you want to achieve with the audience. What exactly do you want listeners to do, to think, or to feel?

WHAT KIND OF AUDIENCE WILL YOU HAVE?

For most internal business presentations, it is fairly easy to assess the listeners. Most will be aware of your experience and why you are talking to them; you won't have to establish credibility. They will be interested in your subject, since it will presumably have a bearing on the business as a whole. And as business associates, they will be fairly homogeneous in their backgrounds or experience. Still, it's worthwhile considering answers to the following questions:

- Who are the key decision makers or opinion makers, and what are their needs and concerns?

- What will the audience already know and what should you explain?

- Where might resistance to your ideas come from and how can you counter it?

  With a formal speech to outsiders, the task of assessing the audience is more difficult:

- The listeners are more likely to come from diverse backgrounds or occupations. The only common bond you can assume is the one that draws them to the organization that has invited you to speak. It's a good idea, therefore, to try to pinpoint some shared concern they will probably have, whether it is economic, political, or cultural.

- Your speech may not be the attraction. The audience may be assembled for reasons other than to hear you—for example, they may be coming for some organizational business that follows the speech or simply for the fellowship of the group. You can't assume that they will be interested in the topic. A light or anecdotal approach may be more appropriate than a speech heavy on specialized facts or subtleties.

- You may have to establish your own credibility. Although as a guest speaker you will no doubt be introduced by someone who will outline your background, it might be wise to include in your speech a few indicators of your relevant experience—without blowing your own horn.

Assessing the Conditions

HOW MUCH TIME DO YOU HAVE?

Whatever the length of time allocated to your presentation, stick to it. If listeners expect a half-hour talk and you speak for only 15 minutes, they may feel cheated, especially if they have given up valuable time—or paid money—to attend.

Far worse than being too brief, however, is being long-winded. Even 10 minutes beyond the expected length can seem like an eternity to an audience. Psychologists have suggested that most people's attention span is not longer than 20 minutes, and many people's thoughts begin to wander before that. If your presentation is scheduled right before a meal, the audience may be even more restless. (Can food for thought compete with lunch?) On the other hand, if it is scheduled right after a heavy meal, the audience may be sleepy. According to a survey by New Jersey–based Motivational Systems, 4 out of 10 top executives admitted to having dozed off—or "fallen dead asleep"—while listening to a business presentation, and others might have as well but were too embarrassed to admit it ("Street Talk," 1989). If you anticipate these problems, you can plan to counteract them by building more changes of pace into the presentation and accentuating possible dramatic elements.

Of course, it's difficult to tell in advance exactly how long you will take, but timing yourself in rehearsal will provide a guide. When preparing your presentation, mark off a rough timing guide and include in the plan some "nice to know" but not necessary detail. Then when you are speaking, you can choose to omit or keep the detail, depending on how close you are to your guide. If it looks as if you are going to be way behind, summarize the remaining material and end on time rather than push on relentlessly through the whole speech.

WHAT IS THE PHYSICAL LAYOUT AND TECHNICAL SETUP?

- Find out how large the room is and whether you will have a microphone. If it is a large room or you have doubts about the audience's ability to hear you, ask for a microphone. Using a relaxed, normal tone of voice always beats straining or shouting. A lapel microphone is better than a fixed one, since it will allow you to move around.

- If a door into the room is placed so that anyone coming in late will distract the audience, try to arrange for an alternative entrance during the presentation or see if latecomers can be kept out. Although these solutions are not always possible, it's annoying to see a good speech disrupted when all eyes turn to observe latecomers.

- Check to see that any audiovisual aids you need will be on hand and in good working order.

- Find out if you will be speaking in front of a lectern or a table. A portable lectern is usually available in facilities where people give presentations. If you prefer to use one, ask for it.

Using a lectern can be both an advantage and a disadvantage. It allows a speaker to look at notes unobtrusively—to move just the eyes up and down rather than the head. It can also hide nervous hands. On the negative side, it presents a physical barrier between speaker and audience, increasing the sense of formality and distance. If you are giving a short, informal talk or presentation, you are probably better to do without a lectern.

Organizing the Material

A common prescription for speakers is, "Tell them what you are going to say, say it, and then tell them what you have said." If this sequence seems repetitive, remember that listeners, unlike readers, cannot review what has gone before. As an aid to memory, therefore, it's a good idea to build in some repetition. Think of a presentation as having

✔•⌐**Practise**

Exercise 16: CEO Speech to Investors

- an introduction that previews
- a body that develops
- a close that reviews

Since the body takes up most of the presentation, it should be developed first.

PLANNING THE BODY

1. **Identify the theme.**   Just as it's sensible to work out a thesis before writing an essay or to clarify your subject before writing a report, so in a speech you should begin with the theme of your presentation. In an informative talk, it will be factual ("How we plan to market Softee soap" or "Discoveries from our European sales trip"); in a persuasive talk or speech, it will have an argumentative edge ("Why we should move toward computer-integrated manufacturing" or "The need to improve internal communications"). The theme needn't be your eventual title; rather, it's a planning device, a linchpin to hold together the various facts or ideas you want to discuss.

2. **Choose the basic method of organization.**   Your options are similar to those for a written report. Select whichever method makes your material most manageable for you as the planner and most interesting and dynamic for the listener. There are several possibilities:

   - order of importance
   - chronological order
   - geographic or spatial order
   - classification or division
   - comparison

   Another simple way to organize is to consider the message as a solution to a problem. It's the common "get 'em on the hook, get 'em off the hook" approach. The introduction points out the problem and the rest of the speech explains how to solve it. The explanation, however, will still need organizing in one of the preceding ways.

   How direct or indirect you should be depends on your analysis of the audience. In most instances, the direct approach works best. When the receiver's mind has a sense of order, it can more easily assimilate the details. For example, with a problem/solution approach, if you not only point out the problem in the introduction but also indicate the solution, the audience will be prepared for the explanation that follows. The direct approach is especially useful for a business presentation when you and the audience are in general agreement about objectives and goals.

   If the audience is likely to be opposed to your ideas, however, you might want to be more indirect, building gradually to your solution and keeping the most effective argument until the end. Another option is to direct the audience by pointing out in the introduction that you will be proposing a solution but not disclosing the specifics until you have laid the groundwork.

3. **Create three main sections.**   Keith Spicer (1988), an accomplished speaker, maintains that three is the magic number for an effective presentation. Certainly students have long been accustomed to a three-part exam answer, and a three-part structure underlies much of our literature, music, religion, and art. Although two, four, or five parts can also work, the three-part body is a good rule of thumb. You can organize around categories ("the three stages in our marketing campaign") or points ("three ways to improve productivity").

4. **Help the audience remember your points.**   Use numerical reminders frequently, for example, "My second discovery in reviewing costs," or "The third reason we need to enlarge the sales force."

5. **Support your points with specifics.** In an informative presentation you will naturally be presenting facts. In a persuasive one, anecdotes, quotations, and dramatic examples may be as effective as evidence or statistics. You may appeal to reason or emotion, but keep in mind that your aim is to gain support rather than simply to state the facts. With listeners you don't know, a story, especially a relevant personal anecdote, will draw in an audience and help establish your credibility.

   You may wonder: "Should I give evidence or arguments contrary to my position?" As pointed out in Chapter 6, if you are talking to the converted, to people who share your view, you can simply keep to the points that reinforce it. On the other hand, if you are talking to a group that is skeptical, you will add to your credibility by being balanced in your presentation. Discuss alternative points of view and give contrary evidence while pressing your own case. Even if the audience is on your side, a two-sided argument will strengthen your case over the long term.

6. **Draw word pictures for the audience.** Your points will have more effect if you put them in visual terms. Let the listeners *see* the implications of your findings or the consequences of following or not following your suggestions. Draw a picture for them. Images have impact.

PLANNING THE BEGINNING AND ENDING

Once you have planned the body, you will more easily be able to work out the opening and closing.

1. **Spark the audience's interest.** The more captive the listeners and the less they know about your topic, the more you will have to work to capture their attention. If you are not well known to them, personally or by reputation, the opening lines are doubly important. Here are some common attention-grabbers:

   ■ **A joke.** This approach is only for those who have a good sense of timing. If you can't tell a joke well, don't try. Few moments are more embarrassing than the long pause after a joke that doesn't work. A joke is not a mandatory opening; nor will any old joke do. While a good joke will warm a crowd, it must be related to the topic or the occasion for it to be effective.

   ■ **A topical anecdote.** If you do not feel comfortable telling a joke, a short description of an incident related to your topic or the context can build rapport with the audience. The incident might have something to do with the organization the audience belongs to, with your own preparation for the speech, or even with an occurrence earlier in the day—anything that is lighthearted and will bring you and your listeners together. Naturally, the more topical it is the more the audience will appreciate it and the more it will remove the impression of a "canned" presentation—one prepared well in advance for an unspecified audience.

   ■ **A startling fact or statistic.** This can be a dramatic opener, if relevant, and can help make the topic itself seem more important. For example, an opening statistic on the number of working hours lost because of alcoholism could raise interest in a speech on ways to combat alcoholism in the workplace.

   ■ **A quotation.** This approach works well only if the quotation itself is startling or dramatic. Quoting the trite words of a well-known person will not do—unless your main purpose is to refute them.

These are not the only ways to begin a speech or talk, but whatever tactic you use, think of your listeners and what will draw them into your address.

2. **Reveal your plan.**   Tell how you are going to proceed and what the main sections of your presentation will be. This will help listeners to remember main points and also reassures them that you have a plan and don't intend simply to ramble on.

3. **At the end, close quickly.**   Summarize the main points of your presentation and then finish in a forceful way. A call to action—the next step for the audience to take—will effectively end many presentations. The ending can be uplifting or funny, dramatic or moralistic, a quotation or a colourful phrase. But at least try to end with a flourish rather than a fizzle.

Using Audiovisual Aids

Explore

Presentation 1: Oral Presentations using PowerPoint

Explore

Presentation 2: Slides from a Presentation

Explore

Presentation 3: Creating Effective PowerPoint Slides

Practise

Exercise 17: Creating an Effective PowerPoint Presentation

Visuals help not only to clarify material and give it impact but also to keep an audience alert. Visual aids are especially useful for internal business presentations, which are often held in stark, single-coloured seminar rooms lit with fluorescent lighting. The problem with these "classroom" surroundings is that sameness makes people drowsy; hypnotists know that a person who has a fixed focus over a period of time will begin to feel sleepy. Along with their other merits, visual aids force a shift in focus from the speaker to the medium and thus combat sleepiness.

Visual aids can have a negative side, however. If you are a dynamic speaker, they may lessen the momentum by shifting the focus away from what you are saying. They can also be overused. A constant stream of transparencies or slides can annoy an intellectual audience, especially if the message is readily understood without them. Despite these potential drawbacks, however, you should get used to handling visuals as a supplement to talking.

Today's presentation graphics programs have revolutionized the use of visuals, making it easy to create presentations on a computer and display them with a multimedia projector. Presentation programs offer a wide range of features:

■ Graphics features make it easy to incorporate charts, diagrams, drawn objects, and artwork into your presentations.

■ Multimedia capabilities allow you to include sound, music, and videos.

■ Animation features allow you to "build" the presentation, adding text or graphics as you speak.

■ An annotation feature allows you to draw or write on a slide during your presentation to call attention to a specific point or recapture your audience's attention.

■ You can print speaker notes to use as a prompt during your delivery or handouts to give to your listeners as "take-home" items for further reference.

■ You can publish your presentation on the Internet or an intranet or send it as an attachment to an email message.

Here are some pointers for designing effective visuals:

■ Be sure to limit any screen to six lines of print. Any more and the reader will be distracted and lose focus.

■ Use a large font that is easy to read from the back of the room. A useful rule of thumb is 36 points for titles and 24 points for body text.

- Use a horizontal (landscape) rather than a vertical (portrait) layout so that heads in the audience don't block the view.

- In a bland and monochrome room, design slides with colours to add life. However, use no more than three in a single illustration. Avoid a combination of green and red, since colour-blind people can't distinguish them.

A note of caution: In preparing your multimedia materials, be careful to avoid common pitfalls:

- Don't use audiovisual effects simply to repeat the obvious. Audiovisuals work best when they supplement your speech and lose impact if they merely duplicate what you are saying.

- Avoid overkill. Don't overload your slides with special effects that might appear gimmicky.

- Don't just read from the visuals. Remember that your listeners can read faster than you can talk. They will become impatient if they are waiting for you to get through what they have already read.

Delivering the Presentation

There are four ways of speaking to a group:

1. **Reading from a prepared text.** Choose this approach when the exact words are important—when any confusion, ambiguity, or mistakes could have serious consequences. Academics usually read papers to other academics, who may query the particular points or even the phrasing. Business and government leaders will usually read from a text when the issues are major ones and they want to avoid misinterpretation by the audience—and any reporters. People introducing guest speakers often read biographical information to make sure they have the correct details.

   Unfortunately, unless the speaker is trained, a reading voice tends to lull the audience. The presentation also lacks spontaneity, the sense of a speaker grappling to express ideas and creating a subtle suspense. Unless you have no other practical recourse, therefore, do not read. If you must read a prepared script, try these techniques:

   - Type the speech on every third line in large print so that it is easy to read at a glance.
   - Fill only the top two-thirds of a vertical page with print, so that you don't have to bob your head up and down noticeably as you glance from page to audience and back.
   - Format the key words in each sentence in boldface, and practise emphasizing them.
   - Mark on the script places where you can change your pace or tone to give variety and drama.
   - Look up from the page as often as you can. Try to begin and end sentences while looking at the audience so that you can accentuate your message. In other words, look down between sentences to recall your points and then look up to deliver them.
   - Practise reading the speech aloud beforehand so that you know the material well enough to maintain visual contact with the audience.

2. **Memorizing.** Although an actor can memorize speeches and deliver them flawlessly, very few others can. The danger is that in a rush of nerves a speaker may forget the text and become more hopelessly lost than if the speech had never been committed to memory. If you have ever been in an audience when a memorized speech came

◉─Watch

Perils of Pauline: Giving a Formal Speech

unstuck, you will recall squirming at the speaker's silent agony. For most presentations, you would be wise not to put your memory to the test by relying totally on it. It's better to memorize only the order of ideas and perhaps some colourful phrases or opening and closing sentences.

3. **Impromptu speaking.**   Few things are more nerve-racking than being asked to address a group on the spot without any advance preparation. If you have the gift of the gab, you might rise to the challenge brilliantly; however, for most inexperienced speakers it's a matter of instant sweaty palms. Luckily, in business you will rarely have to give an impromptu presentation unless it's a very informal occasion (such as a birthday party or other celebration); for business meetings most organizers have the courtesy to give advance notice.

   If you are asked to give an impromptu talk, remember that the audience will not expect much. Be short and to the point, making a few specific remarks that relate to the occasion. If you treat the task with good humour and pleasantness, the audience will likely respond to you in the same way. You can also try to anticipate those occasions when you might be asked to say a few words, planning your approach just in case. (As Will Rogers reportedly said, "A good impromptu speech takes two weeks to prepare.")

4. **Extemporaneous speaking.**   This kind of presentation is prepared in advance but delivered fresh—that is, the exact wording is figured out as the speaker goes along. It combines the benefits of prior organization and spontaneity. Whether the business occasion calls for an informal talk or a formal speech, extemporaneous speaking is usually the best method.

   Sometimes, if you know the material well, you can speak without any notes, relying on your memory of a prepared outline. If you feel uncomfortable without some memory aids, try putting the outline on small cue cards. Don't try to squeeze the entire speech onto cards; use only the key points and any quotations. If it will give you more confidence, write the opening and closing sentences out in full. Then, if you have prepared well, you will probably find that you don't have to use the notes. The mere fact of having them there will relieve you of any anxiety about forgetting.

DELIVERY TECHNIQUES

Look confident. Don't worry about being nervous before a speech. Most speakers are, even seasoned public speakers. The trick is not to appear nervous, since speaker nervousness is somehow contagious. Conversely, a seemingly confident, relaxed speaker will make an audience relax. How do you appear confident? Here is a guide:

1. **Have good posture.**   A speaker who walks purposefully and stands erect conveys a sense of command. Try not to slouch or to drape yourself over the lectern.

2. **Wear clothing that is appropriate and comfortable.**   There's no point in allowing what you are wearing to distract an audience from what you are saying. Unless special clothing is a deliberate part of the drama you are creating—a kind of costume—it's better to be on the conservative side. In any case, if you wear jewellery, avoid any that jangles; if you tend to put your hands in your pockets and can't break the habit, remove loose change.

3. **Establish eye contact.**   As you speak, think of the audience not as a group but as a number of individuals. (Some speakers say it creates confidence to think of the audience as individuals without clothes.) In any case, look for someone who is especially

attentive and establish eye contact. Later, switch to other parts of the room and do the same with different individuals. Try to hold your eye contact for a few seconds with one person before moving to another. Eyes that flit about a room give an impression of nervousness.

This technique will help you feel comfortable with the audience and establish rapport. It will also help you adapt to audience response if necessary—to explain in more detail if you notice quizzical looks or even to leave out some details if you notice fidgeting.

4. **Slow down.**   It's natural, when you are nervous, to speak quickly—to try to get it over with in a hurry. Unless you are normally a slow speaker, take the opposite tack. Before you start to speak, pause for a minute to get your bearings and look over the audience. Take a few deep breaths to relax. Smile. Then begin slowly and deliberately. At appropriate spots, when you are changing your emphasis, pause again. Silence can speak: an occasional deliberate pause will generate suspense over what is to follow—and wake up the audience.

5. **Speak clearly and with varied tones.**   Don't mumble. Articulate your words. When you don't have a microphone, project your voice to the back of the room. When you do have a microphone, stay about 15 cm away from it. If you are not in the habit of public speaking, you will likely have to concentrate on articulating the words and pronouncing word endings.

Nervousness tends to flatten the voice. To counter this effect, deliberately widen your range. Exaggerate the tones and stress key words in each sentence. In general, give a downward emphasis to the ends of sentences. Tentative speakers often let their voices rise at the end of sentences, suggesting that they are not confident. When you are rehearsing make sure that you have a downward thrust when emphasizing your points.

Although you don't want to push beyond your natural range, remember to use the lower end of your natural register. Low-pitched voices are generally the most pleasing and convincing. Breathing from the stomach rather than the upper chest will help increase both the resonance and the depth of your voice.

6. **Be natural with gestures and movement.**   Some people talk with their hands; others don't. While gestures can be an effective way of reinforcing points or expressing moods, there's no point trying to change your style to something you are not comfortable with. Artificial gestures can distract from your presentation. So can repetitive or fidgety movements. However, if you like to use your hands, be assured that they will make you seem less stiff and constrained. In any case, keep from gluing your hands together throughout your talk or from planting them in your pockets. If you leave them free, you will probably use them naturally for emphasis.

A tip: if your hands feel awkward hanging at your sides—like five-kilogram hams rather than helpers—try a tension-release exercise. Just before you walk up to speak, press your wrists hard against your sides for 30 seconds. Release. Notice how light your hands feel. They will seem to float up, ready for use.

Is it helpful to move around while talking? Although constant walking about can be distracting, taking the odd step here and there, if you feel natural doing so, can be useful. It makes the listeners shift focus and helps them stay alert. Don't feel you have to move during a presentation, however; many good speakers prefer to stand still the whole time.

7. **Practise.**   Go through your presentation as often as you can, not only to check the timing but also to strengthen your delivery. If possible, rehearse in front of a video camera; playing the tape back will allow you to see and hear nervous mannerisms

and other weaknesses. If you don't have access to a video camera, try standing in front of a mirror with a tape recorder. The more you repeat the exercise and the more familiar you are with the material, the more confident you will feel about delivering it.

A practice tip: if you stumble, don't start again. Make yourself carry on to the end, however badly you do it. The point is to get used to expressing your ideas in different ways, so that you relax with the wording of your thoughts. If instead you go back and keep repeating material until it is "word perfect," you will likely end up with a memorized tone to your presentation. Rest assured that if you have to struggle for a word during your actual delivery you will add to the sense of spontaneity.

COPING WITH NERVES

It's natural to feel somewhat nervous. It's even desirable. Top speakers and actors know that nervousness releases adrenalin, giving a burst of energy that will help them perform well. Trouble comes with an excess of nervousness. It can produce not only mental stress but also physical discomfort. Chest and voice muscles can tighten, making talking and even breathing difficult.

The strategy is to relax those muscles deliberately. Before you speak, practise breathing deeply from the stomach. Put your hand on your stomach to make sure it is expanding and contracting. Try to loosen the throat muscles by humming a song. When not in view of the audience, make exaggerated faces so that your mouth and jaw are loosened.

When you do get up to speak, stand and survey the audience for a few seconds before beginning. Take a couple of deep breaths, and establish eye contact with a friendly-looking face. Above all, don't apologize or say that you are nervous. If you look confident, the audience may never think otherwise.

By far the best strategy for stage fright, however, is to practise. You will find that the adrenalin rush is a little less each time you repeat a performance. You won't lose all nervousness, but you will feel in control of it.

HANDLING QUESTIONS

With many business presentations, getting feedback through questions will increase the likelihood of achieving the desired results with the audience. When you are giving a speech or presentation, consider whether you should encourage questions and whether they should be raised during the speech or afterward. If you want questions, let the audience know at the start how you will handle the process.

The advantage of taking questions throughout a talk is that the audience becomes more involved rather than sitting back as passive listeners. The disadvantage is that constant interruptions can diminish momentum and allow focus to be lost. Probably a good guideline is to assess the formality of the occasion; save spontaneous questioning for the most informal talks and provide a question period for more formal presentations. For some highly formal speeches, you may choose to have no questions.

When you invite questions, it's important to control the process. Anticipate the kinds of questions you may be asked and figure out how you will answer them. You may decide to have some extra backup information on hand. Remember also what the purpose and focus of your presentation are and don't let yourself get sidetracked. Here are the main problems that can arise with questions along with some suggestions on how to handle them:

■ **A confused question.**   Reformulate or paraphrase the question in simple terms before you answer it. This practice can be useful for all questions, since it gives both you and the audience time to think.

- **A hostile question.**   The trick is not to be defensive or hostile yourself. See first if you can rephrase the question so that it is not emotionally loaded. Then try to use facts to answer it. If you appear unruffled and try to address the matter, the audience will appreciate your poise.

    When answering, address the audience as a whole rather than looking at the questioner. This will divert attention from the source of hostility and reduce the chance of the questioner persisting.

- **A two-part or complex question.**   Separate the parts and answer one part at a time. If this sequence might take too long, answer one part and suggest that you would be pleased to discuss the other issues informally later.

- **An off-topic question.**   Mention that you think topic X is an interesting one you would like to discuss if you had the time but that your focus at this presentation is Y. If you can, suggest that you would be prepared to handle topic X at another time.

- **A question you cannot answer.**   If you haven't got the answer, admit it. If possible, say that you will get a response to the questioner later.

- **A scene stealer.**   Occasionally members of the audience will use a question-and-answer period as a platform for their own opinions rather than to ask a question. If someone starts to launch into a speech, try to take advantage of a pause and politely interrupt. Ask the speaker to state the question briefly so that others have time to raise their questions. Then in your answer steer the audience's attention back to the points you want to stress—to the focus of your presentation.

- **An underground questioner.**   This person can be disruptive. Instead of asking an open question, this individual makes critical comments or asks snide questions in an undertone loud enough for others to hear. The best approach if this behaviour persists is to single out the offender. You can say, "Do you want to ask something?" or "Can you speak out so that everyone can hear?" or "Can the person giving a talk in the back row share the question with other members of the audience?" Such a direct approach will usually silence disrupters.

- **A reticent audience.**   Sometimes a question period needs help getting started, particularly with a large crowd. If you anticipate that this will be the case, arrange for someone you know in the audience to ask the first question. Keep eye contact with all parts of the audience when you respond, encouraging people sitting in different locations to speak up. Another option is to ask the first question yourself. For example, you can say, "You may be wondering . . ." and then address the issue.

When a lengthy or contentious question-and-answer period finishes, it's a good idea to bring the audience's attention back to the main point of your talk. A brief closing statement will place the final emphasis where you want it to be.

Introducing and Thanking a Speaker

Introducing and thanking are the bookends of a formal speech. Unfortunately, people asked to perform these tasks often forget that their role is a secondary one. They talk for too long.

Introducing

Your task is to let the audience know why the speaker has been asked to talk on the subject and to present the speaker to the group. When the topic is already known to the audience but the speaker is not, some introducers rely on the HAM formula:

- **Home:** speaker's birthplace or present hometown
- **Accomplishments:** highlights of the speaker's personal or professional life that are relevant to the topic
- **Moniker:** name, nickname, title, and/or position of speaker, depending on the relative formality or informality of the occasion

Leaving the name until last—"Please welcome Mary Hunter"—builds a little suspense in the introduction. Make sure to check in advance the pronunciation of any unfamiliar names and practise saying them correctly.

For other occasions, especially when the speaker is well-known, you may choose to emphasize his or her experience or the importance of the topic. Whatever form it takes, a good introduction is courteous, specific, and brief.

As mentioned earlier, it is perfectly acceptable to read from notes when presenting the biographical facts about a speaker, since the details need to be accurate. Try to get away from those notes, however, at the beginning and end of the introduction.

Thanking

The most gracious thank you often takes no more than a minute but demonstrates that the thanker has paid attention to the speaker. If your job is to thank, be alert during the speech and try to comment on one aspect or one point that was of particular interest to you and possibly to other listeners. One concrete remark is better than a number of generalized phrases of gratitude. Conclude in the easiest way possible—by expressing your thanks on behalf of the audience.

By working on the techniques in this chapter and becoming comfortable with them, you will discover that oral presentations are not simply a way of dishing out information or ideas but a means of interacting with an audience. You will discover how you can affect listeners not only by your words but also by the manner of your delivery.

As in all other endeavours, however, you need to practise. Instead of shrinking from chances to speak to a group, plunge in and try. Brief informal talks are the easiest way to start, but in more formal meetings you can also get your feet wet by introducing or thanking a speaker or simply by making announcements. Practice may not make you perfect, but it will certainly make you better. And who knows? When you do a lot of it, you may even come to enjoy it.

Managing Meetings

Business managers often feel that their energies are trickling out in a continuous round of unproductive meetings. Bad meetings are enormous time-wasters. Yet when well planned and well run, a meeting has certain communication advantages. It's especially useful for

- a question-and-answer or information-and-feedback session
- group problem solving and decision making

Watch

Perils of Pauline: Conducting a Meeting

Practise

Exercise 2: Planning a Meeting Agenda

- face-to-face discussion
- team building

Good meetings can improve morale, productivity, and commitment. Here are some guidelines for meetings that work.

Before the Meeting

As with all forms of communication, good planning is essential. Well before the proposed meeting date, give careful thought to the following:

1. **What's the reason or expected result?**   If there is none, cancel the meeting.

2. **Is a meeting the most suitable channel and medium?**   For example, a memo or an email message can convey information at much less cost and may achieve the same results—if feedback is not needed.

   If individual opinions about an idea are needed, perhaps a few telephone calls or a conference call can get the result in less time and with reduced effort.

3. **Who are the essential participants?**   Exclude anyone who cannot contribute, since a large group makes discussion more difficult.

   Generally, a meeting with between 5 and 15 participants works best for problem solving. If it's smaller, it may not include enough differing viewpoints to anticipate all the problems or possible solutions. On the other hand, a meeting with more than 30 participants is effective only as an information session with questions and answers.

4. **When's the best time?**   Arrange a time that fits participants' schedules, so that some won't be wandering in late or leaving early. Consider the frame of mind of the participants—when they will be freshest and least distracted by other concerns. A meeting to develop new ideas would not be productive at the end of a busy week or right before another stressful or important event.

5. **Where's the best place?**   If a meeting is held in a private office, the person who "owns" the space will be perceived to be in control of the meeting. This advantage may or may not matter, depending on the nature of the meeting and how well the participants get on. A controversial subject is nearly always better discussed in a "neutral" space, such as a special meeting room. Some businesses schedule important meetings away from the office, so that participants won't be distracted or interrupted by telephone calls.

   Check the size and shape of the room. An overcrowded room can become hot and stuffy, even with air conditioning.

   Seating arrangements also make a difference to the tone of the meeting. As pointed out in Chapter 1, a circular table for a small meeting gives a sense of equality and encourages interaction among participants. If the person chairing the meeting sits at the head of a long table, he or she will tend to dominate.

   In a large meeting, the more separated physically the leader is from the group the more formal the impression. When there's a need for audience participation, the ideal seating arrangement is U-shaped or, at least, V-shaped. Either arrangement allows the leader to move into the group and encourages participants to talk to each other face to face. (See Figure 9-1.)

   When booking a room, arrange for any audiovisual aids or extra materials. Just before the meeting, double-check to be sure the setup is satisfactory.

Figure 9-1   Seating Arrangements

Large Meetings

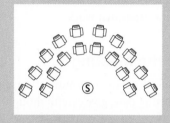

- Appropriate for formal presentations
- Focus is on speaker
- Speaker's distance from audience increases sense of formality

- Appropriate for two-way or informal presentations
- Proximity of speaker to audience increases sense of interaction
- Encourages discussion among audience members

Midsize Meetings

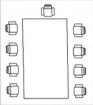

- Emphasizes authority of person at head of table
- People closest to head perceived to have more importance than others
- Discussion more controlled by person at head

- Emphasizes equality
- Encourages free flow of discussion among all members

Small Meetings

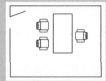

- Emphasizes status of person behind desk
- Can inhibit easy discussion

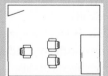

- Downplays status
- Promotes easy discussion

6. **What's the agenda?**   Decide the exact number of issues you want to discuss and then rank them. Check with key participants to see if they have other useful agenda items. Allocate a time period for each.

Ordinarily it's best to put the major item first so that it will be discussed when participants are fresh. Alternatively, you might put first those items for which a quick decision can be made and then move to the major issue for discussion, concluding with minor items.

Occasionally you might even choose to leave until the end a controversial proposal you want passed quickly. This approach carries a risk. The participants may approve the proposal out of sheer meeting fatigue, but they may also be annoyed by the lack of discussion or feel manipulated.

Distribute the agenda and any background reading material to participants before the meeting. That way they will have time to think about the issues and come prepared.

During the Meeting

If you are chairing a meeting, you have three essential tasks:

1. **Focus the discussion.**   Get participants to agree on the order and timing of the agenda. Then gently but firmly keep the meeting on target. Record ideas as they arise, preferably where others can see them—on a flip chart, transparency, or slide. You may also arrange for another participant to assume the task of recorder. When time is running out for a particular item, see if the group is ready for a decision or if the item needs to be deferred to a later date when more facts will be available. If consensus has been reached or a decision arrived at, reiterate the position clearly and specify who is responsible for any further action.

2. **Encourage full participation.**   The trick is to stimulate discussion and make participants feel their contribution is worthwhile. When the person in the chair also has the most senior position, there's a danger of domination, of unintentionally stifling discussion. Others may keep quiet or stay with "groupthink" unless specifically encouraged to put forth alternative opinions.

One way to encourage participation, if you are the boss, is to appoint a meeting facilitator to run the meeting. The facilitator's sole responsibility is to handle the process of discussion, not to contribute ideas. Your authority will not be undermined, since you still set the agenda and contribute to the discussion and you still have responsibility for any decisions or plans arising from the discussion. With a facilitator, you may see participation increase. Moreover, your organization will benefit from having a larger pool of experienced meeting managers.

If you do keep the chair, consider occasionally asking each member of the meeting in turn to comment on an issue. Explicitly encourage dissenting views. If you are running the meeting and the boss or someone several layers senior to the others is a participant, consider getting his or her argument beforehand rather than during the meeting. This will allow you to encourage the more junior members to voice their opinions during the meeting rather than simply defer to rank.

3. **Control aggression.**   Sometimes emotions run high and if left unchecked they can create hostility. You can help by encouraging participants to stick to the facts so that their comments don't become a personal attack on another member of the group. Try to remain neutral rather than taking sides in the dispute.

If you anticipate conflict between two people, try to seat them beside rather than facing each other, so that they find it harder to do battle. Even when there's no open hostility, you should see that the vocally strong don't dominate or exclude more reticent members. Create a constructive atmosphere in which ideas are encouraged and developed rather than criticized. A process of recording all ideas before evaluating them can often work in meetings, as it does in brainstorming sessions.

Even beyond these three tasks, managing a meeting well requires a host of subtle communication skills. From time to time you are likely to find one or more participants creating problems for the most well-planned meeting. Here are some common meeting spoilers:

- **The interrupter.**   Sometimes people are unaware they are interrupting. Often they are simply enthusiasts who do not mean to cut someone else off. In such cases, you can simply maintain eye contact with the first speaker while raising your hand in a "just a minute" gesture toward the interrupter. When someone interrupts repeatedly, you can politely suggest that you want to hear the rest of the first speaker's remarks. Such a comment is usually enough to stop interrupting behaviour. If it isn't, speak to the interrupter privately during a break in the meeting or afterward.

- **The diverter.**   This person brings up off-topic matters or breaks the flow with joking asides. Your job is to steer the discussion tactfully back on track, reminding the group of the issue at hand. If you think the diverter has a hidden agenda, you have several choices:

  – Ask if there's another problem that should be taken care of immediately.

  – Agree to leave time at the end of the meeting for new matters.

  – Discuss the hidden concern privately at the end of the meeting.

- **The nonstop talker.**   Some people seem to go on and on, sapping the forward energy of a meeting. They have trouble coming directly to the point. One way to respond is to listen attentively until the talker pauses for a breath and then politely interrupt with a comment such as "Your point is that . . ." or "So you think we should. . . . Would someone else like to comment?"

At the end of the meeting, if people are tired you can simply adjourn. You can also provide a quick review. Focus on conclusions or decisions resulting from the discussion and on any action plan. The review is especially important if there will be no written follow-up. It will give participants a sense of accomplishment resulting from the meeting.

After the Meeting

Formal minutes are a useful follow-up to a formal meeting. Usually someone who isn't a participant in the discussion is the best person to record the minutes—to act as the meeting's secretary. If you have the job of writing minutes or overseeing the job, ensure that the minutes

- indicate the date, time, and place of the meeting

- name the participants and person in the chair, along with the "regrets"—names of any absentees

- summarize the proceedings, following the order of items as they were discussed

- record each proposal and amendment

- name the proposer and seconder for every motion

- indicate whether each motion was carried or defeated in a vote

Informal meetings don't have formal minutes, but it's often useful to send a brief report to participants summarizing the conclusions and proposed actions emerging from the discussion. Be specific about who will be responsible for follow-up tasks.

Internet Issues

With the decentralization of large corporations, we have witnessed the growth of global networks that enable business associates to engage in long-distance electronic presentations, meetings, and conferences. The trend today is toward "virtual meetings," online interactive meetings where participants from a variety of locations meet without moving away from their home bases. The immediacy and convenience of these electronic meetings combined with falling communications costs make them the option of choice for many companies.

Although the technology changes almost daily, some group communication systems used in business today include the following:

- **Teleconferencing,** a meeting of geographically separated people via telephone, with video capability increasingly becoming an added feature.

- **Web conferencing,** a form of synchronous communication in which participants can exchange ideas and information in real time with cameras in different locations sending audio and video signals to other locations. In a Web conference, each participant has a computer and is connected to other participants via the Internet. Web conferencing is useful for live events where greater interactivity is required. Ideally, the number of participants is reasonably small (between 10 and 20). Although the video tends to be static, two-way interactivity can occur in real time via telephone lines.

- **Video conferencing,** an online meeting conducted by combining Web and phone technologies. In a video conference, two or more locations can interact in a real-time video conversation conducted online.

- **Webcasting,** an asynchronous multimedia event in which a manager can conduct a meeting or make an e-presentation. The event can be watched as live streaming video or as an on-demand download. Webcasts are used for large, company-wide meetings and for announcements and seminars. Although they are less interactive than Web conferences or video conferences, participants can respond through Q&A tools and surveys.

A word of caution: technology isn't foolproof. If you're faced with the prospect of conducting or participating in an online event, be well prepared. Be sure to get the training you need to operate any equipment or run any programs you will be using. Careful preparation will help minimize the inevitable glitches that accompany high-tech occasions.

Remember, as well, the basic rules for television:

- Avoid wearing white, which tends to glare, or patterns, which are distracting.

- Use only restrained gestures, as any movement tends to be exaggerated on camera.

- Keep any background noise to a minimum.

- Avoid embarrassment by remembering that even whispered comments will be readily picked up by a microphone.

Exercises

1. In small groups, practise saying the following sentences with clear articulation and ending with a downward intonation:

   a) Right now, treasury bills are a sound investment.

   b) I feel confident in this talented candidate.

   c) We need to respond to employees' feelings.

   d) I suspect the union will now want to negotiate.

   e) Please correct the mistake on the second forecast sheet.

2. Take a short nursery tale or a passage from it, about half a page in length. Underline the key words in each sentence. Then read the passage to the class, emphasizing the key words. If possible, photocopy the material so that others can easily check your technique.

3. Prepare a short (two- or three-minute) informative talk on one of the following subjects:

   a) How to build a fire outdoors

   b) How to change a tire

   c) How to handle an irate customer

   d) How to create the world's best sandwich

   e) How not to impress a first date

   f) How to dress for business success

   g) How to be a smart shopper

   h) How to . . . (any other task)

   Give your talk to the class. Others in the class will make notes on (a) your organization; (b) your delivery; (c) audience attention.

4. Pick a page of any published article. Practise reading it aloud clearly, varying the tone and speed so that it more closely resembles forceful talk. Read the page to the class and record your presentation. Listen to your delivery. How could you improve it?

5. On a slip of paper, write your name and a topic you know something about. Put the slip in a hat and draw someone else's. Prepare a short introduction for the person whose name you have drawn. (You may have to talk to the person first for background information.) Then prepare a three-minute speech on your own topic. To complete this exercise, you will have to

   ■ introduce your selected speaker and thank the speaker after the talk

   ■ give your own short speech

   If possible, presentations should be videotaped for later viewing and discussion.

6. Select one of the following speech topics, create a theme, and select two different methods of organizing the material. Then plan a three-part structure for each method. (You need only give the headings.)

   a) Leisure activities

   b) Business opportunities: Where are they?

   c) What young people want in a job

   d) Trends in health care (or manufacturing or technology)

   e) Why we need to act on pollution

7. Have each person in the class write on a slip of paper and put in a hat the name of a well-known person from business, politics, or entertainment. Then, in turn, draw a slip from the hat and prepare to give a one-minute talk on the topic. "If I were [name], I would change . . ." You are allowed five minutes to prepare. Remember that in such a short talk you have time to mention, explain, and/or illustrate only one point.

8. Suppose a dinner is being given in honour of another member of the class who will be leaving an organization to which you both belong. (You are free to choose the person and the organization, whether it be a business, school, or club). In front of the class, give a one-minute testimonial talk. Your talk may be serious or lighthearted.

9. Assume that a leading public figure is coming to talk at your college and you have been selected to introduce him or her. Create an imaginary topic for the guest's speech and then give a short introduction to the class. Remember that this is a formal occasion.

10. For a report you have prepared for this class or any other, give a brief presentation in which you emphasize the important points. Assume that members of the class are interested colleagues. Use some form of visual aid in your presentation. If possible, have the presentation videotaped. Other members of the class should mark down the positive aspects of the presentation as well as areas of organization or delivery which you could improve.

11. Put a lighthearted topic on a slip of paper that will be collected in a hat along with slips from other students. Draw a slip and give a one-minute impromptu talk on the topic you have selected. Try to use a specific image or incident to focus the talk.

PEARSON mycanadianbuscommlab

Visit www.mycanadianbuscommlab.ca for everything you need to help you succeed in the job you've always wanted! Tools and resources include the following:

- Composing Space and Writer's Toolkit
- Document Makeovers
- Grammar Exercises—and much more!

Job Search

10

Learning Outcomes

This chapter of *Impact* will help you to

1. assess your qualifications and preferences in seeking a job;
2. develop strategies for researching the job market;
3. understand different resumé formats;
4. design a resumé suited to your own background and experience;
5. write an effective cover letter;
6. prepare for all aspects of the job interview process;
7. understand different facets of a Web-based job search.

"We use a handful of leadership qualities to assess a person's readiness for promotion to the executive level. The ability to communicate effectively, both in writing and orally, is key."

—Jane Peverett, corporate director and former president and CEO, British Columbia Transmission Corporation

Job-hunting can be full of frustration and disappointments, especially when many people are chasing the same job. Although the Internet is a great assistant, you will most often need both oral and written skill—and a little luck—to land that elusive job!

Job Search and Research

It is estimated that somewhere between 15 and 30 per cent of all job openings are advertised. Employers seem to prefer the "hidden job market," where jobs are filled through referrals and networking on a personal basis. The implication for you as a job seeker is that you cannot simply look at the classifieds or check online job boards. You will have to go out and search. But first, give some thought to your interests, your skills, your personality, and your preferences to try to determine the kind of job that suits you. Then you can more readily examine your goals, both short term and long term.

Assessing Your Qualifications and Personality

What kind of job do you want? What are your qualifications? Just as important, what is your personality? Peter Drucker was an internationally renowned expert on management whose 1952 article on the importance of personality type in choosing a job still holds true. Drucker points out that people who are unsuited for their jobs most often have the ability but not the personality for them, and he suggests that before applying for any job you should make some decisions based on your type of personality:

- Do you belong in a routine, secure job or a challenging, less-secure job?
- Do you belong in a large organization with a hierarchy of regular channels or in a small organization with informal, direct contacts? Do you enjoy being a small cog in a big and powerful machine or a big wheel in a small machine?
- Will you be happier and more effective as a specialist or as a generalist?

Analyzing your own personality and temperament—what you really like as opposed to what others like or you think you should like—will help you decide which is the right kind of job to look for.

Researching the Job Market

How do you find a job? Naturally you should look at the employment ads in newspapers and keep in touch with employment agencies. Most academic institutions have career services. Take advantage of their contacts, counselling, and information about careers and specific businesses. But you need to go farther in the job hunt and conduct your own research. Here are the most promising approaches:

1. **Conduct an Internet search.**   A quick Web search will provide you with dozens of sites with online tools to help you identify career options and search for current job openings, either by job title or by region. You can register at these sites and post your resumé and a cover letter. The "Internet Issues" section at the end of this chapter provides guidelines for conducting an online job search and producing Web-based resumés.

2. **Read the financial sections of newspapers and business magazines.**   Most of these are available in local libraries. They often feature articles about up-and-coming businesses and about sectors that are expanding. These are areas where new jobs are likely to be created. You may find that a company has plans to locate in your area, in which case try to apply before an opening has been advertised.

3. **Obtain the annual reports of companies.**   Visit a business library or try writing or phoning the companies directly. In the interest of good public relations, many companies will be glad to send a copy. Many organizations also post their annual reports on websites, and a Web address may be all you need to access valuable information about a company.

4. **Conduct an information interview.**   Talk to anyone you know who works or has worked in the field you are investigating. Ask your friends and acquaintances for the name of a good person to contact. If you don't find any contacts this way, try a cold call to someone in a position to help you. Most people will either spare a few minutes themselves or refer you to someone else in the company.

   When you come to the information interview, be prepared. Don't waste your contact person's time on questions you could easily have found the answer to elsewhere. Here are some useful questions:

   - How did you become involved in this type of work?
   - What are the most rewarding aspects of the work? The least rewarding?
   - Can you describe a typical day or assignment?
   - What is the best preparation for this kind of job? What is the best kind of training or experience for it?
   - What is the best way to gain entry to this kind of work?
   - How would you assess the job prospects in this area?
   - Would you advise young people to pursue this kind of career?
   - Can you refer me to other people doing your kind of work or someone specializing in it?

The Job Application

A job application is not so much an information sheet as a type of sales pitch in which the product being sold is the writer. Like all persuasive communication, it requires creative thinking. As you prepare, keep in mind that if the position you want has been advertised, your application may be one of hundreds. The employer will be looking for reasons to eliminate most and to focus on only a few.

Think of the resumé and cover letter as a package. Ideally, you should create a different package for each firm you apply to. This approach may be a little impractical if you are sending out a number of applications at the same time, as students often do. A workable compromise is to create a distinctive application package for each type of job and then adapt certain elements to give an individualized look. A personalized application will be more effective than an obvious blanket application designed to cover a wide area of the job market.

Experts in job search and relocation say that scattering applications to a lot of companies seldom works. The most effective approach is to try to get a personal introduction to someone in a specific company. Face to face is the best way to sell yourself.

When contacts fail to get you in the door, however, a written application may be the only resort. Target 5 companies at a time rather than sending a "broadcast" letter to 150. Through research, determine what kinds of skills and experience the organization or the particular department needs. Get a sense of the corporate culture and of the ways you could contribute. Relate to the company's agenda, not your own.

The Resumé

Whether you send a resumé to get an interview or leave it behind after one, it is a vital part of the employment process. Write it before drafting a cover letter.

Although a resumé should give a lot of information about you, you need to determine your main selling points and then select and order facts in a way that will impress your reader. Here are some guidelines:

1. **Match your skills and experience to the needs of the organization.**   There's no point emphasizing talents that have no bearing on the job you want. This is where your earlier research helps; you have to determine what kinds of skills and experience are best suited to the job. On the other hand, many of your past accomplishments, which may on the surface seem irrelevant, can add to your qualifications if presented properly.

2. **Stress what sets you apart from the crowd.**   If an employer has a choice of applicants, all with much the same background—perhaps an office administration diploma, an engineering degree, or experience in computer programming—personal attributes will make the difference. These attributes could be a high energy level, curiosity, leadership, entrepreneurial spirit, or any quality that helps you to stand out.

3. **Get the employer's attention.**   Don't write an autobiography. Some career-planning specialists suggest that employers and recruiters typically scan a resumé in 10 to 20 seconds. That brief period is crucial in deciding whether your application package will receive further consideration, so make sure to introduce vital information quickly.

4. **Don't falsify anything.**   It will come back to haunt you.

Watch
Perils of Pauline: Successful Resumés

Explore
Resumé 1: Chronological

Explore
Resumé 2: Combination

Practise
Exercise 18: Combination Resumé

Explore
Resumé 3: Scannable

FORMAT

If an employer does not provide a required format, you have many options. Some information is essential—namely an account of experience and qualifications—but the way the information is arranged and categorized is up to you. Here are some common formats:

1. **Chronological.** This style, also referred to as standard or traditional format, emphasizes education and employment experience, ordered chronologically from most recent to least recent. This format gives the reader an easy grasp of your educational background and your employment history, and it is usually the best option for students who are entering the workforce directly from secondary and post-secondary backgrounds. For an example of a chronological resumé, see Figure 10-1.

2. **Modified.** An effective variation of the standard format is to highlight only significant achievements under each category of work experience. This approach works if previous jobs involved many little assignments that aren't relevant to your present objectives. For each job, a subheading labelled "Achievements" will indicate that you are giving only a partial list of all you did. For an example of a resumé modified in this way, see Figure 10-2.

3. **Functional.** One drawback to the chronological format is that it makes gaps in your employment record more obvious. If you have had a variety of work experience that does not on the surface relate to the position you want, it is probably better to use a functional resumé format. This format emphasizes the functions you have performed, the responsibilities you have assumed, or the relevant skills you possess. Instead of organizing work experience chronologically, you can organize information according to the type of work experience, such as "Marketing Experience" or "Accounting Experience." It's often more effective, however, to stress your skills or accomplishments through headings such as "Initiative," "Creativity," or "Research Skills." This approach is especially useful for people whose experience comes primarily from volunteer activities or for applicants who are switching career paths or returning to the workforce after raising a family. See Figure 10-3 for an example of a functional resumé.

4. **Unconventional.** Departing from traditional resumé styles can be effective, but it is risky. You must be cautious in assessing the reader. If the job is for an accountancy firm, bank, or a conservative organization where dependability, order, and systematic thought are more important than imagination, you are best to stick with a more conventional format. By contrast, if the employer is in advertising, promotion, graphic design, or another occupation where imagination or innovation is a primary qualification, you might try to vary the format to suggest your creativity. In any case, your primary question to yourself should be, "How can I best reveal those qualities the employer is looking for?"

Whatever format you use, design the resumé so that it is easy to read:

1. **Create wide margins** and leave space between sections so that the text stands out boldly—with the black set off by the white surrounding it.

2. **Use boldface and/or capitals** for the section headings.

3. **Create bulleted lists** for economy of space and ease of readability.

4. **Be consistent** in placing and setting off the details for each section.

5. **Use boldface or italics** (but not underlining) to set off an important point.

6. **Stick to one or two font faces,** as more than that will look cluttered and unprofessional.

Figure 10-1   Chronological Resumé

JULES FOURNIER

1721 Millhaven Crescent		Ph: 802-223-0000
Ottawa ON K4V 2N1	jfournier@grolen.net	Fax: 802-223-0001

College graduate with solid background in economics and political science seeking challenging position in industrial development field.

EDUCATION:	**Carleton University**	2007–2011
	Bachelor of Arts	
	Honours in International Relations	
	Zhejiang University, Hangzhou, China	Summer 2007
	Exchange Program	
WORK EXPERIENCE:	**Westway Books & Music**	Summers 2007–2009
	Brockville ON	

Stock maintenance, customer service, cashier duties, and special orders. I also co-managed the Magazine and Newspaper Department for two years and was appointed manager of the travel section in my final year.

	Carleton University	2007–2010
	Ottawa ON	

Selected to work in the Writing Resource Centre as a writing tutor for students in all years and disciplines.

Hired by the External Relations Office as a caller for the alumni fundraising drive.

	New Age Café	2003–2007
	Ottawa ON	

Employed part-time and full-time in the summer. Duties included hosting, serving, opening and closing, and cash.

COMPUTER BACKGROUND: I have a solid background in Microsoft Word and Photoshop and have also used Excel, Access, and PowerPoint in the preparation of essays, reports, and assignments. Experienced Internet user with knowledge of Windows and the Web.

I also won a *Toronto Star* High School Newspaper Award for layout design using Adobe CS5.

TRAVEL: Jamaica, China, Singapore, Bahamas, and extensive travel in the United States and Canada.

JULES FOURNIER   2

POSITIONS HELD:	**Co-Chairperson** Youth Partnership with Jamaica Carleton University	Spring 2010
	Volunteer Counsellor Youth Centre, Brockville	Summer 2009
	Orientation Guide Carleton University	Fall 2008
ACTIVITIES:	Varsity ski team Intramural basketball Tennis Hiking Hockey	2008–2011

REFERENCES:

Professor James Townsend
English Department
Carleton University
Ottawa ON K4V 2N1
jtownsend@carleton.ca
802-443-0000

Professor Ellen Decarie
Psychology Department
Carleton University
Ottawa ON K4V 2N1
edecarie@carleton.ca
802-443-0001

Julian Romero
Manager
Westway Books & Music
193 Main Street
Brockville ON K7L 42T
westway@cogeco.ca
802-223-0000

Serena Collom
Owner/Manager
New Age Café
192 West Street
Ottawa ON K4V 3H5
newage@hotmail.com
802-223-0002

Figure 10-2   Modified Resumé

JANE MCGREGOR

914–55 Banrigh Road   jmcgregor@sympatico.ca
Scarborough ON M1W 3V4   (416) 491-7124

PROFILE
Training and development specialist with excellent communication skills and the ability to analyze needs and implement solutions for all levels of an organization.

EDUCATION
Bachelor of Arts: McMaster University
Les Cours Spéciaux de la Faculté des Lettres: Université de Dijon, France
Data Processing Fundamentals: Seneca College

EXPERIENCE

Infomarket   2009–2011

Manager, Education Services

Assumed responsibility for company-wide professional development in management and sales

Reported to the vice-president, Corporate Development

Achievements:

- Directed a series of seminars for senior executives at the request of the president
- Designed a sales program which benefited the sales teams of six U.S. clients and the Infomarket sales force
- Developed a basic computer course for all non-technical employees to increase staff morale and improve productivity
- Created and managed a seminar to enhance product knowledge

Datacrown   2007–2009

Senior Education Analyst, Education Services

Responsible for the development, maintenance, and delivery of technical courses to Datacrown clients

Reported to the director, Planning and Development

Achievements:

- Managed the activities of the education coordinator, the technical educator, and the technical analysts who delivered the programs
- Oversaw the design and implementation of new classroom facilities and a new calendar, two significant changes that enhanced the marketing of products and services

Jane McGregor   2
_____

Edufax Learning Systems   2005–2007

    Training Consultant

    Conducted skill development seminars for Edufax clients including

- Interpersonal Managing Skills
- Professional Selling Skills II & III
- Strategies for Effective Listening
- Account Development Strategies
- Focused Selection Interviewing

INTERESTS

Watercolour painting, weaving, cross-country skiing, aerobics

REFERENCES

Available upon request

INFORMATION

Your resumé should include enough information to interest the employer in interviewing you. Here is a list of the most common kinds of resumé information. Be prepared to omit, add, or alter according to the job and how you choose to present yourself.

Name and address.   Usually this information is placed at the top of the resumé. Be sure to include the full mailing address, including postal code. It is important to add your telephone number, fax number (if you have one), and email address. If you are a student with a different mailing address for winter and summer months, give both addresses and the dates when you will be at each location.

Objective.   This category is helpful if you are a student trying to suggest that you have definite career goals. It may also be useful if you want a specific job in a large organization with a number of different job openings. On the other hand, if you are willing to try a variety of jobs, you may omit this category from your resumé as long as your accompanying letter gives a more specific focus to your search.

In any case, for an unsolicited application, it's usually better to give not the position you would like (for example, sales manager), but the area and general level of responsibility (for example, "a management position in marketing" or "management trainee"). Students who are willing to take a junior or entry-level position but expect opportunity for advancement can state this expectation. An application to a bank might say "management training position with the goal of future employment in international banking"; a student applying to an accountancy firm might say, "seeking student placement with the goal of becoming a practising chartered accountant."

Profile.   Some well-known job-placement consultants recommend that, instead of a statement of objectives, a capsule "Profile" of one or two positive sentences precede the more detailed listing of your experience or qualifications. This summary is your chance to hit the reader directly with your most important attributes for the job, an advantage if

Figure 10-3   Functional Resumé

MARIA RIVERA

428 Fort Street
Victoria BC V8X 5A6   mriv@shaw.ca   **(250) 546-1808**

Objective: Clerical position in an office setting with opportunity for
                          growth and development.

Profile: Camosun College graduate with Office Administration Certificate,
                          possessing strong computer skills and a record of
                          reliability and hard work.

Computer Skills:

Word	Excel	Simply Accounting
Adobe CS5	Access	
PowerPoint	Photoshop	

Office Skills:

Keyboarding: 45 wpm with excellent accuracy
Bookkeeping   Business Communications
Desktop Publishing   Switchboard

Communication Skills:

Completed two post-secondary Business Communications
courses with an "A" grade in report writing, editing, and
proofreading.

Punctuality and Reliability:

Excellent attendance record in high school and college;
achieved top marks for participation in group projects and
class projects.

Interpersonal Skills:

Demonstrated ability to work well with others in group
activities and fundraising initiatives for class field trip.

References:

Professor Catherine Keenan	Professor Lois Moore
Coordinator, Office Administration	School of Business
Camosun College	Camosun College
Victoria BC V8X 1J8	Victoria BC V8X 1J8
250-544-5522 Ex 1190	250-544-5522 Ex 1293

competition is fierce, as is often the case today. The resumés in Figures 10-2 and 10-3 provide examples. While it is perfectly proper to keep this kind of statement for your cover letter, if your resumé is separated from the letter when it is filed or passed on to others it will benefit from having a compact summary of your "selling points" near the top.

Education.   If your job experience is scanty or nonexistent, this section usually comes first since your educational qualifications are your primary selling point. Begin with your most recent educational attainment or your most advanced or relevant degree or diploma. If you have post-secondary education, it isn't necessary to include your high school unless you have some particular reason for doing so. Be sure to name any degree or diploma, along with the name of the institution that granted it. If courses you have taken are a selling point, list those relevant to the job you are applying for. (This advice pertains especially to students seeking their first permanent job.)

Work experience.   In a chronological resumé, the record of jobs held is given in reverse order, starting with the most recent. In a functional resumé, experience may be arranged according to type of work, for example, sales, marketing, and administration. Students without a great deal of work experience should include volunteer and part-time jobs in order to add depth to this section.

However you arrange your work experience, follow this guide:

1. **Make the information action-oriented.**   Use verbs as lead-ins to the facts. For example, say

   - *reviewed* customer service procedures and *recommended* changes
   - *organized* employee training seminars
   - *acted* as keyholder
   - *repaired* electronic circuits
   - *prepared* budgets for the Promotion Department
   - *trained* new employees in the Delivery Department

   Be sure to use parallel structure for all items in your list, as in the preceding example. If you're not sure how to check for parallel structure, see Chapter 7 and the Appendix for detailed discussion and examples.

2. **Stress accomplishment.**   A job description hasn't much impact. Instead of listing your duties for each job, tell what you have achieved. After all, duties represent an employer's expectations; listing them doesn't necessarily signify that you have fulfilled them. Rather than say "duties were to supervise customer accounts and keep the books," say that you "supervised the Customer Accounts Department and kept the books."

3. **Be honest.**   A small lie in your resumé is enough to destroy the employer's trust in you, even if it is discovered after you get the job. Integrity is an attribute never worth sacrificing. This advice does not mean that you should lay out your faults or draw attention to errors. It does mean that you should not misinform the reader.

Other interests or accomplishments.   In outlining outside activities, you will have to use your judgment on what to include. Many employment counsellors say that a person with varied interests makes the best employee in the long run. Clearly, though, you don't want outside interests to dominate your resumé. If you have a long list of possible items, concentrate on those that reveal unusual talents or personal qualities relevant to the work you want, such as leadership, imagination, or perseverance.

Personal information.   Most personal information, other than your address and telephone number, is unnecessary and should be left out. The law now forbids employers to ask about religion, race, colour, age, sex, marital status, or disability. Employers anticipate your familiarity with human rights legislation and do not expect to see this kind of information on your resumé.

References.   Although it's not mandatory, listing your references and their contact information can save the employer valuable time. This might tip the scales in your favour if other candidates don't make this information available. Remember to contact referees in advance and ask permission to use their names, and be sure to give full name, title, company, complete mailing address including postal code, telephone number, and email address. Some applicants prefer to wait until the employer is seriously interested, especially if they are currently employed and don't want others to know they are looking around. If you don't want to provide names on the resumé, say that references will be supplied on request. However, make sure you have your list prepared so that you can hand it to a potential employer during a job interview or send it with your follow-up letter.

The Cover Letter

A cover letter, also called an *application letter*, should do more than state "Here's my application and resumé." It should be the primary attention-getter, making the reader want to examine the resumé and grant you an interview. Can you imagine a prospective employer, with a stack of applications on the desk, wanting to read the following applicant's resumé?

✕ Dear Sir

I am applying for the job in your Sales Department which you advertised. I am graduating from college this year and would like a job in sales. The enclosed resumé gives my qualifications for that kind of work. I hope you will think I am suitable and that I will hear from you soon.

Yours truly

Joe Sinclair

Not only is this an *I*-centred letter but it provides no particular reason for the employer to hire the applicant. Your cover letter must do a better job. Aside from what you say, the way you say it matters; a well-written letter reveals important communication skills.

The type of letter you write will depend in part on whether the company is actually advertising a position. The unsolicited cover letter in Figure 10-4 is a letter of inquiry to a company that may or may not have openings. In this instance, your task is to interest the company in your background and qualifications rather than to apply for a specific job.

The solicited cover letter shown in Figure 10-5 targets specific qualifications for an advertised position.

The following guidelines for a cover letter, like the AIDA guidelines for other kinds of sales letters (see Chapter 6), are not hard and fast rules. Applicants should not be like cookie cutters, producing identical products. Feel free to express your own personality, as long as you remember the reason for writing and the reader you hope to influence.

✱ Explore
Career Letter 1: Application Letter—Unsolicited

✱ Explore
Career Letter 4: Application Letter—Unsolicited

✱ Explore
Career Letter 2: Application Letter—Solicited

✱ Explore
Career Letter 3: Application Letter—Solicited

Figure 10-4   Unsolicited Cover Letter

31 Lombard Drive
Edmonton AB T6H 1C3
April 1, 2011

Mr. Ewen Jacobs
Personnel Director
Computer Systems Inc.
125 Microchip Road
Calgary AB T2M 4H1

Dear Mr. Jacobs

Since Computer Systems is a fast-growing company, you are likely in need of young and energetic people with a solid background in information technology. In one month I will be graduating from the University of Alberta with a Computer Science degree and would like to join
your company as a programmer.

As you will see on the enclosed resumé, I have had work experience in programming and information systems. Last summer I implemented programs for the design of loudspeakers at
Nortec Industries, and in November I demonstrated Morris computers at the Alberta Computer
Show. Throughout the school year I have worked part-time at the University Computing Centre
as an IT technician.

At your convenience, I would like to meet you to discuss how my qualifications could benefit
Computer Systems. I will be in Calgary during the week of April 19 and will call in advance to
confirm an appointment.

Sincerely

Michelle Robert

Michelle Robert
Enc.: resumé

Figure 10-5   Solicited Cover Letter

1420 Grenstone Road
Belleville ON K8G 2Z9   October 14, 2010

Mr. Leo Pirelli
Director of Sales & Marketing
Fortune Travel Agency
4490 Emmett Avenue
Welland ON L3C 7C1

Dear Mr. Pirelli

The position of regional sales manager advertised in today's *Toronto Star* is an exact match for my background and career goals. As you will see from the attached resumé, my experience in the travel industry has prepared me for this challenging position, and I would welcome the opportunity to work for a prestigious and well-respected employer such as Fortune Travel.

My academic background includes a degree in Business Administration from Queen's University, where I completed eight marketing courses with honours. I also have two years of experience in advertising and public relations, including the design and implementation of a marketing plan for Interprovincial Business Systems. My communication skills have always been a major asset and I take pride in my ability to work well with others in a managerial and supervisory capacity. These skills will allow me to make a positive contribution to your sales and marketing effort.

I will be in Welland during the week of October 23 and would appreciate the opportunity to discuss my qualifications with you then. I will call you next week to confirm a convenient time.

Sincerely

Cheryl Wong

Cheryl Wong
Att: resumé

GET THE READER'S ATTENTION

Try to say something that will make the reader want to read on. This could be an outstanding qualification or a reason for your interest in the firm. Here are some examples:

✓ The article in *Canadian Business* on recent developments at Acme Industries suggests that you may be expanding. Are you looking for a dynamic salesperson?

✓ I believe my skill as a writer and my experience as a peer tutor would be useful attributes in your Public Affairs Department.

Name-dropping is another attention-getter. If someone respected by the employer has suggested you make the application or is willing to vouch for you, mention the person at the beginning of your letter, for example, "Arthur Stone suggested that I get in touch with you," or "Arthur Stone has told me that your company regularly hires students as summer office help."

STATE YOUR PURPOSE

You want the reader to know early in the letter that you are applying for a job. Don't beat around the bush and merely imply that you want employment—be specific. If you are responding to an advertised opening, say so. If your application is unsolicited, indicate the type of work you are applying for. Remember that a reader who is uncertain about your purpose is unlikely to act.

GIVE A BRIEF SUMMARY OF YOUR SELLING POINTS

You may create a second paragraph for this, but keep it as short as possible. A cover letter should not exceed a page. The shorter the better—as long as it creates interest in you. Here are some tips:

1. **Link your skills to the employer's needs.**   Don't just restate part of your resumé, but adapt it to the company or organization. Focus not on how the job would help you but on how you could help the employer. If you were a surveyor looking for summer help, which sentence from a surveying student would appeal to you most?

✗ I would like to work for a surveyor this summer to upgrade my qualifications and gain some practical experience.

✓ I believe the surveying courses I have taken will help me make a useful contribution to your summer surveying work.

2. **Sell yourself without seeming egotistical.**   This may seem to be a tall order, but you can emphasize strengths in a sincere way. First of all, don't boast. State your attributes simply and positively, without exaggeration or a lot of intensifying adjectives. For example, instead of saying "I am extremely responsible," or "I am exactly the person you are looking for" (a statement that presumes you can read the employer's mind), reveal why you can do the job well. In other words, try to use facts that speak for themselves rather than merely making claims:

✗ I have extraordinary talent in mathematics.

✓ I have consistently achieved honours standing in mathematics.

✗ I am a very good salesperson.

✓ Last summer, although one of the youngest salespeople in the store, I had the second-highest sales record.

3. **Avoid an *I*-centred approach.**   When writing a cover letter, it's impossible to avoid using *I* repeatedly. After all, the letter is about you. You can make the first-person pronoun less prominent, however, by placing something in front of it. Rather than putting it in a position of emphasis at the beginning of the sentence, bury it in the middle.

✗ I worked for an accountancy firm last summer.

✓ Last summer I worked for an accountancy firm.

   You needn't switch the order in all instances, but you can easily prevent a string of *I* beginnings.

4. **Place any weaknesses in a subordinate position.**   Most of the time your cover letter or resumé will not mention a weak area of your background. In the case of an advertised job opening, however, you may be asked to provide specific information that is not a selling point for you—information such as present employment or work experience in a specific field. If you must include something you don't want to emphasize, try putting it in a subordinate clause, with a main clause emphasizing a more positive point.

✗ Unfortunately I have never worked in a job requiring accounting.

✓ My background in accounting includes four undergraduate courses that required major projects and honours seminars.

5. **Don't apologize.**   If you don't think you can do a specific job, don't apply for it. If you think you can, be confident in outlining your qualifications. Avoid apologetic phrases such as "I'm sorry," "I regret," or "unfortunately" when referring to your background or skills.

ASK FOR AN INTERVIEW

Applicants often forget to do this directly. You need to press for an interview politely. You can indicate specific days or times when you will be available.

   If practical, mention that you will telephone the employer rather than asking the employer to get in touch with you. Exceptions to this practice occur when your application is one of hundreds routinely received (for example, an application for a summer job with a government department or with a large manufacturing plant). If the hiring company is going through specific channels, such as a student placement service, you are best to abide by their terms and not try to do an end run around the designated route. For the most part, however, a telephone call will not be considered a nuisance. As long as you are courteous, you will appear eager rather than pushy. In case you can't reach the person you want by phone, include in your letter some way for the employer to reach you.

   Two final tips:

■ **Don't mention salary expectations unless asked.**   The interview is a more appropriate time to discuss money, after you have had a chance to assess job opportunities; moreover, you will be better able then to gauge the employer's reactions.

■ **Don't thank in advance.**   Although intending to be polite, you may seem presumptuous.

Application Letters for Unusual Cases

In rare instances, a resumé may not be a benefit. If someone has been out of the workforce for many years and has done little in the community, a resumé might be embarrassingly bare. Similarly, if a person wants to move to a completely different line of work from any past jobs—for example, a salesperson who wants to work as a chef in a summer resort or a stockbroker who wants to learn the theatre business—a resumé may be unsuitable. In both cases, an extended application letter with explanatory comment might be a sensible substitute for a cover letter and resumé.

Follow this approach only as a last resort—if a resumé is truly unsuitable. If you are a student without much of a job record, or a homemaker who has not had paid employment for many years, you do not necessarily fall into this category. Take some time to think about yourself and your experiences. In most instances you can create a good resumé by drawing attention to the skills and knowledge you have gained in other endeavours.

The Job Interview

✔●┤Practise
Exercise 11: Script for Informational Interview

👁┤Watch
Perils of Pauline: The Job Interview

If you have been asked for an interview, you can usually assume that you are being considered seriously for the job; businesses don't want to waste time—and money—on people they have no wish to employ. In a buyer's market, you can also assume that you will be competing with others for the available position. Preparing for the interview will help you put your best foot forward.

Researching the Company

If you are going to an interview with a manufacturing company, learn all you can about its products and customers. If the employer is an advertising agency, know something about the advertisements for its main accounts. Annual company reports are a useful source of information for large companies. For large and small firms, you may find a receptionist who will help you if you are polite rather than demanding. The Internet, the local library, your college library or career counselling service, or even a customer or supplier is a useful source for research.

Preparing Answers to Likely Questions

👁┤Watch
BCVL: Interviewing Skills

In a survey of employers, the University and College Placement Association (later to become Canadian Association of Career Educators and Employers—CACEE) asked what employers value most in potential employees. Here are the five factors employers named as most important in selecting an employee ("Interviewing Skills"):

1. **Ability to communicate.**   Almost any open-ended question will test this ability, but recruiters may deliberately ask some difficult ones just to see how well you can respond. Here are some common questions:

    ■ Tell me about yourself and why you think you can do this job.

    ■ Why are you applying to this company?

    ■ Why did you take your particular program of studies and what courses did you enjoy the most? The least?

    ■ What are your strengths and weaknesses? (Tread warily in revealing weaknesses; don't mistake the recruiter for a confessor.)

    ■ Tell me about your last job; what did you accomplish or learn in it?

    ■ Why did you leave it?

2. **Willingness to take initiative**

    ■ What have you done that shows initiative?

- What do you do in your spare time?
- What accomplishments have given you the most satisfaction?

3. **Willingness to accept responsibility**

- What is your attitude to overtime work?
- Can you give examples from your background that demonstrate your ability to accept responsibility?
- Can you give an example of a job you have held that required you to demonstrate your responsibility?
- How old were you when you became self-supporting?

4. **Leadership potential**

- What offices have you held at school or elsewhere?
- What has been your most difficult assignment in dealing with people?
- Describe a situation where you had to show leadership.
- What kind of people do you like to work with most? Least?
- How many people have you ever had to manage?

5. **Ambition and motivation.**   Recruiters like people who have a sense of purpose and have thought about their careers. They look for motivated employees. On the other hand, they are wary of a young employee who is an arrogant know-it-all and unwilling to learn. These questions are common:

- What would you like to be doing in five years? Ten years?
- How would you describe your energy level?
- What would you hope to accomplish in this job?
- What are your salary expectations?

Planning a Few Questions

Be ready to ask the interviewer questions of your own about the organization you are applying to. The thoroughness of your research will demonstrate your interest in the company and is sure to impress your interviewer. Here are some questions that might work in some situations, but keep in mind that you will have to adapt them depending on the nature of the employer and the interview:

- What computer hardware and software are you currently using?
- Does the company provide professional development opportunities?
- What are the organization's plans for future growth or change?
- Does management encourage the policy of promotion from within the organization?
- What does the department hope to achieve in the next two to three years?
- Are lateral or rotational job moves available to provide broader experience?
- How often are performance reviews given and how are they conducted?

Developing Poise

Even if you're nervous, try to look calm and relaxed. Remember to smile, especially when you greet the interviewer and when you leave. If you seem pleasant rather than grim, the recruiter will naturally respond more favourably.

Figure 10-6   Follow-Up Letter

4729 Queen's Crescent
Sackville NB E4L 1B3
June 28, 2011

Ms. Ellen Akroyd
Personnel Manager
Telesystems Associates
439 Queen Street
Fredericton NB E4L 1B3

Dear Ms. Akroyd

Meeting with you today to discuss the sales representative position has made me
especially eager to work for Telesystems.

It was a pleasure meeting members of your sales staff and discussing with them the
expanding customer base that Telesystems is experiencing.

I hope to hear from you soon about the possibility of joining your sales team.

Sincerely

Jill Trenholme

Jill Trenholme

Here are a few more tips to impress recruiters:

- Dress neatly in a manner appropriate for the job.
- Shake hands firmly—no limp handshakes.
- Look the interviewer in the eye, especially when greeting and thanking, and when listening to the interviewer's comments and questions.
- Speak clearly and correctly. Poor diction or grammar will be a strike against you in many managerial jobs.
- Project a sense of vitality in your voice and manner. A flat voice and lifeless manner are not impressive.
- Avoid simple "yes" or "no" answers; your job is to communicate.
- Don't condemn others, such as former bosses or co-workers.

Writing a Follow-Up Letter

When you have completed an interview, remember to send a brief thank-you letter to the interviewer. You can use this opportunity to show your enthusiasm for the company or staff or to emphasize a qualification the interviewer considered important. Even if you don't get the job this time, you will help create a positive climate for any future dealings.

Figure 10-6 is an example of an effective follow-up letter.

Internet Issues

The Internet is a major job-hunting resource. In addition to researching companies on the Web, applicants can check listings and post resumés with job boards such as Monster, Workopolis, Working, and Yahoo! HotJobs. Although it's probably unwise to make the Internet the sole focus of your search, here's a quick look at some online features that can be helpful:

1. **Internet research sites** are a powerful source of information about companies, fields of employment, and specific geographical areas. An effective Web search can be a time-consuming process, but the Internet is a major research tool that can be instrumental in conducting your search for employment.

2. **Job boards** such as Monster, Workopolis, Kijiji, Yahoo! HotJobs, and Job Bank (the Service Canada website) have online tools to help you identify career opportunities and search for current job openings by field, occupation, or region. Applicants can submit resumés and cover letters electronically either to the site or to a specific employer.

3. **Scannable resumés** are one method adopted by some companies to cut down on the labour-intensive process of sorting through the large number of resumés they receive. Computer scanners filter resumés by key words and store the information on a database. The employer can then search the database for specific skills, education, or experience and select resumés that match the criteria for a particular job.

   Here are a few tips for creating a scannable resumé:

   - Remove all formatting.
   - Choose a common font and use 14-point font size.

- Include a section at the top of the resumé containing 20 or 30 key words relating to your skills and experience as well as the job description (for example, "clerical" or "communication skills").

4. **Electronic resumés** include those sent by email, submitted to online job boards, or posted on Web home pages. Formatting electronic resumés requires specific knowledge to ensure that the resumé transmits and scans properly. A cardinal rule is to keep your formatting simple, as your recipient may be looking at your resumé in a different program or browser.

5. **Multimedia resumés,** for those with a high-tech flair, can be created as a presentation using text, graphics, sound, and even video. The resumé can then be produced on a CD for distribution to potential employers.

Exercises

1. Investigate the job market in an area where you are interested in getting employment. Compile a list of 10 companies that would be good prospects for employment. Include the contact information of the companies and the names and titles of the appropriate people to apply to (for example, the personnel director). You may substitute the names of people with whom you would like to have an information interview. In compiling this information, you will find it helpful to use the Internet, your college's career service, the library, and the telephone.

2. Draw up a list of questions that you would like to have answered during an information interview with a company on the list you compiled for Exercise 1.

3. Create a chronological resumé and accompanying cover letter for a summer job or permanent job in a field you are interested in. Be sure to include any volunteer work, part-time jobs, and positions of responsibility you have held at school or elsewhere. Remember: any work that shows you are reliable is useful information for an employer, and any accomplishment that shows initiative or leadership will help set you apart from the crowd.

4. With your resumé as a backup, write two separate cover letters for two different employers or jobs. Change the emphasis or approach according to the differing needs of each.

   Remember that the letters must reflect the facts of the resumé. The point of this exercise is to show how your record can be adapted while sticking to the truth.

5. What response would you give in an interview situation if you were asked the following questions?

   a) If I were to contact your professors, what would they say about your punctuality, your work ethic, and your academic excellence?

   b) Can you give me an example of your ability to handle pressure calmly and react well in an emergency?

   c) What do you consider your major weaknesses?

   d) What are your salary expectations?

   e) If you were in a position to hire a co-worker, what type of person would you avoid?

   f) Which of your courses did you enjoy most during your last year of study? The least?

   g) During your previous work experience, which manager did you like the most? The least?

   h) What activities do you engage in outside of school and work?

   i) What do you expect to be doing five years from now? Ten years from now?

   j) What kinds of professional development activities would you like to pursue while you are working in this field?

6. Which of the following questions are in violation of current Canadian legislation protecting the rights of job applicants? In each case, discuss how you would respond if the question were asked.

   a) Are you bilingual?

   b) Do you have any dependants?

    c) What is your opinion about a dress code?

    d) Do you smoke? Drink alcohol?

    e) What is your year of birth?

    f) Are you self-supporting?

    g) Would you be willing to submit to a drug test?

    h) Do you have any disabilities or handicaps?

    i) What clubs or organizations do you belong to?

    j) Are you bonded?

7. In groups of three or four, take turns practising for a job interview. Try forming a group with others who are interested in the same field of employment. One person should play the applicant and another the interviewer; the third (and fourth) should assess the positive and negative aspects of the applicant's performance. If possible, videotape the role-playing for critique and discussion.

8. Create a functional resumé and accompanying cover letter for a permanent job in a field of interest to you. In groups of three or four, evaluate the application packages, pointing out possible improvements to the information provided, the order of information, the wording, and the layout. Make the needed revisions.

PEARSON
mycanadianbuscommlab

Visit www.mycanadianbuscommlab.ca for everything you need to help you succeed in the job you've always wanted! Tools and resources include the following:

- Composing Space and Writer's Toolkit
- Document Makeovers
- Grammar Exercises—and much more!

Appendix: Editing Guidelines

A Practical Grammar

You may sometimes say to yourself, "If only I'd learned more grammar when I was young, my writing would be fine!" or "If only I could remember the grammar rule!" Knowing the grammar of a language certainly helps in writing, especially when you are checking your work, but it is less important to know the terminology—the parts of speech and their functions—than to appreciate that the essence of good grammar is clarity. The rules of grammar are really a description of how clear sentences work. If you don't know what your errors are, review this section of the Appendix, which discusses the most common grammatical errors in business writing. Figure out which weaknesses apply to you. You can then check on your work with an eye to spotting and correcting them.

Lack of Sentence Unity

Rule 1   Sentences Must Be Complete.

A complete sentence is an independent clause (able to stand by itself) containing both a subject and a verb:

> I solved the problem.

> The report will be printed tomorrow.

SENTENCE FRAGMENTS

A sentence fragment lacks a subject or a verb, or it contains a subordinating word making the clause dependent rather than independent. Remember this tip: an *ing* word, such as *being*, is not, by itself, a verb.

✗ London being a good city to test-market a new product.

> The verb is lacking, but *being* can easily become the verb *is*.

✓ London is a good city to test-market a product.

> Words such as *although*, *while*, and *whether* at the beginning of a clause make it dependent—unable to stand by itself.

✗ I was late. Although I solved the problem.

✓ I was late, although I solved the problem.

MyCanadianBusCommLab

Developing your basic grammar, punctuation, mechanics, and style skills is vital to improving your writing and to succeeding in your courses. For more help with these skills, go to MyCanadianBusCommLab at www.mycanadianbuscommlab.ca (access included with your purchase of this new textbook) to get further help through additional instruction, activities, and video.

An occasional sentence fragment is acceptable, if it is used for emphasis and the rest of the sentence is easily inferred:

✓ How long can we continue with these losses? No more than six months.

RUN-ON SENTENCES

Sometimes called a *fused sentence*, a run-on sentence is the opposite of a sentence fragment; two sentences are improperly joined as one, sometimes without any punctuation.

✗ I like business this is why I enrolled at Queen's.

When a comma joins two sentences, the mistake is called a comma splice:

✗ These sales figures are higher than last year's, they increased by 10 per cent.

Remember: two independent clauses (clauses that can stand by themselves as sentences) must be separated by one of the following:

- a period
- a coordinating conjunction (*and, or, nor, but, yet, for*, and sometimes *so*)
- a subordinating conjunction (*because, since, although, if, when*)
- a semicolon

Faulty Predication

Rule 2   The Subject of a Sentence Must Fit the Predicate.

Faulty predication occurs when the subject does not mesh with the predicate, which includes the verb and any direct object or complement.

✗ The main point of the report examines the lack of adequate daycare as a cause of absenteeism.
✓ The report examines the lack of adequate daycare as a cause of absenteeism.
✓ The main point of the report is that a lack of adequate daycare causes absenteeism.

The first sentence is faulty because a *point* cannot *examine*. The first revision changes the subject to fit the predicate and the second changes the predicate to fit the subject.

Remember: if you use the verb *to be* by itself, follow with a noun phrase that completes the subject; otherwise change the verb.

✗ The explosion was when the pipeline sprang a leak.
✓ The explosion occurred when the pipeline sprang a leak.
✓ The leaking pipeline caused the explosion.

Lack of Subject-Verb Agreement

Rule 3   The Subject Must Agree in Number and Person with the Verb.

This simple rule is most often broken when the grammatical subject has a modifier and the verb wrongly agrees with the modifier rather than with the bare subject:

✗ The *settlement* of native and Inuit land claims *are* likely to take several years.

Since the bare subject is the singular noun *settlement*, the verb should be *is*.

✓ The *settlement* of native and Inuit land claims *is* likely to take several years.

COMPOUND SUBJECTS

Two nouns joined by *and* take a plural verb:

✓ The carpenter and the bricklayer are coming tomorrow.

When two nouns are joined by *or, either/or,* or *neither/nor*, the verb agrees with the last noun.

✓ Neither my boss nor my subordinates *regret* the change.

If a plural noun precedes a singular one, however, a singular verb may sound awkward. If so, recast the sentence:

✓ Either the creditors or the bank is likely to act.

✓ Action will come from either the bank or the creditors.

Note: the phrases *as well as, in addition to*, and *together with* do not make a compound subject.

✓ Jack and Jill are attending the meeting.

✓ Jack as well as Jill is attending the meeting.

EACH, EITHER, NEITHER, ANYONE, EVERYONE, SOMEONE

These indefinite pronouns take singular, not plural, verbs:

✓ *Each* of the employees *is* contributing to the fund.

✓ *Neither* of my colleagues *wants* the job.

None can take either a singular or a plural verb, depending on the context:

✓ *None* of the staff *are* happy with the decision.

✓ *None* of the money *was* used for new computer software.

NAMES AND TITLES

Even if the name of an organization or the title of a book includes a plural or compound noun, it is considered singular and takes a singular verb:

✓ Dominion Castings *has* a good pension plan.

✓ Deloitte & Touche *is* the accounting firm we use.

Pronoun Problems

Rule 4	A Pronoun Must Refer to a Specific Noun and Must Agree with It in Number and Person.

✗ When *office machinery* becomes costly to fix, *they* should be replaced.

✓ When *office machinery* becomes costly to fix, *it* should be replaced.

✗ When *an employee* has worked here for 25 years, *they* get gold watches.

✓ When *employees* have worked here for 25 years, *they* get gold watches.

THE PERSON DILEMMA

Our lack of a neutral personal pronoun causes problems in the singular: should a person be referred to as *he*, or *he or she*? Convention decrees that you still cannot mix singular and plural:

✕ When *a person* applies for a job, *they* should look *their* best.

Most North Americans think that using the masculine form is sexist, a view not held everywhere.

✕ When *a person* applies for a job, *he* should look *his* best.

One option is to use both pronouns, but this can be stylistically awkward and repetitive:

✓ When *a person* applies for a job, *he or she* should look *his or her* best.

The English rely on *one* and *one's* to get around the difficulty:

✓ When *one* applies for a job, *one* should look *one's* best.

However, *one* doesn't come naturally to many North Americans, who find it a bit pretentious and formal for most occasions.

What to do? A practical solution is to use the plural wherever possible for both subjects and pronouns:

✓ When *people* apply for jobs, *they* should look *their* best.

Where the plural is not possible, you can occasionally use *he or she*, as this book does, but try to avoid a constant repetition of double pronouns. You should also make clear in your discussions or examples that you are referring to both sexes and, if possible, use neutral terms such as *fire fighter* rather than *fireman* or *server* rather than *waitress*.

As in other areas of communication, be aware of cultural context. Although your writing and speaking should reflect the sensitivities of your community, others do not always share these sensitivities. Be careful, therefore, of attributing sexist attitudes to those from English-speaking cultures outside North America who may use masculine forms to refer to both genders.

VAGUE *THIS* OR *IT*

The indefinite pronouns *this* and *it* must refer to a noun. When they don't have a specific reference, they can cause confusion:

✕ The supervisor decided to reprimand the workers, but *this* was not acted on.

What specific noun does *this* refer to?

✓ The manager decided to reprimand the workers, but *this decision* was not acted on.

✕ Our plan was to conduct a seminar in the boardroom, but the advisory group considered *it* unsuitable.

Does *it* refer to the plan, the seminar, or the boardroom? When a pronoun leaves any doubt about its reference, repeat the noun:

✓ Our plan was to conduct a seminar in the boardroom, but the advisory group considered *the location* unsuitable.

WOE WITH *ME*

Having been trained as a child not to say, "Me and Sheila want to play outside," many adults wrongly use the subjective pronoun *I* when the objective pronoun *me* is correct. This mistake usually happens when two people are being referred to.

✕ The congratulatory letter mentioned Helen and *I*.

A simple guide if you are not sure about what case to use is to try the sentence without the first name (Helen) and then use the pronoun that comes naturally:

✓ The congratulatory letter mentioned *me*.

✓ The congratulatory letter mentioned Helen and *me*.

Remember that the objective case follows a preposition:

✓ *Between* you and *me*, Bernhard is a phony.

✓ She gave the tickets to John and *me*.

One exception: when a pronoun following a preposition also modifies a noun or noun phrase, use the possessive form:

✕ She objected to *him* leaving so early.

✓ She objected to *his* leaving so early.

In this case, *leaving* is a gerund, which acts as a noun, so the pronoun takes the adjectival form *his*.

Tense Troubles

Rule 5   Verb Tenses Must Be Consistent with the Time Frame.

TENSE SHIFT

A common error in business proposals is to switch constantly from the conditional *would* to the future *will*:

✕ Implementing this idea *would* improve employee morale and in turn it *will* likely increase profits.

Either tense will do, but be consistent.

HYPOTHETICAL ACTIONS

The conditional verb (*would* or *could*) is often improperly used to describe a hypothetical action in the past. Use a conditional verb only in the consequence clause, not in the *if* clause:

✕ If he *would have* smiled, I *would have* invited him.

✓ If he *had* smiled, I *would have* invited him.

When writing about a hypothetical action in the future—one that is unlikely to happen—use the subjunctive in the *if* clause and the conditional in the consequence clause:

✓ If the president *were* to adopt this plan, the plant *would* show a profit within six months.

✓ If I *were* you, I *would* read that report before tomorrow's meeting.

A quick tip: use *would* in only one clause.

WRITING ABOUT THE PAST

Actions that precede other past actions should have the past perfect tense—indicated by *had* and the past participle. Notice the ambiguity in the following sentence:

✗ When the owners *toured* the plant, the manager *went* back to his office.

Did the manager avoid the owners? Or did he go back to his office afterward?

✓ When the owners *had toured* the plant, the manager *went* back to his office.

Muddled Modifying

Rule 6   Modifiers Must Show Clearly What They Modify.

To modify a noun, use an adjective; to modify a verb, adverb, or adjective, use an adverb. (Adding *ly* to an adjective often forms an adverb.) Sportscasters seem to have forgotten this rule.

✗ He played *good* today.
✗ He threw the ball *real well*.
✗ He finished the project *quick*.
✓ He played *well* today.
✓ He threw the ball *well* (or *really well*).
✓ He finished the project *fast* (or *quickly*).

Remember, however, to use an adjective after the verb *to be* (and its variations) as well as after some sense-related verbs—*taste, smell, feel, look,* appear, *seem, become.*

✓ The pie tasted *good* even though it looked *bad*.
✓ The material feels *soft*.
✓ A massage feels *good*.

MISPLACED AND SQUINTING MODIFIERS

Meaning in an English sentence is partly conveyed by word order. A misplaced modifier can cause confusion:

✗ He made his brief to the commission, *which was disorganized and long-winded*.
✓ He made a *disorganized and long-winded* brief to the commission.

A squinting modifier seems to look two ways, creating doubt about whether it belongs to the phrase before it or after it:

✗ She decided *after her vacation* to look for another job.

To avoid confusion, relocate the modifier:

✓ *After her vacation* she decided to look for another job.
✓ She decided to look for another job *after her vacation*.

A dangling modifier is not connected to anything:

✗ *Walking into the lobby*, the office was intimidating.

Who is doing the walking? Surely not the office.

✓ Walking into the lobby, *he* thought the office was intimidating.

Problems with Pairs (and More)

Rule 7   Comparisons Must Be Equivalent.

The two parts of a comparison should match grammatically, whether the second part is stated or implied.

✕ Young employees often understand more about computers than their bosses.

This sentence unintentionally compares computers and bosses; it should compare the employees' understanding with the bosses' understanding.

✓ Young employees often understand more about computers than their bosses do.

✕ Baggs was a tedious man and so were his speeches.

✓ Baggs was tedious and so were his speeches.

CORRELATIVES

The two parts of correlative constructions, *not only . . . but also* or *both . . . and*, should be equivalent. The coordinating term must not come too early; make sure both the parts that follow are grammatically the same.

✕ Margaret is *not only* good with figures *but also* with people.

✓ Margaret is good *not only* with figures *but also* with people.

✕ I like *both* going to movies *and* to concerts.

✓ I like going *both* to movies *and* to concerts.

or

✓ I like going to *both* movies *and* concerts.

✕ The manager hired Heather *both* for the marketing *and* sales jobs.

✓ The manager hired Heather for *both* the marketing *and* the sales jobs.

PARALLEL PHRASING

Rule 8   Similar Ideas Should Have Similar Wording.

For clarity, items in a series need to be phrased in the same way.

✕ We had increased sales, better productivity, and profits were higher.

✓ We had increased sales, better productivity, and higher profits.

Even when similar ideas take more than one sentence to express, your message will be more easily understood if you use similar wording:

✕ Carolyn Fisher is a good manager. She is energetic and well organized. The ability to motivate people is another of her attributes.

✓ Carolyn Fisher is a good manager. She is energetic and well organized. She also knows how to motivate people.

A Guide to Punctuation

Punctuation marks are conventions—convenient, common symbols. Writers use them to give readers easy passage through a piece of writing. Long ago, when there weren't such conventions, it often took hours to decipher a page. Anyone who has read a piece of prose without punctuation will know the difficulty.

Punctuation gradually alters with the times, as does grammar, and the trend today is toward less punctuation. In some instances, use of punctuation may also vary according to the writer's judgment about what is clearest. Yet the rules are still useful. Faulty punctuation can make a passage almost as hard to read as one with no punctuation, since it sends the reader the wrong signals. Ironically, although punctuation is probably the most frequent problem in writing, it is the easiest and most straightforward part of the writing process to learn. Most of the rules can be applied mechanically. For those that cannot, the sound of a sentence—its natural breaks and pauses—is often a helpful guide.

Punctuation rules and guidelines vary somewhat from one dictionary, handbook, or style guide to another. The discussion of punctuation rules in this section of *Impact* follows the guidelines in the *Publication Manual of the American Psychological Association* (6th ed.). If your teacher or employer uses a different guide, find out what it is and follow it. If you get conflicting advice from different sources, be consistent: Choose one approach and stick to it.

' Apostrophes

1. Use an apostrophe to show possession. The simplest way to remember whether the apostrophe should come before or after the *s* is to follow this rule:

   a) Turn the possessive element into an "of" or "belonging to" phrase:

her parents decision	⟶	the decision (of her *parents*)
Ross car	⟶	the car (belonging to *Ross*)
the childrens coats	⟶	the coats (belonging to the *children*)
managements proposal	⟶	the proposal (of *management*)

   b) If the noun in the "of" or "belonging to" phrase ends in *s*, add an *apostrophe*:

   her parents' decision

   Ross' car

   (It's also correct to write *s's* for the possessive of proper nouns ending in *s*, as in *Ross's car*.)

   If the noun in the "of" or "belonging to" phrase does not end in *s*, add an apostrophe + s:

   the children's coats

   management's proposal

   Remember that possessive pronouns (*yours, hers, his, its, ours, theirs*) never take an apostrophe.

   Remember too that possession may be shown without an apostrophe if the possessor is preceded by *of*:

   the rules of the game, the page of the report

This form is most often used with nonhuman entities or things, rather than with people.

2. Use an apostrophe to show contractions of words or numbers:

isn't, don't, I'm, it's, spring of '86

Caution: don't confuse *it's*—a short form of *it is*—with the possessive pronoun *its*, which never has an apostrophe.

3. Use an apostrophe to form the possessive of nouns in a series:

Bill and Martha's house is located in the west end of town. (ownership is shared)

Ellie's and Samantha's husbands won awards at the national conference. (ownership is separate)

4. Do not use an apostrophe to form the plural of an abbreviation or number:

CDs

1990s

threes and fives

40s and 50s

[ ] Brackets

Don't confuse brackets [ ] with parentheses ( ).

Bracket any additions you make to a quotation. For example, if you need to insert words to make sense of a quotation, surround those words in brackets:

Jones said, "The costs of indexed pensions are more than they [taxpayers] realize or their grandchildren will be able to afford."

Use brackets around the word *sic*, to show that any misspelling or misuse of the preceding word or phrase is in the original quotation:

Their sign said, "Ban all nuclear missles [*sic*]. Ban the bomb."

: Colons

A colon is a sign that something is to follow. Note that a colon is followed by one space, not two.

1. Use a colon after an independent clause to introduce an explanation, expansion, or restatement of the clause. (Tip: if you can say "that is" or "namely" after the first clause, use a colon.)

We made one mistake: rushing the job.

This is his advice: hire an accountant.

2. Use a colon before a vertical list introduced by a complete sentence:

The following employee transfers took place in June:

- Mary Aster to Victoria
- Hugh Koster to Calgary
- Max Cohen to Westminster

If the list runs horizontally, use a colon only if the part preceding it is a complete sentence:

✗ We want: three chairs, two desks, a credenza.

✓ We want three chairs, two desks, and a credenza.

or

✓ We want the following furniture: three chairs, two desks, and a credenza.

3. Use a colon to introduce a direct quotation when the part preceding the quotation is an independent clause:

I remember Diefenbaker's scornful remark: "Polls are for dogs."

4. Use a colon before a direct quotation of more than three lines, and indent the quotation.

5. Use a colon between numerals when giving the time:

3:20 p.m. or 15:20

6. Use a colon between a title and subtitle:

Managing Change: A Guide for the New Leader

, Commas

Commas are the most problematic of punctuation marks, not only because they have so many uses, but also because they are sometimes discretionary. Although a long complex sentence with no commas is sure to confuse, a sentence with a string of commas will seem fragmented and laborious. The following guidelines will help you steer a course between too many and too few. Ultimately, however, the clearest choice is always best.

1. Use a comma between elements in a series of three or more items:

Give me a computer, several disks, and a painkiller.

The final comma sometimes avoids confusion:

✗ The company suffered from old machines, inefficient manufacturing processes, increased competition and management turnover.

Had management turnover increased?

✓ The company suffered from old machines, inefficient manufacturing processes, increased competition, and management turnover.

2. Use a comma between adjectives that precede and modify the same noun:

a heavy, unlabelled package

her interesting, diverse responsibilities

but

favourite little restaurant

In the last case, *favourite* modifies not *restaurant* but *little restaurant*; therefore, no comma is needed. A simple test is to see if you can reverse the adjectives. If you can reverse them, use a comma.

3. Use a comma before a coordinating conjunction (*and, or, nor, but, yet*) connecting two independent clauses if the clauses are long and the subject changes.

   The report indicated a need for increased control over spending, and the president followed the recommendation to establish new guidelines for all departments.

   Note: *however, therefore,* and *thus* are not coordinating conjunctions, since they can go in various places other than between two independent clauses.

   ✗ I felt like shouting, however, I managed to stay calm.

   ✓ I felt like shouting; however, I managed to stay calm.

   ✓ I felt like shouting; I managed to stay calm, however.

   ✓ I felt like shouting; I managed, however, to stay calm.

   The first example has a frequent error—a comma splice—since it wrongly treats *however* as a coordinating conjunction.

4. Use a comma after a long introductory phrase or clause:

   In the middle of the coldest winter on record, the pipes froze.

   Since the order was submitted after the budget was approved, the committee turned it down.

5. Use commas to set off an appositive or naming phrase that gives inessential identifying information:

   My boss, Enid Miller, is on holiday.

   Mr. Hughes, our vice-president, will make the decisions.

   However, do not use commas if the naming phrase is essential to identify the person:

   My daughter Brenda is a skilful promoter.

6. Use commas to set off a nonrestrictive clause (one that is not essential to the meaning of the sentence).

   Mavis Jones, who comes from Halifax, will join the firm in June.

   Arthur immediately contacted the assistant manager, who gave him the information he needed.

   However, if a clause is essential to the meaning of the sentence, do not use commas to set it off. Failure to observe this distinction can cause serious muddles, as suggested by these two sentences:

   All part-time employees, who aren't in the regular benefits plan, should obtain this insurance.

   All part-time employees who aren't in the regular benefits plan should obtain this insurance.

   In the first sentence, all part-time employees are directed to buy insurance. In the second sentence, only those who aren't in the regular benefits plan are told to get it.

7. Use a comma before a short direct quotation (unless it's just one or two words):

   Duffy said, "Let's take a break."

   Do not use a comma before an indirect quotation:

   Duffy said we should take a break.

8. Use a comma before a tag question:

She's a good organizer, isn't she?

9. Use a comma between parts of a date:

Tuesday, February 3, 2011

10. Use a comma to separate three digits in most numbers:

$3,000,000

Note, however, that the metric system uses spaces or hyphens rather than commas for dates and numbers:

2011 12 03 or 06-12-11

$3 000 000

11. Do not use a comma between the two parts of a compound verb:

✗ The deficit plunged the company into debt, and caused a public relations crisis.

✓ The deficit plunged the company into debt and caused a public relations crisis.

12. Do not use a comma between a subject and a verb:

✗ The parents who came to the meetings the most often, seemed to have the best relationships with their children.

✓ The parents who came to the meetings the most often seemed to have the best relationships with their children.

Dashes

Some people treat the dash as an all-purpose mark and toss it into their writing frequently. A dash can effectively substitute for many other punctuation marks, especially the comma, but it should not be used constantly. Dashes are more common in informal notes and messages or personal correspondence than in formal business documents. A page full of dashes will make writing seem breathless; it won't give the impression of calm reason most business writing strives for. To create a dash, key two hyphens or insert an "em dash" on your computer.

1. Use a dash to emphasize the phrase that follows. The dash creates stronger emphasis than a comma or parentheses.

We got their approval—at last.

2. Use a dash on both sides of an interrupting phrase if you want to emphasize the phrase.

The management team—not the board of directors—was responsible for that decision.

Ellipses Points

1. Use ellipses (three periods) to show that part of a quotation is missing:

He maintained that "Kelso is a profitable business . . . with a great future."

If the omission is at the end of the sentence, the ellipses are followed by a fourth period.

2. Use ellipses to show that a series of numbers continues indefinitely:

   2, 4, 6, 8 . . .

! Exclamation Points

Use an exclamation point for an exclamatory statement—a loud or dramatic utterance:

   What an impressive speech!

However, be sparing with exclamation points in both paper-based and email business messages. Netiquette rules governing online communication suggest a limited use of exclamation points. Capital letters and exclamation points are the electronic version of shouting and are considered discourteous and inappropriate in email correspondence.

Try to restrict exclamation points to informal correspondence, as they soon create a tone of exaggeration and emotionalism.

✗ Last chance! Act now! Don't delay!

✓ Act now, before this valuable offer expires.

- Hyphens

Hyphenation rules are tricky, and they change from time to time and place to place. There is a tendency away from hyphenation, and many words that were once hyphenated lose the hyphen as they become more commonplace. Dictionaries do not always agree on hyphenation rules, so stick to one style guide or dictionary and be consistent.

1. Hyphenate compounds acting as nouns:

   lieutenant-governor, mass-producer, father-in-law

2. In the case of compound adjectives, rules depend on whether the compound precedes or follows the noun. For example

   a well-known writer

   the writer was well known

3. Do not hyphenate compounds including an adverb ending in *ly*:

   a quickly diminishing supply of capital

4. Use a hyphen to separate compound numbers under a hundred when they are written as words:

   sixty-five, thirty-two

5. Most words formed with prefixes are written as one word. Exceptions are the prefixes *self*, *all*, *ex*, and any prefix to a name, number, or abbreviation:

   antisocial, multilingual, midterm, intramural, extracurricular, ultramodern

   but

   self-sufficient, all-encompassing, ex-wife, pro-Conservative, pre-1960s

6. If two or more words modify the same base word, hyphenate each modifier:

   The pro- and anti-strike groups agreed to talk.

   The skiers started at 2-, 5-, and 10-minute intervals.

7. Hyphens can be used to divide a word at the end of a line.

( ) Parentheses

Be sure not to confuse parentheses ( ) with brackets [ ].

Use parentheses to set off incidental material or references:

Housing starts were up 20 per cent in March (despite gloomy forecasts) but are now levelling off.

In his speech, Fraser predicted increased drilling activity (Empire Club, May 10, 2011).

If the insertion is within a sentence, put any punctuation after rather than before the parentheses; if the insertion is itself a sentence, put the period within the parentheses.

Despite the gloomy economic forecast (see Figure 2), sales revenues are up 10 per cent.

Sales revenues this year increased by 10 per cent, despite the forecasts. (See enclosure for a breakdown of forecast figures.)

Periods

1. Use a period to mark a "full stop" at the end of a sentence.
2. Most abbreviations ending in lowercase letters take a period: *Mrs., Dr., St.,* etc.
3. Abbreviations for measurements do not use periods: *rpm, kph, kg, cm, psi, hr*
    If the letters each represent a word, such as *3:00 a.m.* (*ante meridiem*), no space intervenes between the letters.
4. Acronyms (abbreviations that form a word) and other uppercase abbreviations generally omit the periods: *NAFTA, NORAD, CD-ROM, BA, USA.*
5. Use a period and a space for initials: *J. R. R. Tolkien, Lester B. Pearson.*

? Question Marks

Use a question mark at the end of a direct question. Do not use it for an indirect one:

✓ How will you increase productivity?

✗ I wonder how you will increase productivity?

✓ I wonder how you will increase productivity.

When phrasing a courteous request or a rhetorical question for which you don't expect a verbal answer, use a period instead of a question mark:

✓ Will you please send me the form next week.

Never directly follow a question mark with a comma, period, or semicolon.

" " Quotation Marks

1. Use quotation marks to set off short quotations:

    Helen said, "Let's try to get that account."

    For quotations of 40 or more words, indent the text 0.5 in. from the left margin, but do not enclose it in quotation marks.

2. Use single quotation marks to enclose quoted material within a quotation:

   As Chalmers suggests, "Let's follow the old adage that 'a penny saved is a penny earned' to keep this company afloat."

3. Use italics, not quotation marks, for emphasis, words used as examples, technical terms, or words that could be misread:

   American and Canadian forces traditionally pronounce the word *lieutenant* differently.

   What is the meaning of *increase exponentially*?

   Examples are words such as *streaming* and *Webcasting*.

4. Use quotation marks around a word or expression used in a special sense or purposely misused:

   Evidently he "misspoke" when he earlier denied the crime.

5. Use quotation marks to enclose the titles of poems (unless the poem is an entire book), short stories, articles, songs, and chapters in books.

   For movies, paintings, plays, ballets, and television programs, use italics.

6. Put periods and commas inside quotation marks:

   "Lend me your iPod," he said, "and I'll download it now."

   Put other punctuation marks outside quotation marks unless they are part of the quoted material:

   He claimed, "I can double productivity"; only Sheila believed him.

   The moderator said, "What is the point of this exercise?"

   Did the teacher instruct students to "delete any comments they disagreed with"?

; Semicolons

1. Use a semicolon between closely related independent clauses (clauses that can stand by themselves). The semicolon suggests a closer link than a period and is especially useful before conjunctive adverbs, such as *thus, however, therefore*. Use it sparingly, however, or your writing will seem dense.

   Preparing the lunch took 4 hours; eating it took 40 minutes.

   I realize I need exercise; however, I'll lie down first to think about it.

2. Use a semicolon between items in a series if there are already commas within each item:

   ✗ The honoured employees were Helen Smith, the controller, Jean Hardy, her assistant, and Dr. Jack Hughes.

   ✓ The honoured employees were Helen Smith, the controller; Jean Hardy, her assistant; and Dr. Jack Hughes.

   The semicolons in the second sentence remove any confusion about the number of employees.

3. You may even use a semicolon before a coordinating conjunction in a long sentence, especially if there are internal commas within some of the clauses:

   The mediator settled the strike; but, despite their relief at getting back to work, not many workers were happy with the contract.

A Checklist of Misused Words and Phrases

accept, except   *Accept* is a verb meaning *agree* to something; *except* is either a verb meaning *exclude* or a preposition:

> I *accept* your offer.
>
> John's boss *excepted* him from the general criticism.
>
> He agreed with everyone *except* John.

accompanied by, accompanied with   Use *accompanied by* for people; use *accompanied with* for objects:

> She was *accompanied by* her assistant.
>
> The payment arrived, *accompanied with* an explanation.

advice, advise   *Advice* is a noun, *advise* a verb:

> He was *advised* to ignore the consultant's *advice*.

affect, effect   As a verb, *affect* means influence; as a noun, it's a technical psychological term. The verb *to effect* means *to bring about*. The noun *effect* means *result*. In most cases, you will be safe if you remember to use *affect* for the verb and *effect* for the noun:

> Interest rates *affect* our profit.
>
> The *effect* of higher government spending is higher inflation.

all together, altogether   *All together* means in a group; *altogether* is an adverb meaning entirely:

> She was *altogether* certain that the supervisors were *all together* at the meeting.

allusion, illusion   An *allusion* is an indirect reference to something; an *illusion* is a false perception:

> In his speech he made an *allusion* to the president's report.
>
> He thought he saw a ship on the horizon, but it was an *illusion*.

alot   Write as two separate words: *a lot*.

alternate, alternative   Used as an adjective, *alternate* means *the other of two choices*. As a verb, *to alternate* means *to do first one thing and then another*. *Alternative* means a choice between two things.

> He was chosen as an *alternate* for the leadership conference.
>
> The domestic model is a good *alternative*.
>
> The teachers will *alternate* from week to week.

among, between   Use *among* for three or more people or objects, *between* for two:

> *Between* you and me, there's trouble *among* the maintenance crew.

amoral, immoral   *Amoral* means *nonmoral* or *outside the moral sphere*; *immoral* means *wicked*:

> As an art critic, he was *amoral* in his judgments.
>
> Not to report the danger would be *immoral*.

amount, number   Use *amount* for money or noncountable quantities; use *number* for countable items:

No *amount* of persuasion or *number* of petitions will budge him from his position.

anyways   Nonstandard English; use *anyway*.

as, because   *As* is a weaker conjunction than *because* or *since* and may be misinterpreted as meaning *when*:

✗ He left *as* his rival arrived.

✓ He left *because* his rival arrived.

✓ He arrived *as* I was finishing.

✓ He arrived *when* I was finishing.

as to   A common feature of bureaucratese; replace it with a single-word preposition such as *about* or *on*:

✗ They were concerned *as to* the new budget.

✓ They were concerned *about* the new budget.

✗ They recorded his comments *as to* tax changes.

✓ They recorded his comments *on* tax changes.

bad, badly   *Bad* is an adjective meaning *not good*:

The meat tastes *bad*.

He felt *bad* about forgetting the handouts.

Badly is an adverb meaning not well; when used with the verbs *want* or *need*, it means *very much*:

She thought he managed the meeting *badly*.

I *badly* need a new office chair.

beside, besides   *Beside* is a preposition meaning *next to*:

She sat *beside* her assistant.

Besides has two uses: as a preposition it means *in addition to*; as a conjunctive adverb it means *moreover*:

Besides recommending the changes, the consultants are implementing them.

Everyone was getting impatient; *besides*, it was late and we needed a break.

can't hardly   A faulty combination of the phrases *can't* and *can hardly*. Use one or the other instead:

He *can't* balance the budget.

She *can hardly* stay awake.

canvas, canvass   *Canvas* is a type of heavy cloth; *to canvass* is *to survey* or *to solicit votes*.

capital, capitol   As a noun, *capital* may refer to a seat of government, the top of a pillar, an uppercase letter, or accumulated wealth. *Capitol* refers only to a specific American—or ancient Roman—building.

complement, compliment   The verb *to complement* means *to complete*; *to compliment* means *to praise*:

> The colour of the office carpet *complements* the new chairs very well.

> I *complimented* her on her outstanding report.

> The adjective *complimentary* also means *free*:

> He gave us *complimentary* tickets to the game.

continual, continuous   *Continual* means *repeated over a period of time*; *continuous* means *constant* or *without interruption*:

> The strikes caused *continual* delays in building the road.

> In August, it rained *continuously* for five days.

could of   Incorrect, as are *might of, should of,* and *would of*. Replace *of* with *have*:

✗ He *could of* done it.

✓ He *could have* done it.

✓ They *might have* been there.

✓ I *should have* known.

✓ We *would have* left earlier.

council, counsel   *Council* is a noun meaning *advisory* or *deliberative assembly*. *Counsel* as a noun means *advice* or *lawyer*; as a verb it means *give advice*:

> The town *council* meets on Tuesday.

> He is a *councillor* for the city of Peterborough.

> We respect his *counsel*, since he's seldom wrong.

> As a *counsellor*, you may need to *counsel* some people after hours.

criterion, criteria   A *criterion* is a standard for judging something. *Criteria* is the plural of *criterion* and thus requires a plural verb:

> These are my *criteria* for selecting the applicants.

> The *criterion* for success is dedication.

data   The plural of *datum, data* is increasingly treated as a singular noun. Most dictionaries accept the use of *data* with a singular verb and pronoun:

> Once the *data* has been verified, we will publish it.

disinterested, uninterested   *Disinterested* implies impartiality or neutrality; *uninterested* implies a lack of interest:

> As a *disinterested* observer, he was in a good position to judge the issue fairly.

> *Uninterested* in the proceedings, he yawned repeatedly.

due to   Although *due to* is increasingly used as a compound preposition, meaning *because of* or *owing to*, prevailing opinion still prefers the use of *due* as an adjective:

✗ The golf tournament was cancelled *due to* bad weather.

✓ The cancellation of the golf tournament was *due to* bad weather.

✗ *Due to* his rudeness, we lost the contract.

✓ The loss was *due to* his rudeness.

farther, further   *Farther* refers to distance, *further* to extent:

He paddled *farther* than his friends.

Let's wait until we are *further* along in our research.

good, well   *Good* is an adjective, not an adverb. *Well* can be both: as an adverb, it means *effectively*; as an adjective, it means *healthy*:

The apple cake tastes *good*.

She is a *good* tennis player.

She plays tennis *well*.

He is *well* again after his long bout of pneumonia.

hanged, hung   *Hanged* means *killed by hanging*. *Hung* means *suspended* or *clung to*:

He was *hanged* at dawn for the murder.

He *hung* the picture.

He *hung* from the mast in a safety harness.

hopefully   Use *hopefully* as an adverb meaning *full of hope*:

She scanned the mail *hopefully*, looking for her cheque.

In formal writing, using *hopefully* to mean *I hope* is still frowned upon, although increasingly common; it's better to use *I hope*:

✗ *Hopefully* we'll make a bigger profit this year.

✓ *I hope* we'll make a bigger profit this year.

imply, infer   *Imply* refers to what a statement suggests; *infer* relates to the audience's interpretation:

His letter *implied* that he was upset.

I *inferred* from his letter that he was upset.

irregardless   Incorrect; use *regardless*.

its, it's   *Its* is a form of possessive pronoun; *it's* is a contraction of *it is*. Many people mistakenly put an apostrophe in *its* in order to show possession:

✗ We can see *it's* advantages.

✓ We can see *its* advantages.

✓ *It's* time to leave.

Note that there is no such word as *its'*.

less, fewer   Use *less* for money and things that are not countable; use *fewer* for things that are countable:

Now that he's earning *less* money he's making *fewer* large expenditures.

lie, lay   *To lie* means *to assume a horizontal position*; *to lay* means *to put down*. The changes of tense often cause confusion:

present	past	past participle	present participle
lie	*lay*	*have lain*	*am lying*
lay	*laid*	*have laid*	*am laying*

✗ I plan to *lay* down for an hour.

This is a common error. Remember that hens *lay* eggs and humans *lie* down.

✓ I plan to lie down for an hour.

However, note the correct form to describe action in the past:

✗ Last weekend I *laid* down for a nap.

✓ Last weekend I *lay* down for a nap

✗ I *was laying* down when he called.

✓ I *was lying* down when he called.

like, as   *Like* is a preposition, but it is often wrongly used as a conjunction. To join two independent clauses, use the conjunction *as*:

✗ I want to develop *like* you have this year.

✓ I want to develop *as* you have this year.

✓ Arthur is *like* my old boss.

majority, plurality   *Majority* means *more than half*; *plurality* means *the highest number of votes.*

media   A plural noun requiring a plural verb. The singular noun is *medium.*

myself, me   *Myself* is an intensifier of, not a substitute for, *I* or *me.* Don't use the reflexive form (*-self*) unless the pronoun occurs elsewhere in the sentence.

✗ He gave it to Jane and *myself.*

✓ He gave it to Jane and *me.*

✗ Jane and *myself* are invited.

✓ Jane and *I* are invited.

✓ I would prefer a swivel chair *myself.*

nor, or   Use *nor* with *neither* and *or* by itself or with *either*:

He is *neither* overworked *nor* underpaid.

The file was *either* lost *or* destroyed.

off of   Remove the unnecessary *of*:

✗ The fence helps keep trespassers *off of* the premises.

✓ The fence helps keep trespassers *off* the premises.

phenomenon   A singular noun: the plural is *phenomena.*

principal, principle   As an adjective, *principal* means *main* or *most important; the head of a school* is the *principal.* A *principle* is *a law* or *controlling idea*:

Our *principal* aim is to reduce the deficit.

Our *principal*, Prof. Smart, retires next year.

We are defending the policy as a matter of *principle.*

rational, rationale   *Rational* is an adjective meaning *logical* or *able to reason. Rationale* is a noun meaning *explanation*:

That was not a *rational* decision.

The president sent around a memo explaining the *rationale* for his proposal.

real, really   The adjective *real* shouldn't be used as an adverb in Canadian English, although this use is common in some parts of the United States; use *really* instead:

✗   It was *real* valuable.

✓   It was *really* valuable.

✓   We got *real* value for our money.

set, sit   To *sit* means *to rest on the buttocks*; to *set* means *to put or place*:

After standing so long, you'll want to *sit* down.

Please *set* the machine on the desk.

their, there   *Their* is the possessive form of the third person plural pronoun. *There* is usually an adverb meaning *at that place* or *at that point*:

They parked *their* cars *there*.

to, too, two   *To* is a preposition as well as part of the infinitive form of a verb:

We went *to* town in order *to* buy equipment.

Too is an adverb showing degree or meaning *moreover*, *also*.

I want to go *too*.

The work is *too* hard.

Two is the spelled version of the number *2*.

while   To avoid any misunderstanding, use *while* only when you mean *at the same time as*. Do not use it as a substitute for *although*, *whereas*, or *but*:

✗   *While* he's getting fair results, he'd like to do better.

✗   I left the meeting *while* she decided to stay.

✓   He glowered *while* he was listening.

-wise   Never use *-wise* as a suffix to form new words when you mean *with regard to*:

✗   *Sales-wise*, the company did better last year.

✓   The company's sales increased last year.

your, you're   *Your* is a pronominal adjective used to show possession; *you're* is a contraction of *you are*:

You're likely to miss *your* train.

Exercises

In addition to the following exercises, a wealth of online material exists on the subjects covered in this Appendix. Here are some educational websites that offer a wide range of articles, exercises, quizzes, assignments, and tests on grammar, punctuation, and style:

Advice on Academic Writing—University of Toronto:
www.writing.utoronto.ca/advice

Writer's Guide—University of Victoria:
http://web.uvic.ca/wguide/Pages/StartHere.html

HyperGrammar—University of Ottawa:
www.arts.uottawa.ca/writcent/hypergrammar/

Guide to Grammar and Writing—Capital Community College, Hartford, Connecticut:
http://grammar.ccc.commnet.edu/grammar/

Writing Resources—George Mason University, Fairfax, Virginia:
http://writingcenter.gmu.edu/writing-resources.php

Purdue Online Writing Lab (OWL)—Purdue University, Lafayette, Indiana:
http://owl.english.purdue.edu/owl

1. Correct faulty predication, sentence fragments, and comma splices in the following sentences:

   a) Since the train was late, we took the bus, however we arrived on time.

   b) The reason the report lacks information on the research is because of the secrecy surrounding so much of the activity.

   c) One example of faulty sampling is when the group sampled is not representative.

   d) Having little chance to upgrade her skills, on account of heavy family responsibilities.

   e) We were late for the meeting, we didn't miss much.

   f) Communications bypassing is when a word has a different meaning for the speaker than for the listener.

   g) I got the information I needed, you don't need to search for it.

   h) The campaign is important, therefore we should plan carefully.

   i) Although the meeting was adjourned early, since she felt ill and the important matters were covered.

   j) Please reread this file, it contains a few mathematical errors.

2. Correct any problems with pronouns and pronoun-verb agreement in the following sentences:

   a) He explained the procedure again, for the benefit of Jean and I.

   b) The problem with him being ill is that we can't finish the report.

   c) Each of us have a different aspect of the case to research.

   d) The manager's report criticized the Sales Department's performance and it caused concern among staff.

   e) Both of us have difficulty making early morning meetings, but neither of us have a problem with lunch meetings.

   f) Between you and I, the advertisement is a bad one.

g) When one travels through the north in summer months, you need protection from black flies.

h) I wonder if each of the partners are planning to attend the conference.

i) When the invitation came to Pierre and I, I sent the reply on behalf of us both.

j) The challenges are great, but it doesn't discourage us.

3. Correct any problems with verb tense and subject-verb agreement:

a) When he ate the giant hot dog, he went back to playing baseball.

b) Since the photocopier arrived, I no longer need carbon copies.

c) If the manager would have talked to us earlier, the problem could have been solved.

d) Either of the accountants are willing to check your books.

e) Neither of the problems are too difficult; but either one or the other are likely to pose a challenge to students at your level.

f) My supervisor, as well as the manager, are on holidays, but both are due back next Monday.

g) We looked at several accounting firms, but Jones & Hume are best suited to our needs.

h) Neither of the debtors have made an effort to pay us.

i) Simplifying the process will create savings and would improve our balance sheet.

j) If Canada was part of Europe, we could increase our leather exports.

k) We think that application of those new computer programs require a basic understanding of statistics.

l) The latest version of the instructions haven't been translated yet.

4. Correct the faulty or confusing modifiers in these sentences:

a) Although the interview was tough, fortunately I handled it good.

b) In the consumer tests, the samplers said that the cake tasted well but the cookies were too salty.

c) Talking to an angry customer, the experience was stressful and unpleasant.

d) I want signs for the two entrances, which are inexpensive and easy to see.

e) Thinking about the client's attitude, our proposal should be more detailed.

f) Although she usually plays good tennis, yesterday the lighting was bad and she couldn't hit good.

g) The office in the west end of the city, which needs extensive repairs, is vacant.

h) The deputy minister will talk about cleaning up the St. Lawrence River after lunch.

i) He almost ate the entire pie, but fortunately I arrived when one piece was still left.

j) She made arrangements at the morning break to have muffins with the coffee.

5. Correct the faulty comparisons and correlatives:

a) She both handles promotion and advertising for our company.

b) He not only designed the building but the landscaping as well.

c) Fortunately, Bill's accounting problem is not as troublesome as my other clients.

d) It's as important to keep the children's interest during the show as their parents.

e) We hope that our sales for March will be as high as last year.

6. Use parallel phrasing in the following sentences:

   a) We want Mary to do the planning, Jerry to handle purchasing, and the books should be kept by Joan or Sam.

   b) Please make arrangements to paint the office this week, install the carpet next week, and by the end of the month see that you hang the new curtains.

   c) George and Peter are away at a conference, Jill is on holiday, and sickness accounts for the absence of five other employees.

   d) We have to develop a concept, devise a marketing strategy, and create the advertising copy, but handling the client will not be our responsibility, fortunately.

   e) Writing the proposal will be fairly easy, but it will be more difficult to complete the job on time.

7. Revise the following sentences, correcting the grammatical errors named.

   a) **Sentence fragment:**   The new boss, having little time to spare for trivial matters, owing to a shortage of staff.

   b) **Comma splice:**   We rushed to deliver the cheques, since it was Friday, unfortunately the bank was closed.

   c) **Faulty predication:**   The subject of my report for Harry is about the cost of printing in our branch office.

   d) **Wrong verb tense:**   If the typist would have stayed longer and typed those three pages, I could have finished the project.

   e) **Subject-verb disagreement:**   Our lawyer, together with his associates, have presented a formidable case for collecting damages.

   f) **Pronoun disagreement:**   Despite a busy winter, neither of the partners are taking their holidays in the summer.

   g) **No pronoun reference:**   Fred Barnes told Ed Smith that he had received a promotion.

   h) **Faulty pronoun case:**   After we had aired our grievances, our supervisor invited Ted and I to lunch at his club.

   i) **Faulty modifiers:**   My old car ran as good as this one, but it didn't look as well because it was painted bad.

   j) **Misplaced modifier:**   After weeks of partying and water-skiing, Mr. Smythe decided that his son should settle down to work.

   k) **Dangling modifier:**   Walking along the dark street late at night, the tall buildings looked imposing and a little frightening.

   l) **Squinting modifier and faulty comparison:**   Although Jean is a better speaker as a result of training, I write better than her.

8. Although you don't need to name any grammatical errors, correct the following faulty or confusing sentences:

   a) As the report was finalized, the committee made its decision.

   b) You need more collateral, then we will be happy to increase the loan.

   c) Neither of them remember, unfortunately, who was our third prime minister.

   d) Squash as well as other racquet sports are good exercise and will keep a person fit.

   e) Being good in mathematics, accounting was her best subject last year.

f) Payment of the expense claims for the last two months have been delayed, owing to a computer breakdown.

g) I wore my old Greb boots to the construction site, which kept my feet warm and dry.

h) Upward mobility, they say, is when you turn in jeans for a jogging suit.

i) When the office staff saw the auditors arriving, they knew they would take over their offices for the week.

j) Lawyers seem to have more financial problems than accountants.

k) We need to hire fewer people, encourage early retirement, and expenses should be reduced in office administration.

l) Jokingly, he said that the reason he needed glasses was not because his eyes were worse but because his arms were too short.

9. Correct the faulty grammar in the following memo:

Scott has decided not to hire more salespeople until spring at that time he will have a better idea of his sales picture. This fits in good with our overall budgeting plans, but I realize it may change if his departmental sales pick up much more. Scott reported last weekend he was understaffed.

Between you and I, I'm more optimistic than him about economic trends, however I appreciate him being cautious. If we would have hired more personnel last autumn we would have had a hard time keeping them through the slump. Moreover, comparing last year's forecasts with our actual sales, the experience is sobering.

This year, sales either will rebound over the Christmas season or we will be in the red again. We not only need to watch our internal costs but to keep a closer eye on cash flow. Like Scott, each manager will have to do their bit to avoid inessential hiring. I am confident, however, that with an improved economy, a lean staff, and by making a determined sales effort we will be profitable this year.

10. Put commas where needed in the following sentences:

a) We need a new blue covering for that unattractive uncomfortable chair.

b) When I was away the office had a fire in its newly furnished boardroom.

c) I asked him to call my accountant Susan Hughes but he forgot to my dismay.

d) Students who are caught plagiarizing assignments will fail the course.

e) Last Friday June 4 I held a meeting with Bill Hines Reg Hawkes and Sarah Rykert our new research director.

f) The prospects are not good however despite our early optimism.

g) Last week she said "Consumers are more confident" but this week she is predicting that the economy will soon be "sluggish."

h) Your forecast is shocking needless to say but you are a pessimist aren't you?

i) My boss who is always supportive suggested that I apply for the job in Lethbridge Alberta.

j) I recommend therefore that we keep the old computers buy the furniture and restore the panelling and wood trim.

11. Add apostrophes where needed:

a) Mr. Coates secretary is having lunch with the other bosses secretaries.

b) Its a challenging job and Ill keep my fingers crossed that Marys application succeeds.

c) The Hawkins house is located next to the Jennings property.

d) A new womens club has opened downtown but its entrance fees are high.

e) That fact that John Frasers little shoe store has grown into the huge chain of Frasers outlets restores ones confidence in the countrys spirit of entrepreneurship.

f) My mother said "Mind your young sisters manners when you go to that reception."

12. Add quotation marks (and other punctuation where needed) to the following sentences:

a) When he asked Are you free on Saturday night I replied No Im expensive.

b) She said there was a good opportunity however I was not as certain.

c) If you pay for the gas he said I will drive you to Montreal.

d) Can we really believe the slogan Practice makes perfect.

e) Have you read the article Managing Innovation.

13. In the places marked by a caret (^) add a semicolon, a colon, a comma, or no mark:

a) We think ^ however, that the proposal is sound.

b) I like Susie ^ however, she doesn't like me.

c) For my presentation next Friday please arrange for ^ a flip chart, an overhead projector, and a tape recorder.

d) He invited three guests ^ Mr. Jones, Mrs. Hunter, and Mr. Zavitz.

e) My new book is called *Interaction* ^ *A Guide to Productivity*.

f) My reason is simple ^ it's too costly.

g) I called Arthur Hanna, the lawyer who works for us ^ but he was at a conference with Jed Hughes ^ our accountant ^ and won't be back for a week.

h) The press conference will take place at the Holiday Inn ^ Yorkdale ^ on Monday morning.

i) Please send notice of the meeting to our lawyer ^ Jane Higgins ^ and her partner ^ Dan Spivak.

j) A prompt reminder of their overdue accounts should go to our clients ^ who have not paid their December bills.

14. Add semicolons, colons, and commas where appropriate:

a) We bid on the contract nevertheless we didn't get it.

b) We invited three influential lawyers Harold Stark QC Melvin Thomas and Sylvia Raski.

c) We plan to give long-term service pins to Ann Arbour our accounting supervisor Al Smith the sales manager and Pete Stuart head of maintenance.

d) Last night I stayed up until 3 30 since I was engrossed in reading *Murder on the Metro A Tale of High Finance*.

e) The plant will likely not need chemical engineers you should however check with Jim Jackson the general manager.

f) Please paint the reception area the manager's office and the computer lab by next weekend one coat should be enough.

g) Guy quoted Trudeau's remark "The state has no place in the nation's bedrooms."

h) The woman who gave me the job is the aunt of my best friend who lives in Fredericton.

i) The friendly old supervisor I've often talked to you about gave me a ticket to the hockey game between the Ottawa Senators and the Toronto Maple Leafs on Saturday night.

j) Here is our strategy hang tough and keep cool.

15. Punctuate the following sentences:

a) On Friday June 10 at 9 30 a m the premier will meet the union leaders however he is not expected to make an announcement afterward.

b) The weary student asked whats the meaning of this assignment and I certainly didn't have an answer.

c) I wish people would stop repeating that trite expression have a nice day.

d) Jeffs article Magnum Corporation A Study in Entrepreneurship is a good one but its not likely to be published.

e) When the Lewis car lost its muffler Sam had to take it to Susans fathers garage.

f) Thats a nineteenth century attitude Ann said but at least its not hypocritical.

g) On a cold winter night in March Mr Gallant went on a holiday his first in five years and he never returned.

h) People who are shy often have spouses who do most of the talking for them or so it seems.

i) The treasurers report see Appendix A gives details of our finances and unfortunately we still have a large debt to be paid off.

j) What a disaster he shouted but then hes always overreacting.

16. Correct the punctuation in the following memo. Capital letters show where sentences begin, but you may create added sentence breaks if you wish.

Date: June 3, 2011

To: J Walker

From: M Smythe

Subject: Date of Opening for New Office

Alan's plans for opening our new office make good sense however I think the date is not late enough Will it matter to you if we move the opening date back two weeks to Tuesday August 1

My concern arises from two potential problems First the furniture company cannot guarantee delivery of our order before July 28 Second Ace Movers is fully booked until the last week in July They may have cancellations for an earlier date but its safer I think to change our schedule I would rather not switch to another moving company because Aces prices are considerably lower than those of its competitors As well other companies who have used Ace report good results Reliable Movers who moved us last time have gone out of business I plan to hold the Ace people to their slogan let us take the fuss out of moving

mycanadianbuscommlab

Visit www.mycanadianbuscommlab.ca for everything you need to help you succeed in the job you've always wanted! Tools and resources include the following:

- Composing Space and Writer's Toolkit
- Document Makeovers
- Grammar Exercises—and much more!

References

Chapter 1

Brownell, J. (1990, Fall). Perceptions of effective listeners: A management study. *The Journal of Business Communication, 27*(4), 401–415.

Burgoon, L. K., Bullet, D. B., & Woodall, W. G. (1989). *Nonverbal communication: The unspoken dialogue.* New York, NY: Harper & Row.

A conversation with Roger D'Aprix [Videotape]. Towers, Perrin, Forster & Crosby.

Hung, C. L. (1994, March 16). *Canadian business alliances in Pacific Asia and the role of communication.* Paper presented at the Pacific Region Forum on Business and Management Communication, Simon Fraser University, Vancouver, Canada. Retrieved from http://www.cic.sfu.ca/forum/CLHung.txt.html

Mehrabian, A. (1981). *Silent messages: Implicit communication of emotions and attitudes.* Belmont, CA: Wadsworth.

Nolen, W. E. (1995, April). Reading people. *Internal Auditor, 52*(2), 48–51.

Pace, W., & Boren, R. (1973). *The human transaction.* Glenview, IL: Scott, Foresman.

Rogers, C. R. (1995). *On becoming a person.* Boston, MA: Houghton Mifflin.

Shannon, C., & Weaver, W. (1963). *The mathematical theory of communication.* Urbana, IL: University of Illinois Press.

Chapter 2

Flower, L. (1993). *Problem-solving strategies for writing* (5th ed.). Cambridge, MA: International Thomson Publishing.

Lengel, R., & Daft, R. (1988). The selection of communication media as an executive skill. *The Academy of Management Executive, 2*(3), 225–232.

Chapter 3

Goldsborough, R. (1999, September/October). Words for the wise. *Link-Up, 16*(5), 25–26.

Mitternight, H. L. (1998, March). Winning the hearts—or at least the eyes—of the online audience. *Communication World, 15*(4), 36–38.

Chapter 4

Abernathy, D. J. (1999, April). You've got email. *Training and Development, 53*(4), 18.

Canada Post. (2004, November 1). *Canadian addressing guide.* Retrieved from http://www.fnesc.ca/Attachments/BCeSIS/PDF's/addressing_guide-e.pdf

Sanchez, P. (1999, August 1). How to craft successful employee communication in the information age. *Communication World.* Retrieved from http://www.allbusiness.com/human-resources/workforce-management/378502-1.html

Chapter 6

Maslow, A. H. (1987). *Motivation and personality* (3rd ed.). New York, NY: Harper and Row.

Rogers, C. R. (1995). Communication: Its blocking and its facilitation. In *On becoming a person* (pp. 329–337). Boston, MA: Houghton Mifflin.

Shelby, A. N. (1986, January). The theoretical bases of persuasion: A critical introduction. *Journal of Business Communication, 23*(1), 5–29. doi:10.1177/002194368602300102

Wheeless, L. R., Barraclough, R., & Stewart, R. (1983). Compliance-gaining and power in persuasion. In R. Bostrom (Ed.), *Communication yearbook 7* (pp. 105–145). Beverly Hills, CA: Sage.

Chapter 8

American Psychological Association. (2010). *Publication manual of the American Psychological Association* (6th ed.). Washington, DC: Author.

Ogilvy, D. (1985). *Ogilvy on advertising.* New York, NY: Random House.

Chapter 9

Spicer, K. (1988). *The winging it logic system: How to think and make sense.* Toronto, Canada: Doubleday.

Street talk. (1989, July 10). *Marketing.*

Chapter 10

Drucker, P. F. (1952, May). How to be an employee. *Fortune,* 126–127.

Interviewing skills theory. (n.d.). *University of British Columbia Science Co-op Programs.* Retrieved from http://www.sciencecoop.ubc.ca/info/interview.html

15

50

Presentation
↓
logo
↓
Timhootoy
↓
sample advertising
only (@12 8pic)
↓
SEBI
the man also na
cowa

Index